Advance Praise for *Appalachia's Alternative to Mainstream America*

"An important and beautifully written memoir of the non-native back-to-the-landers who helped shape the Appalachian resistance movement of the late twentieth century."
—**Ronald Eller,** distinguished professor of history emeritus, University of Kentucky

"*Appalachia's Alternative to Mainstream America* is much more than a memoir. It's a meditation on how we live; a guide to activism and rural community; and it demonstrates Paul Salstrom's guts, ingenuity, and ability as a storyteller. At a time when so many lack political imagination, Salstrom shows us that not long ago he and others joined a local society based in 'barter and borrow' that looked back to rural tradition and forward to a new America."
—**Steven Stoll,** professor of history, Fordham University, and author of *Ramp Hollow: The Ordeal of Appalachia*

"In this interesting memoir, Paul Salstrom contends that America's culture of individualism threatens the destruction of the environment, the food and energy supply, and democracy itself. The best alternative, he argues, is a retreat to the traditional rural Appalachian culture of small farms, self-reliant neighbors, and a low-cash reciprocal economy. This message will be stoutly resisted, of course, but Salstrom's thought-provoking analysis of the past gives us much to ponder about the future."
—**Ronald L. Lewis,** Stuart and Joyce Robbins Chair in History and professor of history emeritus, West Virginia University

"In his engaging memoir, Paul Salstrom takes us 'back to the land' in Appalachia with a colorful cast of characters during the 1970s. They thought they were breaking new ground, but what they discovered was an ancient way of life based on neighborly borrowing and sharing. This is no *Hillbilly Elegy*. Salstrom is convinced that traditional rural values offer a way forward for our unsustainable modern economy. Read this book and you might be convinced, too."
—**John Mack Faragher,** professor of history emeritus, Yale University, and author of *California: An American History*

"In this memoir Paul Salstrom, author of a groundbreaking work on Appalachia, takes us along on his personal journey through the upheaval and idealism of the 1960s and 70s. In some ways it's a story typical of young folks of that era searching for and experimenting with ways to bring about a better, more just world; in Salstrom's case his path led to Appalachia, West Virginia in particular, where he came to admire the lives and culture of rural farming communities. But Salstrom's story became unique when he left his cabin on a West Virginia mountainside to study for a PhD in history. Combining his experience in Appalachia with economic theory, he developed his own theory positing that Appalachian culture with its traditions of sharing, reciprocity and barter might be a model for mainstream America challenging usual perceptions of Appalachia as a backward, primitive region. This memoir takes us through the steps he took, from personal experience with Appalachian people to admiring their way of life to a scholarly theory of how that way of life could and should be applied more generally to American economic and cultural life. It's a provocative theory as well as a fascinating story."
—**Altina Waller,** professor emerita, University of Connecticut, and author
of *Hatfields, McCoys, and Social Change in Appalachia, 1860–1900*

"It seems impossible for the breadth and depth of experiences in Paul Salstrom's memoir to have been lived by a single soul. The flip of a few thin pages and we cross paths with Chuck Berry and Ansel Adams, Abbie Hoffman and Dorothy Day, an eccentric European high-wire acrobat and a natural-gas pipeline walker named 'Mud River' Ray Elkins, both hunkered down in West Virginia's Lincoln County. Yet Salstrom's intrepid, justice-minded journeys weave these characters and locales into a single personal narrative often propelled by the big questions of a fraught, hopeful, tumultuous era: what if we could stop this war? Where can we find an antidote to toxic mainstream materialism? Could peeling back the centuries-old stereotypes of Appalachia provide us with a roadmap for the future? The answers, of course, are complicated, but Salstrom is a generous, witty, insightful inquisitor, and provides his reader with not only the meticulous historic details of people and places, but also a taut thread of humor, mysticism, and immense humanity. I loved this book."
—**Josh MacIvor-Andersen,** author of *On Heights & Hunger* and editor
of *Rooted: The Best New Arboreal Nonfiction*

Appalachia's Alternative
to Mainstream America

Appalachia's Alternative to Mainstream America

A Personal Education

PAUL SALSTROM

The University of Tennessee Press | Knoxville

Manufactured in the United States of America.
First Edition.

Frontis: Photo by Justin Campbell on Unsplash

Library of Congress Cataloging-in-Publication Data
Names: Salstrom, Paul, 1940– author.
Title: Appalachia's alternative to mainstream America :
a personal education / Paul Salstrom.
Description: First edition. | Knoxville : The University of Tennessee Press,
[2021] | Includes bibliographical references and index. | Summary: "Longtime
Appalachian resident, scholar, and historian Paul Salstrom recounts the education
in homesteading, subsistence farming, gardening, and community-based mutual
aid that he discovered in rural Lincoln County, West Virginia, beginning in the
early 1970s. These experiences inspire a reflective history of Appalachia's 'neighborly
networking' form of life and an impassioned case for its value to contemporary
America. Salstrom notes that the 'back-to-the-landers' of the 1960s and 1970s have
by no means disappeared, finding new expression in farm-to-table and other related
movements. But today is different, Salstrom argues. Pandemics, climate change, and
deepening political divisions signal a crisis of common sense in mainstream America
and cast new light on these old, landed practices, which may yet stand a chance of
generating local sufficiency in food and energy production"—Provided by publisher.
Identifiers: LCCN 2021038748 (print) | LCCN 2021038749 (ebook) |
ISBN 9781621907152 (paperback) | ISBN 9781621907169 (pdf)
Subjects: LCSH: Salstrom, Paul, 1940– | Farm life—Appalachian Region, Southern. |
Local exchange trading systems—Appalachian Region, Southern. | Cooperation—
Appalachian Region, Southern. | Reciprocity (Psychology) | Appalachian Region,
Southern—Social life and customs. | LCGFT: Autobiographies.
Classification: LCC S521.5.A67 S25 2021 (print) | LCC S521.5.A67 (ebook) |
DDC 338.109756/9—dc23
LC record available at https://lccn.loc.gov/2021038748
LC ebook record available at https://lccn.loc.gov/2021038749

For Miriam Ralston
and
Eve Ananda Salstrom Ralston
and
Future generations

CONTENTS

ILLUSTRATIONS

PREFACE

"You're not getting back on this bus!" the driver told me after our rest stop at Chattanooga, Tennessee. He blocked the bus entrance with his body. Why? Only later did I realize why. It was spring 1960 and the news was full of student sit-ins at segregated southern lunch counters. On the bus, I had sat in the back with five or six black workers as we sped south through Tennessee—myself being a curious nineteen year old asking those black workers what they thought about the sit-ins at lunch counters, and about race relations in general.

About a year later it dawned on me that was the reason I'd been expelled from the Greyhound bus. But I never grew as involved with civil rights as I did with the peace movement. And during the second half of the 1960s, despite the Vietnam War raging, my participation in protests drastically dropped as I focused instead on "alternatives"— exploring ways to change how we lived our lives, hoping to see "a new society growing in the shell of the old." That's how Dorothy Day of the Catholic Worker movement described "alternatives."

During the 1960s, I often worked with a social-change visionary named Bob Swann while he developed the now-popular Community Land Trust method of land holding. Then he launched "micro-finance" experiments and a supplemental local currency. It's because of Bob Swann there's an "Alternative Economics" chapter in this book.

When the 1960s sputtered out and the 1970s started with Richard Nixon as president, circumstances landed me in rural West Virginia— not in one of the impoverished coal-mining counties where John F. Kennedy campaigned in 1960 for president, but instead in old-fashioned, agricultural, traditional Lincoln County, just north of southern West Virginia's six worst-off coal counties.

When our local roads weren't dirt they were mud, snow, or both. During my first year there (1972) our rural-route mailman was still delivering his mail route on horseback. He'd cram the out-going mail down in his left saddlebag and then fish down in his right saddlebag for the new mail he was delivering.

But don't jump to conclusions. Compared to the coal-mining counties south of us, Lincoln County was doing quite well. Gradually it dawned on me that the rural way of life there might end up being "a new society in the shell of the old" if and when America's mainstream economy ever falters or breaks down. That the daily bartering and borrowing I saw all around me might someday become a model for millions of Americans elsewhere—a sort of Plan B that Americans could resort to if and when we need a Plan B.

Now fifty years later, the climate crisis and coronavirus-19 pandemic are prompting many Americans to start thinking about a Plan B.

People in rural Lincoln County in the 1970s were earning their livelihoods at least partly (and sometimes mostly) by doing favors for each other—by giving or lending what someone else needed, and receiving back favors when they themselves needed something. Often it was just lending a helping hand when someone needed it and getting a helping hand back when they needed it themselves.

Most of them had very little money but they seemed to have enough. If lots of money came their way, it didn't necessarily help them. One of our aging friends named Gobel Greenhill had black-lung disease (from lifelong coal mining) and started receiving large compensation checks from the federal government. He didn't go to a bank and open a savings account. Instead, he bought four brand-new pick-up trucks, one for each of his four children.

Of course, not everything in Lincoln County was sweetness and light. Patriarchy still more or less reigned, and of course provincialism. At our local country store, people's jaws dropped when my younger brother John and I went shopping with his tall, strong, jet-black young African-Swiss visitor, dressed chic for "roughing it." Her baritone voice and thick German accent scored the knock-out blow and the other shoppers just stood there with their mouths open.

In the late 1960s I had pursued an array of experimental alternatives, but when fate landed me in rural Lincoln County, I found myself sharing an alternative way of life that wasn't experimental at all. It had been going on there for two hundred years. And despite two centuries of slowly depleting the local natural resources that it depended on, it was still functioning quite well. Besides its resource base, it depended on people constantly trading favors with each other in a spirit of mutual aid—which could be called "voluntary reciprocity" because if you didn't do people any return favors, they would quit doing you any favors—assuming you were physically able-bodied enough to at least lend a hand. If you weren't physically able to, then they'd keep on doing you favors gratis.

But then came another change. After several years of sharing rural Lincoln County's neighborly solidarity, the later 1970s turned me into a printer and editor in the Ohio River city of Huntington, West Virginia—along with a young woman who I had met in early 1974, Miriam Ralston, who became a printer and editor as well. During our late 1970s at Appalachian Movement Press in Huntington we found ourselves in the midst of Appalachia's new protest movements *and* its new "alternative" movements, keeping us busy for several years printing and editing.

When our daughter was born in spring 1978 we re-located back to rural West Virginia, but not back to Lincoln County since our cabin-in-progress on a hilltop there was still without a roof and floor. (It still is.) Instead we moved up the Ohio River to rural Mason County, where we met an amazing woman 87 years old, Maude Hunter Dyke. She was the last of her generation on both sides of her family and a one-woman treasure-store of Appalachian tradition (Chapter 12 will tell her story).

By then I was returning to college after a twenty-year absence, which led to teaching American history five years at West Virginia University in Morgantown, and then teaching Appalachian history and all sorts of other history for twenty-seven years (and counting) at a small liberal-arts college in rural Indiana.

Now that so many years have passed and I've reached age 80, I find myself glancing back through my life. By now in 2021 it's grown clearer why Americans will probably need to live simpler lives in closer contact with the earth, but *how* can they? How they can, I think, is how I saw rural Appalachian people living in the 1970s. It starts by offering to lend people a helping hand.

Mind you, I'm not writing a how-to-do-it manual (although I may mention some things I know from personal experience). Nor is this a blueprint for a sustainable end result. It's a first-hand memoir of see-ing Americans live successfully under circumstances like those which many more Americans may find themselves living under in the future. If a large-scale "return to the land" does happen in America's future, I hope its participants will be as successful as most of the people in this book.

ACKNOWLEDGMENTS

Many thanks to Liv Charlton, Tom and Sara Gibbs, Ronald L. Lewis, Tom and Judy Rodd, my brother John Salstrom, Steven Stoll, David Vancil, and Bill and Lucy Wieland for reading earlier drafts of this book and offering suggestions which have made things clearer. The book's semi-final draft was then read by the psychologist Douglas Sperry, one of my Indiana colleagues. Doug made several major suggestions which have single-handedly upgraded the book.

I'd also like to confer my own "lifetime achievement" appreciation on some persons I've known who set a high example with their truly worthwhile achievements: Ansel Adams, Diane Arbus, Moe Armstrong, Chuck Berry, Yogi Bhajan, Ralph Borsodi, Yvon Chouinard, Lenore McComas Coberly, Bill Coperthwaite, Dorothy Day, Mildred J. Loomis, Staughton and Alice Lynd, Elaine Mikels, Arthur E. Morgan, Olaus and Mardy Murie, Wally and Juanita Nelson, John C. Plott, Bob and Marj Swann, Eric Weinberger, and Tom Woodruff.

So many acknowledgements for information and photos are in order that I'll simply hope the book itself makes clear who helped, and how they did so. But finally, thanks to the director of my college's library, Rusty Tryon; to Aaron Parsons at the West Virginia State Archives; and to Scot Danforth, Thomas G. Wells, Linsey Perry, Jon Boggs, Stephanie Thompson, and the rest of the fine team at University of Tennessee Press.

CHAPTER 1

My Appalachian Preview

It was past nightfall on April 1st, 1960 in Chattanooga, Tennessee. I had heard about the southern lunch-counter sit-ins going on, and I had sat with some black workers in the back of the southbound Greyhound bus and asked them what they thought about the sit-ins and about race relations in general. I was just curious, but they were non-committal. In fact, most of them seemed rather "distant," and I wasn't clueless why. Then came our Chattanooga rest stop, and when we returned to the bus, I was *totally* clueless why the bus driver blocked my re-boarding. I had a ticket for somewhere further south, some Georgia town near the starting point of the Appalachian Trail.

"You're not getting back on this bus!" he growled. I wasn't just surprised but stumped. He offered no explanation and I couldn't think of one. Despite my awareness of the lunch-counter sit-ins, I wasn't aware how *many* ways the South was segregated.

It was night but I thumbed rides on south. Finally, one of those drivers said he thought Mount Oglethorpe was off that-a-way to the left. So I thanked him, climbed out of his car with my rucksack, headed that-a-way on foot and soon found myself in an overgrown pasture. There I called it a day (night).

Next I knew, a very red cardinal was chortling "What Cheer, Cheer, Cheer!" four feet from my face. It was dawn, cold and frosty but under a clear sky. And sure enough it *was* a flank of Mount Oglethorpe, confirmed a few hours and nasty laurel thickets later when I reached the 38-foot stone obelisk somehow installed on the mountain's 3,288-foot summit in honor of James Oglethorpe, the founder of Georgia.

I ate some lunch and started north on the trail—totally clueless that it wasn't actually The Trail anymore (the Appalachian Trail). Only long afterward did I learn that in 1958 the Appalachian Trail Conference had shifted the Trail's southern starting point thirteen miles eastward to the summit of Springer Mountain—because (so they said) development was encroaching from the south up onto Mount Oglethorpe.

My twelve-day hike northbound showed me some of the old Appalachia, including an extremely old man with a long white beard wearing homemade clothes and toting a shotgun. We crossed paths in a thick fog (a cloud) high on a mountainside. He said he was turkey hunting, which sounded 180 degrees out-of-season in April but I prudently didn't say so since he was armed. (Later I found out Appalachian states do have a "spring gobbler" hunting season.) The old fellow looked like Rip Van Winkle. Lord knows what I looked like to him, what with binoculars dangling from my neck and a large rucksack on my back. We scrutinized each other and traded a few words and went our very separate ways.

Another day a huge wild boar came barreling right at me, plowing up the trail with its tusks. A few yards away it suddenly saw me and veered around to my right and resumed plowing up the trail behind me. Whew.

Another day, at sunrise, a break in the trees showed a tiny homestead about 2,000 feet below in a green cove. I faintly heard a screen door banging itself closed (if you know that sound) so I raised the binoculars and saw a teenage girl carrying two buckets out to a water pump in her back yard. I called down "hello" and she stopped in her tracks and looked up my way, scrutinizing the wooded ridge I was at the top of.

There was plenty of time to think (the Appalachian Trail is usually boring). I found myself rehashing my recent college career at the University of Chicago. Early on, one of my fellow male students told me that all male students automatically had student draft deferments. So I went and asked the Registrar. She said "Yes you do" and told me it wasn't actually legal but that every college in America sent the Selective Service System the names, home addresses, and Social Security numbers of all their full-time male students, and then those students automatically had student draft deferments as long as they stayed full-time students. What the law actually required, she said, was that every student who wanted a deferment had to personally sign a request for it, but she said no college enforced that. I told her I wanted my student deferment ended immediately and she promised it would be—which later became "academic" because I didn't stick around. I dropped out, spent a month steel-working to earn some money, and hit the road.

I had been brought up by my parents to care about fairness and resented the University of Chicago illegally acquiring a draft deferment for me. I'd been reluctant to go to college at all unless it was far away from my home town. I had applied unsuccessfully to the University of Edinburgh in Scotland and to a newly-founded college in rural Australia. Then in mid-summer 1958 after high school graduation came news I'd been awarded an Illinois State Scholarship, something brand new that year. They told me they would pay my full tuition for four years at any college in Illinois, and that only my flunking out could end the scholarship.

Trouble was, I couldn't think of any Illinois college I wanted to attend. As high school seniors we had been bused down to Champaign-Urbana to tour the University of Illinois, but its countless identical little red-brick dorms jam-packed with students seemed like a dreary prospect.

Summer 1958 when the scholarship news arrived was my third in Jackson Hole, Wyoming. The scholarship news reached me at Jenny Lake Campground there. One of my campsite guests right then happened to be a graduate of the University of Chicago's Great Books program, and his infectious enthusiasm sold me on it. He said the upcoming fall would be the very last chance to enter the Great Books program because the university's current chancellor had just abolished it, provoking an enormous but futile student protest on the Midway Plaisance in front of the chancellor's mansion. So I applied to the University of Chicago and was admitted. When I turned 18 and could legally work, I hitchhiked up to Jackson Lake Lodge and got a dishwashing job to earn some money for college room and board.

As soon as I reached Chicago, problems started. Fresh from the Tetons, I found myself crammed into a miniscule cement-block room in a brand-new dormitory—crammed in there with a roommate non-stop telling me he planned to fill all the top student jobs before he graduated. First he'd be manager of the campus radio station, then he'd be editor of the campus newspaper, and finally student-body president. I listened, but didn't look forward to hearing updates all year. So I walked south across the Midway to the stately old gothic Burton-Judson dormitory and found a large empty two-room suite on the second floor, with a huge bay window looking out on the Midway. I invited a fellow freshman who I'd just met to move in there with me and we promptly did so. Then I phoned the student housing office and reported my changed location. There was a stifled female gasp, then silence. Next came the angry male voice of someone obviously in charge, telling me "This is the very last thing you will ever get away with at the University of Chicago."

Whatever. But things went downhill from there.

I had placed out of Humanities 2 (a year of English literature) so I wouldn't have to take it, but I did have to take Humanities 1 (a year of art, music, and world literature). The instructor was a tall young red-headed fellow with a crew cut. My grades were generally B's all quarter but he gave me an "F" for the quarter overall, apparently because he had blushed beet-red after I answered one of his questions. On our classroom screen he had projected a fallen statue of a Greek nymph, headless as I recall, and he asked us what the statue represented. No one spoke up, so I said art actually happens in the mind of the beholder, and the statue could just as easily represent "torso on a bed" as whatever its sculpture might have named it. Wrong answer apparently. The red-headed instructor turned beet red for a good five minutes and I got "F" at the end of the quarter.

The upshot of my freshman year was that when I returned to the university from the Tetons in fall 1959 (—whoa, actually from two September weeks in the Canadian Rockies which nearly proved fatal thanks to Canada's *totally fictitious* official topographic map of the high country northeast of Banff)—anyway, one of the university's deans summoned me to his office and told me I no longer had my Illinois State Scholarship. The rules of the Illinois Scholarship Commission no longer applied, he told me, because the university had taken control over all the scholarships of its students. I pointed out to the dean that his timing came too late for me to attend college anywhere else that fall. He then said my scholarship would cover one more academic quarter, through December 1959.

During my previous year as a freshman, while making sure I didn't flunk out, I had audited more courses than I was officially taking. Now in fall 1959 I continued that. My favorite again was Richard McKeon's ongoing series of spellbinding Wednesday afternoon lectures on the history of philosophy. I also attended David Grene's semi-weekly evening graduate seminars on translating Greek plays. That fall of 1959 Grene was on the

Philoctetes of Sophocles, next in line for publication in his series of Greek drama translations.

Incredibly, Professor Grene spent half of every year raising pigs in Ireland, and I was equally amazed by Philoctetes, a warrior in the process of being totally banished from Greek society because of a foul-smelling foot wound. His warrior buddies deposit him on an uninhabited island and sail away. But ten years later when they need him, they come back and he gives them an ear-full!. Professor Grene and his graduate students probed the nuances of every important phrase in Sophocles' original Greek, collectively weighing how to word Grene's English translation.

In those days before student loans, tuition at the University of Chicago was only $300 per quarter (which would equal $2,700 today) and a friendly Humanities 1 instructor offered me a loan to cover my remaining years, but I decided to leave UC when my scholarship expired in December 1959. I lived off campus that fall at an apartment on South 55th Street above Congo Village, a bar with live music. There (at the apartment, not the bar) my roommate was about to graduate at my own age, which was 19 by then, but meanwhile he needed a co-renter.

Next door to us, an avant-garde New Left journal named *New University Thought* was being edited and my roommate kept suggesting I get involved with it. I was convinced, however, that the Left contradicted itself. Several students had issued an open invitation to hear them explain socialism. Besides themselves, I was the only person who attended. I asked them how socialism could come about and they told me "By the workers taking over the means of production." But I already knew Marx said the means of production dictated the nature of society. So after the workers take over the means of production, wouldn't the nature of society stay the same as it had been *before* the workers took over the means of production? When I asked them that, they had no answer. I guess I was ready for Dorothy Day's idea of "a new society growing inside the shell of the old society"—a new society with *different* means of production "growing inside the shell of the old society." (She had picked up that saying from the Catholic Worker's co-founder Peter Maurin, a French peasant who had immigrated to the U.S. and advocated going "back to the land." Dorothy and Peter together had launched the Catholic Worker movement and its monthly newspaper on May 1, 1933.)

As it turned out, I would soon cross paths with Dorothy Day in the peace movement, but I never agreed with her that higher education was "the bunk." I had merely lost interest in continuing at the University of Chicago. So I dropped out and started working what turned out to be a dangerous job at Republic Steel Company on South 116th Street in Chicago, working with ten-thousand pound steel billets. One close call which could have been fatal left me with a dented left shinbone.

I saved my steel-working pay for a month, then hitchhiked to New York City and stayed a month in Greenwich Village—a "village" I had always pictured being fifteen miles up the Hudson River from New York City. At first I pictured it as a quaint little village on the riverbank, but then I read something about the "East Village." So I pictured it mostly on the Hudson's west bank but some of it on the east bank. Once there, of course, I stood corrected. And whenever the Metropolitan Opera changed its billing, I paid a dollar to occupy "standing room" along its balcony rail.

Then on April 1st I headed south, as clueless about the South as I had been about Greenwich Village. That's why I didn't understand why the Greyhound bus driver blocked my re-boarding his bus at Chattanooga. I was naïve! It's surprising with just a highway map that I located the Appalachian Trail, even the ex-Trail.

CHAPTER 2

On the ~~Trail~~ Road

Along the Trail (the ex-Trail) "blazes" marred hundreds of tree trunks. Was that *really* why they had moved the official trail thirteen miles east? (Not that I knew they had.) The blazes were hatchet slashes on tree trunks that were painted bright yellow, orange, red and sometimes other colors which must all have meant something to the trail cognoscenti. I just tried to guess which way was north. What spelled my defeat was different: a major snowstorm or ice storm had hit the North Carolina mountains, apparently in March because it hadn't all melted yet by mid-April. The remaining slush was no problem but the storm also left piles of fallen branches mile after mile on top of the trail. Two days of climbing over those and crawling under them and detouring around them, exhausted me.

Finally, about ten miles west of Franklin, North Carolina the trail dipped down to a low gap and crossed a paved road, so I "bailed out" and hitchhiked to Celo Community, located about sixty miles to the northeast, beyond Asheville. Celo was (and still is) a rural 1,100-acre Quaker "intentional community" along the Little Toe River underneath the highest mountains in the eastern United States, Mount Mitchell and the two Black Brothers. My communally-minded Quaker uncle David Salstrom lived there.[1]

My family had visited Uncle David for two weeks in summer 1949. That led a few years later to my receiving an hysterical tongue-lashing from the McCarthyite mother of my best friend. We lived then (in the

---

1. For more on Celo see George L. Hicks, *Experimental Americans* (2001) in which my uncle David Salstrom and his wife Margaret bear the pseudonym "the Nielsons."

early 1950s) in Wisconsin, home state of the Republican Senator Joseph McCarthy. My own family was liberal Democrat. Unbeknownst to me, my best friend's mother was an avid McCarthyite. It turned out she considered Stalinist Russia and Quaker intentional communities to be identical, both being "communist." My best friend instantly became my ex-best friend. As his dad drove me home, he suggested that I be more cautious who I shared my personal opinions with.

Apparently I took his advice, because a year or two later (after my family moved to Rock Island, Illinois) I won Rock Island High School's annual "I Speak for Democracy" contest and then started to worry. I had included (and cited) a glowing paean to democracy from the autobiography of the adventure writer Rockwell Kent—despite my knowing from the book that Rockwell Kent wasn't *just* an adventure writer but was also chairman of the Soviet-American Friendship Committee. I assumed no one connected in any way with Rock Island High School had ever heard of Rockwell Kent (except maybe as a book illustrator) but now I worried that someone at the *state* contest might knew all about him and I'd be skewered for quoting a "pinko" while pretending to "speak for democracy." So one day when my mother told me to take out the trash and burn it, I burned my "I Speak for Democracy" speech too, and next day told the high school people it was lost. Whew.

In April 1960, it turned out my Uncle David was away at Berea College in Kentucky studying to become a college teacher. His friends at Celo put me in his empty house and had me eat meals with another Celo family, so I stayed several days and learned more about rural communal life. Back in 1949 when my family visited Celo, most of the Celoites were supporting themselves by knitting wool Argyll stockings on little knitting machines run by foot petals. By 1960 they had switched over to making vitamins and had also just acquired a herd of 100 milk cows. Plus they were about to start a junior-high boarding school named for Celo Community's founder, Arthur E. Morgan. Morgan had created Celo in 1937 as a non-government project while he was chairman of the government's Tennessee Valley Authority (TVA). The conservative Chicago publisher Henry Regnery gave Arthur Morgan the money to buy Celo's 1,100 acres of land. Morgan turned it into a land trust similar to what are now called *community* land trusts, with the land all owned by the trust but almost all the buildings (mostly houses of course) owned privately.

Celo Community's gravel road along the Little Toe River, about 1960.
Courtesy of Arthur Morgan School, Celo Community.

After a few days at Celo, I hitched rides up and over the Smoky Mountains to Berea, Kentucky to see my uncle. Eastern Kentucky's hillsides
were profusely lush with blooming redbud and dogwood but only a pale
green wisp yet showed of the budding leaves. It was warm and sunny and
Appalachian Spring.

One of my rides was with John Lair, founder of the Renfro Valley Barn
Dance. Mr. Lair was going only as far as Renfro Valley—thirty miles shy
of Berea—but he proudly showed me through the "barn" auditorium, the
radio studio, the restaurant, and the souvenir store.

Then I hitched rides on to Berea, which seemed a lot like what Mr.
Lair had just showed me at Renfro Valley. Except that Berea wasn't just
a theme *park*, it was a whole theme *town* filled with quaint boutiques of
Appalachian arts and crafts and souvenirs.

But ironically, the agenda at Berea College turned out to be the exact
opposite. The college was all about helping its students overcome Appalachia's folksy lifeways by preparing them for modern white-collar careers.
I didn't yet see the irony of Berea, the contradiction between the town's

celebration of tradition and the college's "forward looking" agenda for its students. I didn't yet see that overcoming "backwardness" via white-collar careers, prioritizing your own advancement so as to "get ahead," was eroding what was traditional *out* of Appalachia.

Why? Because Appalachia's arts and crafts and lifeways had all been started and kept going by poor people, not by people in white collars. Those poor people lived by low-budget farming and by crafts, lore, and constant sharing with each other because they had to. If they hadn't been poor they wouldn't have lived that way. When they first settled Appalachia and created its lifeways, most of them were *very* poor—very money-poor—but back then at first they were rich in resources. Appalachia was crammed with natural resources at their fingertips, resources which could sustain them if they husbanded it all and shared it with each other. By sharing it, none of the pioneers or their successors needed to feel they had to control very much personally, or had to compete against each other for their personal economic security or their family's security. They shared the use of their possessions and also their know-how, and often shared their workdays as well. Their sharing could sustain them if they didn't deplete the resources except temporarily. The resources they used were almost all renewable—topsoil of course but also clay; lots of wood; bark for tanning hides; nuts especially chestnuts to eat but also butter-nuts for dye; berries; ginseng and goldenseal and other wild herbs; fish, honey, feathers; and wild animals for meat, grease, leather, fur; and the list goes on—including many more nuts that their hogs ate, particularly acorns.

It turned out that Appalachia held *non*-renewable resources too, particularly the underground fossil fuels—coal, oil, and natural gas. But renewable or non-renewable, the region's rich resources couldn't keep sustaining the people who lived there if they went after personal wealth and careers for themselves by selling off the resources to outsiders and then accepting white-collar jobs to help the outsiders "extract" the resources and ship them somewhere else.

I didn't realize any of this yet. It was only 1960. Only after the '60s and because of the '60s was I ready for traditional Appalachia's answers to America's unsustainable mainstream economy. Not that anyone asked Appalachians for answers to anything. They were just minding their own business, which included trading favors with their kin and neighbors daily. I guess what I didn't have yet in 1960 were my *own* questions, because back then, having "seen through" socialism during my brief college career, I had no idea there was any other alternative to mainstream America. ("Intentional communities" like Celo were an alternative, but they seemed unlikely to proliferate.)

From Berea, I thumbed rides back over the Smoky Mountains to North Carolina. I had decided to skip the Appalachian Trail and instead hike north on the Blue Ridge Parkway before it opened for the season. A few rangers were up on the parkway cruising it in their dark-green pick-up trucks but they didn't mind my walking it. A few nature lovers were up on the parkway too. One middle-aged botanist showed me how to find the early white trillium wake-robins, a wildflower initiation I'll always remember because one of my favorite books as a teenage bookworm had been *Wake-Robin* by John Burroughs.

Eventually the rangers opened the parkway to public traffic and I found myself riding more than walking despite never putting out my thumb to hitchhike. At the town of Shenandoah, Virginia I picked up my general-delivery mail. It was a Sunday but the postmaster heard by the grapevine I was there and opened the post office without being asked. At Washington, DC I paid my respects to Old Abe, my fellow Illinoisan, at his Memorial on the Mall.

Then on as quickly as possible to Maine and its ferry from Bar Harbor to Yarmouth, Nova Scotia. Through the Maritimes including Prince Edward Island and into French Canada, another treasure-store like Appalachia of traditional rural life. At Riviére-du-Loup I decided to skip the Gaspé Peninsula (it was only a week into May) and turned left, going upstream along the south shore of the wide St. Lawrence River. Passed Quebec City across the river at night, passed through Montreal, Ottawa, Sudbury's copper- and nickel-smelting devastation, reentered the United States by ferry at Sault Ste. Marie, crossed the long Mackinac Bridge from Upper into Lower Michigan, on down Lake Michigan's eastern shore and on home to Rock Island, Illinois.

The previous summer (1959), Yvon Chouinard had convinced me to try Yosemite Valley in 1960 rather than spend a fifth summer in the Tetons. That summer of '59 in the Tetons was when Yvon fell 160 feet down the overhanging north face of Teewinot Mountain's Crooked Thumb. A few days later I stopped by his Jenny Lake campsite to see how he was. He showed me a huge gash in his left calf but said he was fine otherwise. His climbing partner Bob Kamps had a deep flaming red burn across the palm of his belaying hand. Bob told me that when Yvon quit falling, he looked to see how much rope was left to play out and there were only three feet left. Since they were roped together, they had both almost fallen thousands of feet.

My trip west to Yosemite Valley was uneventful except for an afternoon in Las Vegas in the custody of Stardust Casino detectives, who took turns grilling me. Once I reached Yosemite Valley, it turned out I didn't personally enjoy its climbing. Handholds and footholds were mostly absent, which meant inching upward by jamming all or parts of yourself into vertical cracks of various widths. (Yvon preferred Teton climbing too, despite the Yosemite Valley climbs he's known for.) I went up just one high-angle valley-to-rim route, the 5.6-rated "Lunch Ledge" route up the crease between the Royal Arches and Washington Column. And I didn't lead the route's gutsy crux pitch since my friend Penny Carr, an experienced Yosemite climber, was perfectly willing to lead that.

Yvon Chouinard got me to organize a beat poetry reading at the Sierra Club's Le Conte Memorial information building. He was still too shy to read anything himself, but a few other California climbers did. Plus, Paul Berner from Seattle read Allen Ginsberg's "Sunflower Sutra" and I read Gregory Corso's "Gasoline." But I didn't like Yosemite's so-called "Teton tea," a really weird *California* concoction. In the actual Tetons, "Teton tea" was just tea from the big campfire teapots fortified with a dollop or two of 150-proof Hudson Bay rum to counteract the cold Wyoming nights.

The prior four summers I'd been up twenty Teton peaks, some by varied routes, and named one of them Buckingham Palace, a name which stuck. My climbing was mostly in 1958 when I had the same climbing partner all summer, and two of the climbs were fairly hard (5.6's), including the Black Chimney on Teewinot Mountain. But my favorite days were ones I spent alone, route-finding and making bird notes aided by the large official topographic map, whose contour lines showed the altitude above sea level. *Accurately*, by the way.

Jackson Hole was in the Transition life zone but the Tetons rose from Jackson Hole through the Canadian and Hudsonian and into the Alpine life zone. My first Teton summer (1956) I had started surveying which birds were in which life zones and when (including time of day), so the rangers told me about Olaus Murie. At park headquarters they let me pour through card-file drawers full of Murie's Teton bird-watching notes that dated back to the 1920s. But the rangers said Murie and his wife Mardy were away that summer in northeastern Alaska with some other conservationists. (Their research camp-out led in 1960 to President Eisenhower creating the Arctic National Wildlife Reserve—now Refuge.)

The next summer, 1957, I reached Jackson Hole by mid-July and dropped by the Murie ranch. A *Life Magazine* photographer was taking pictures non-stop while Olaus told me about his favorite birding spots, first and foremost Alaska Basin in the Hudsonian life zone on the far side of the Teton Range Divide. I had hiked up there the previous summer in mid-August, but he said "right about now" was the best time because the rosy finches would be starting to nest on the Basin's headwall cliffs. He scrutinized my boots (Army surplus, with added lug-rubber soles). Then he asked if I had an ice axe and knew how to use it. I did have one, and being 16 I figured I knew how to use it. But he frowned and dashed into his studio cabin, coming out with an antique ice axe. He wrapped his knobby old knuckles over the axe-head and plunged its scoop into imaginary snow. Then he had me do it a few times.

Next day I loaded my Army-surplus rucksack with camping gear and food for three days. The trail to the Teton Range Divide started up Death Canyon nice and easy, but then it turned right and climbed almost 3,000 altitude feet of switchbacks. Much of the trail was still covered by steep snow chutes. Crossing one of those, I lost my footing and slid downward surprisingly fast, rucksack flapping. Recalling Murie's lesson, I flipped over onto my stomach and gripped a hand over the axe-head and plunged its scoop in the snow. *Voila,* my sliding soon stopped. I felt I'd been initiated into something.

Alaska Basin is a vast amphitheater at about 10,000 feet altitude. Murie had said the rosy finches would be building their nests "right about now" on the basin's headwall cliffs, and they were—thousands of rosy finches flying along the cliffs with long blades of old grass trailing from their beaks, and hovering over the basin's melting snowfields which a month later would become several square miles of flowers six feet high. (Much later it occurred to me Murie had probably named Alaska Basin. He had been in Alaska seven years studying caribou before he came to Jackson Hole in 1927 to study elk.)

Mardy and Olaus Murie in the 1950s.
Courtesy of the Wilderness Society.

When I last saw him, he was hiking up to Alaska Basin again. It was August 1959 and Olaus along with several younger men was climbing the steep switchbacks out of Death Canyon as I was coming down from visiting the Basin. Later his widow Mardy told me Olaus had terminal cancer by then and wanted to see Alaska Basin one more time. Several other conservationists, she said, had volunteered to hike up there with him.

Much later I wrote an essay remembering him but it's never seen print, maybe because it ends by mentioning a letter he wrote me in winter 1962–63. He said he'd seen in a peace periodical that I was in prison for draft refusal and wanted me to know he supported my stand.

I had no any idea Murie cared about peace. When I asked his widow Mardy later, she said some other Wilderness Society leaders told Olaus his efforts on behalf of world peace were "incomprehensible." But not to me. By then I knew Olaus's youthful role model had been Fridtjof Nansen, the famous arctic explorer who in his later life led the League of Nations' refugee work. Nansen became newly re-famous when he received the 1922 Nobel Peace Prize for publicly shaming the western powers into feeding the Ukraine's starving peasants even though their government was communist.

In retrospect, I now realize that my youthful summers camping and hiking in the Tetons prepared me for roughing-it and improvising when I later moved to rural Appalachia and shared its traditional lifeways. But what prepared me to see *wider* importance in rural Appalachia's traditional lifeways—to see their potential as a role-model for future Americans—were my experiences during the 1960s with "alternatives."

CHAPTER 3

Alternatives to
Mainstream America

So summer 1960 took me to Yosemite National Park to climb (and wash dishes at Camp Curry). Then I returned east to the woods along Rock River in north-central Illinois to help my uncle Phil Salstrom start his Rock Wood Carvers machine-woodcarving company. Then after Thanksgiving I hitchhiked west across Kansas and got caught outside overnight in a winter storm with just a flimsy yellow RAF (Royal Air Force) jumpsuit for a sleeping bag. No vehicle had passed for hours. Noticing a round corrugated metal culvert under the road about two feet in diameter, I slid myself inside it feet-first and blocked its opening with my rucksack. I tried to sleep but no sooner would I doze off than a loud "whoosh" of wind would wake me up, only to discover that the culvert was actually calm and windless. Dozing off and jolting awake to that sound of rushing wind continued all night. Strange.

Finally dawn showed at the far end of the culvert. I waited a bit and then climbed back up to the road. A pick-up truck approached across the white emptiness. It stopped and I climbed in with my rucksack and started warming up. The driver was a large middle-aged man who seemed hyper-agitated. He spoke in snippets and asked me over and over if I carried any weapon for self-defense—"a pistol maybe? a knife? at least a little *billy*-club?" He repeated the question every five or ten minutes and I always told him "no, nothing." Once or twice he added "no *blackjack*?" but he always ended with "not even a little *billy*-club? *At least* a *little billy-club*?" Strange man.

Reaching Tucson, I located my summer Yosemite Valley friends who had urged me to join them. We dug ditches a few days to earn money, then drove their old post-war Packard to Seattle for the winter. There I worked two months as an oncology-ward attendant at the University of Washington Hospital. On Sunday mornings I attended the U-District's Quaker Meeting and found out that working as a hospital attendant was often what conscientious objectors did during their two years of alternative service.

My hometown draft board probably had me on its "watch list"—not just for canceling my student deferment while I was still a student, but right from the start when I reached age 18. All young men were supposed to register in-person with their local draft board as soon as they turned 18, but I had turned 18 in the Tetons in mid-August 1958. Once home in Illinois a month later, I did troop into the draft board office and registered, but they were huffy big-time about my being a month late. So I was probably on their "watch list."

Regardless, I decided to try my luck. From Seattle, I wrote my draft board that I considered myself a conscientious objector like my Uncle David had been during World War Two. That led to an official hearing with them when I got to my hometown of Rock Island, Illinois in late March (1961)—a "hearing" at which it turned out they *didn't* want to hear it. The draft board chairman was a vigorous middle-aged man who started the hearing by telling me I was wasting their time because I wasn't Quaker, Amish, Mennonite, Church of the Brethren, or Jehovah's Witness. (I was Augustana Lutheran.) Then he proudly gestured toward an elderly member of the draft board and said he had served in the Philippine War back at the turn of the century. Curiosity got the best of me and I asked the old gentleman, 'Did you see anyone tortured, sir?"

Wrong question apparently. The old fellow meekly answered "We did what we had to do." But then the chairman yelled at me, "We ask the questions here, not you!" The rest of the hearing was brief and *pro forma*.

Summer 1961 found me back in Yosemite Valley as Sierra Club's question-answerer at its Le Conte Memorial information building. There I tried to convince Ansel Adams and some other Sierra Club board members they should set up a process with peace and civil rights groups to explore their commonalities with each other, but Ansel and the others thought it was best for conservationists to stay on their own separate track. One Sierra Club board member did agree with me (Bob West of Los Angeles) but I'm pretty sure nothing came of it.

I learned that Freedom Riders were being signed up in Los Angeles and traveling interracially on Greyhound buses from Los Angeles to Mississippi. I was tempted by that possibility but couldn't bring myself to "abandon ship" and leave Sierra Club in the lurch.

When summer 1961 ended, I hitchhiked east and joined the staff of a peace-movement project I had visited right before coming west. Called Polaris Action, it was located in eastern Connecticut. There I began learning not just how to organize protests but also began learning, from a middle-aged carpenter/builder there named Bob Swann, about non-protest "alternatives" to mainstream America. During those years, Bob Swann was gradually creating the Community Land Trust method of land-holding, among other innovations.

Back then in 1961 the peace movement wasn't yet fully separate from the civil rights movement. We heard about mass evictions of African-American sharecroppers from their small tenant "sharecrop" farms in west Tennessee's Haywood and Fayette counties. Those who were being evicted were among the 700 African Americans who had recently tried to register to vote in those two counties. A tent campground had been hastily erected on a black man's farm and "housed" many of the most destitute of the evicted sharecroppers.[2]

As that news reached us at the peace project in Connecticut, Bob Swann suggested we try to create a leather-working project on-site in west Tennessee, so that some at least of the evicted sharecroppers could earn some money. So three of us young peace activists went to Rindge, New Hampshire's Quaker boarding high school and learned from Bill Coperthwaite (soon to become America's pioneer yurt builder) how to make leather tote bags with braided leather shoulder straps. Bill Coperthwaite was a whiz at many crafts.

We spent three days learning leatherwork from Bill Coperthwaite and then went to New York City and met with the national youth committee of CORE, the organization that was sponsoring the Freedom Rides. They decided to buy one of us a one-way bus ticket to Brownsville in Haywood

2. For more, see Robert Hamburger, *Our Portion of Hell: Fayette County, Tennessee: An Oral History of the Struggle for Civil Rights* (1973).

County, Tennessee and designated me. But I had already been ordered to report for induction into the Army and expected to be arrested and imprisoned at any time, so I asked my fellow leather-work apprentice Eric Weinberger to go there instead. (Eric was also my fellow University of Chicago dropout. In the late 1940's he had started there at age 15 but got fed up and dropped out at age 17.)

Eric did go to west Tennessee using the bus ticket CORE provided. Despite his first few weeks in jail being tortured daily with an electric cattle prod and severely beaten several times, he got the leather project going as the Haywood (Tenn.) Handicrafters League. It eventually sold 3,000-plus leather tote-bags by mail. Meanwhile, its influence spread south into northwestern Mississippi's Delta region (which is the Yazoo River delta, not the Mississippi River delta). There a "Poor People's Corporation" was founded and distributed numerous locally-made tote bags and other leather products, and soon many *non*-leather locally-made products, through its Liberty House retail stores in northern U.S. cities. (The later-notorious Abbie Hoffman managed the smallest of the Liberty House stores, which was in New York City's Greenwich Village.)

In early November 1961 my hometown draft board had ordered me to report for induction into the Army, and late in December an FBI agent arrested me while I was vigiling about that in front of my hometown federal building, the site of the draft board office. Then, surprisingly, came six months of "pre-sentence investigation" until they realized I was out east on a peace walk.[3]

I was ordered to appear in three days in federal court in my hometown of Rock Island, Illinois and was sentenced to three years in prison. The Connecticut peace project—which by then was known as "Voluntown Peace Farm"—kept me on its staff throughout those three years and sometimes it carried out peace projects that I suggested in long, detailed letters.

Since at first I was hunger striking, the FBI agent transported me to the Medical Center for Federal Prisoners near Springfield, Missouri, where I was soon befriended by the songwriter Chuck Berry, the spy Morton Sobell, and Robert Stroud the Birdman of Alcatraz, among others. I was

---

3. That peace walk is described by Thomas B. Morgan, "Doom and Passion along Rt. 45," *Esquire* magazine, Nov. 1962.

there two years until my "good time" release. They told me they would cancel all my good time (almost a year's worth) if I didn't sign my name at the bottom of a list of extra-tight restrictions they had devised for me. I didn't sign and they didn't cancel my "good time" after all. Either they were bluffing or they changed their minds. Although I didn't sign the list of restrictions, they re-arrested me when I moved to New Hampshire in August 1964 to pick apples. Then came nine months of "backing up good time" (convict lingo) at the federal prison in Danbury, Connecticut, where the Living Theater director Julian Beck befriended me. I applied to work on the prison farm, which had been my job for a year at the prison in Missouri, but the U.S. Bureau of Prisons had just abolished all of its job-training for released convicts to become farmers or farm hands, and Danbury Prison had therefore just abolished its farm. So they assigned me to help run the prison's art room.

Once freed in July 1965, I became aware that I had grown emotionally dissociated. Only very gradually did I start feeling emotions again, and only thanks to friends.

And thanks to nature. At Voluntown Peace Farm after prison, I helped start a children's camp in a hemlock forest located behind the Peace Farm, where a Finnish-American camp had once flourished on Beech Pond, the largest *lake* in Connecticut, stretching (the *lake*) well into Rhode Island. There I served as resident caretaker, including of the camp's old-fashioned firewood-heated sauna next to a very cold stream named Bliven Brook.[4]

But then a year later, in fall 1966 came a painful parting of our ways, a parting that ironically came about due to nonviolent peacekeeping, which for several years by then had been my particular interest. Despite the Vietnam War rapidly escalating, I felt that more than protests were needed—that an actual on-site alternative way of dealing with international conflicts was needed, an alternative not just to military conflict but also to military peacekeeping by the United Nations. I thought independent nonviolent peacekeeping projects could gradually pull U.N. peacekeeping in the direction of nonviolence, so I laid out four steps for

4. A vibrant account of the Voluntown Peace Farm and its many activities in the mid-1960s is Chapter 6 in Stephanie Mills' biography of Bob Swann, *On Gandhi's Path* (2010).

the professionalization of nonviolent peacekeeping, including a Peace-makers Academy and two types of internships. A code of ethics similar to doctors' and lawyers' ethical codes seemed desirable as well.[5]

Meanwhile, living and working with us at Voluntown Peace Farm dur-ing summer 1966 was a traumatized Vietnam War medic named Moe Armstrong who would later help create the Vet-to-Vet movement. Moe wasn't a conscientious objector. In fact he had hoped to join the SEALS, but the Marines made him a medic. He had recently been flown back from Vietnam almost catatonic, and now he was in eastern Connecticut searching for the sister of his best buddy, who had died in Vietnam. Moe had begun corresponding with his friend's sister while he was still in Vietnam.

Moe was suicidal, so while searching for his friend's sister he also went to New Haven's Veterans Administration (VA) hospital for help, but they told him they didn't do psychology and couldn't help him—even though when he was first brought back from Vietnam he *had* been helped psy-chologically at the Navy hospital in Oakland, California. Then someone told him about our Peace Farm in the town of Voluntown on the far eastern edge of Connecticut, and one day he just showed up. We told him he could stay and help out.

We didn't "use" Moe whatsoever. Most of the peace movement was obsessed with Vietnam by then (summer 1966) but we kept Moe anony-mous as regards where he had been, and he seemed to get better. A cou-ple years later he became lead singer of the clamorous rock band Daddy Long Legs which made a splash briefly in England, especially with its hit "Tell the Captain." Much later, Moe went back to school for two bach-elor's degrees and then two Master's degrees related to psychology. After 9/11 led to the U.S. war in Afghanistan, Moe helped start Vet-to-Vet and soon became its spark plug. "Each one reach one" became his motto, and "gladly teach / gladly learn."

---

5. My short book on nonviolent peacekeeping was never published, but Arthur Waskow's short book was: *Toward a Peacemakers Academy* (1967). Our efforts led in 1970 to the International Peace Academy (IPA), founded by the philanthropist Ruth Forbes Young and the retired U.N. military advisor Gen. Indar Jit Rikhye. The IPA was not actually an academy, however, and in 2008 it changed its name to International Peace Institute.

Vet-to-Vet hit the ground running, creating many venues for interaction between Vietnam War vets who were still living with Post Traumatic Stress Disorder (PTSD) and Afghan War vets (and soon also Iraq War vets) who were new to PTSD and might want to hear Vietnam vets share their longer experience with that affliction. The Iraq War's "Marlboro Marine" James Blake Miller became the best-known participant at Moe's six-month PTSD in-patient therapy program in West Haven, Connecticut. Miller, however, stayed there only two months and remained troubled by PTSD.

During the summer of 1966 when Moe Armstrong was helping us at Voluntown Peace Farm, most of the peace movement was busy trying to escalate its anti-war protests as fast as the Vietnam War was escalating. Obsession with numbers had led most peace-movement leaders to accept Far Left participants at their anti-war protests without demanding any commitment to nonviolence. That soon led to storefront windows being smashed, police being called pigs, returning veterans being shunned, and now one end result of those "do your own thing" anti-war protests is that the people who protested the Vietnam War are hated even more than the war itself has come to be hated. End of sermon (this one).[6]

Meanwhile, I had re-crossed paths in summer 1965 with the leather tote-bag maker Bill Coperthwaite and he invited me up to Bucks Harbor, near the eastern end of Maine where he was somehow acquiring 500 acres of coastline. There he was building modern America's first yurt made entirely from unprocessed materials—entirely, that is, except for the yurt's woven steel-wire "tension cable" that held it together around its girth, plus little wires we inserted through little drilled holes and then twisted tight, locking together all the crossings of the bouncy alder-tree saplings that were crisscrossed into a lattice and tapered slightly outward to create the yurt's continuous 360-degree round wall. The yurt's roof rafters were pine "tepee" poles reaching from its steel-wire tension cable up to a circular six-foot-diameter smoke hole at the very top.

We covered the outer wall and the roof with birch-bark shingles, which we had to keep damp from the moment we cut them off the birch

---

6. The full story of the peace movement's anti-war coalition with the Far Left from 1965 to 1975 is accurately told by Tom Wells, *The War Within* (1994). In my opinion, that coalition was one long counter-productive squabble.

Bill Coperthwaite about 1987.
Photo by Abbie Sewall.

trees to the moment we put them on the wall and roof of the yurt. If not kept damp, they would start to curl inward. Within a year, in fact, they *did* all curl inward so badly they had to all be taken off and replaced with something else. So much for that idea.

Even before the birch bark curled, I began doubting Bill Coperthwaite's infallibility when he told me we two could be the first human beings to cross Davis Strait from Labrador to Greenland in a two-kayak catamaran. The prevailing wind, he said, could propel us across Davis Strait in twenty-four hours if we simply hoisted a sail. But if a storm hit, he added, we'd have to take down the sail and unlash the two kayaks from each other, since we'd be goners if the kayaks tipped over while they were lashed together. With luck, he said, we could join back up again after the storm and re-lash the two kayaks back together and raise the sail back up.

I had enough sense by then (1965) to tell Bill Coperthwaite "no thanks." But the next summer I was in charge of Moe Armstrong and the five other Counselors-in-Training (CITs) at the hemlock-forested children's camp located behind Voluntown Peace Farm, so I used the Peace Farm's Volkswagen "bus" to drive the CITs up to Bucks Harbor, Maine to let them learn survival skills for a few days from Bill Coperthwaite—digging and baking clams, de-treeing and skinning porcupines to eat them too (—they tasted like rabbit sautéed in spruce sap), and so on. By then Bill had a new brainstorm. He wanted me to go build yurts with him that fall in Fairbanks, Alaska. It sounded slightly less fatal than trying to cross Davis Strait in a kayak catamaran so I told Bill "maybe."

By the time fall arrived, however, I was busy earning money in Strafford, Vermont re-establishing a commercial "sugar bush" (a stand of sap-producing maple trees) on ten acres of sugar-maple trees that hadn't been "sugared" (tapped for sap) for eighty years. The young landowner and I meanwhile set up an economic Sharing Plan that soon grew to ten individual and household members—none of them local Vermonters (too individualistic). For that collaboration the young landlord paid me room-and-board, and the U.S. Department of Agriculture paid me $20 for each of the ten wooded acres that I "economically improved"—$200 total, but it took all fall because I corded all the logs so the young landlord could burn them as firewood. (The next spring, 1967, the stand of maple trees went into profitable production using gravity-fed hoses to gather the sap, but by then I was 3,000 miles away in Haight-Ashbury.)

So Bill Coperthwaite and I didn't start west until late December 1966. After Christmas festivities with my family at Rock Island, Illinois our next stop was Jackson Hole, Wyoming since I still wasn't sure I wanted to go any closer than that to mid-winter in Fairbanks, Alaska. Which was in fact what I decided once I landed a dishwashing job at Teton Village ski resort. (Did I ski? No, not crazy enough!) Also at Teton Village we visited the legendary Teton climbing guide Paul Petzoldt and he hired us to work for him the next summer in Wyoming's Wind River Mountains, where he ran a wilderness-immersion program similar to what he had helped start for Outward Bound in Colorado. Paul Petzoldt called his month-long wilderness immersion in the Wind River Mountains the National Outdoor Leadership School (NOLS). He hired Bill Coperthwaite to run its provisioning for summer 1967 and myself to take photos for a feature article *Life Magazine* planned to publish.

We also visited Reggie and Gladys Laubin (authors of *The Indian Tipi*) at their large tepee on a bluff overlooking Snake River. Reggie and Bill talked tepee and yurt ventilation all afternoon—I should have made notes.

I remained in Jackson Hole that winter and rented a cabin from a rancher while Bill Coperthwaite drove his pick-up-truck-camper on to

Fairbanks. In fact, he was *paid* to drive there. A semi-truck driver bought all his gas and meals for driving the entire Alcan Highway closely behind his semi-truck with his taillights on, since the trucker's own taillights had failed and it was dark almost around the clock that far north in January. Coperthwaite didn't make much progress building yurts until Fairbanks started to thaw, but then he did build a few, in the process teaching some other people how to build them and thereby starting a Fairbanks yurt craze. Today, a lot of Fairbanks' many yurts are seasonal rentals, but some of them are winterized against the worst of Fairbanks weather and are lived in year-round.

Bill Coperthwaite drove back south to Wyoming and carried out his NOLS summer 1967 job, but I was busy that spring and summer in Haight-Ashbury, trying to help solve the Vietnam War with a compromise plan. Jon J. Read, Wally Cox and I corresponded heavily with the retired general James Gavin about his "Enclave Plan" for South Vietnam, which our plan resembled. The front-runner for the 1968 Republican presidential nomination was Nelson Rockefeller, and he had General Gavin in mind for the vice-presidency. Arthur Schlesinger Jr. joined in our barrage of brainstorming letters, so it was bi-partisan since Schlesinger was a Democrat.[7]

The main difference between the two plans was that Gen. Gavin wanted the U.S. to *unilaterally* turn South Vietnam's cities into fortified "enclaves"—which is what the British had done successfully in Malaya in the 1950s—whereas our "Free Cities Plan" wanted the urban/rural dividing up of South Vietnam to occur by agreement with the National Liberation Front (Viet Cong) in exchange for our leaving the countryside to their control—since they already controlled it at night anyway.

But it all came to nothing. Neither of those two peace plans was ever tried. Richard Nixon saw to that after he edged out Nelson Rockefeller for the Republican presidential nomination, and then went on in November 1968 to win the presidential election with the help of treasonous secret negotiations with South Vietnam's president Thieu that came to light several years ago.[8]

---

7. See Jon J. Read and Paul Salstrom, "The Free Cities Plan," The *Humanist,* January-February 1968, pp. 12–15. About Gen. James Gavin's Enclave Plan, see his 1968 book *Crisis Now,* Chapter 3: "Vietnam: History and Resolution."

8. Richard Nixon's treasonous (and successful) secret fall 1968 negotiations with

So it wasn't that I *ignored* the Vietnam War. As soon as I reached the Bay Area from the Tetons that spring of 1967, I learned from a new group called The Resistance about a confidential "channeling" memo issued in July 1965 by Selective Service to all its local draft boards. The memo justified the "channeling" of young men that Selective Service had been secretly doing by then for at least ten years—since the early or mid-1950s. It's a six-page memo, single-spaced, but I'll quote a few sentences about what the memo called "channeling manpower":

> Many young men would not have pursued a higher education if there had not been a program of student deferment [from the draft]. . . . A million and a half [draft] registrants are now deferred as students. One reason the Nation is not in shorter supply of engineers today is that they were among the students deferred by Selective Service in previous years. . . . Throughout his career as a student, the pressure—the threat of loss of deferment—continues. . . . The psychology of granting wide choice under pressure to take action is the American or indirect way of achieving what is done by direction in foreign countries where choice is not permitted. Here, choice is limited but not denied. . . . Selective Service processes do not compel people by edict as in foreign systems to enter pursuits having to do with essentiality and progress. They go [to college] because they know that by going they will be deferred [from the draft]. . ."[9]

Finding out about "channeling" by Selective Service made me all the happier that I had terminated my student draft deferment back while in college. "Channeling" was the reason why young male African Americans were being killed and wounded in Vietnam at a higher rate than

---

South Vietnam's President Thieu to pull South Vietnam out of planned Paris Peace Talks (which were scheduled for January 1969) was discovered in both Washington, DC and Saigon several weeks before the November 1968 U.S. presidential election. Nixon's treachery and its discovery in Washington, DC is documented by Lawrence O'Donnell's book *Playing with Fire* (2017) in its Chapter 30: "The Perfect Crime," pp. 376–419.

9. The full six-page memo was accessed online on June 4, 2020, by entering: Selective Service System "Channeling." See also Amy J. Rutenberg, "How the Draft Reshaped America," *New York Times*, Oct. 6, 2017.

young male African Americans' percentage of America's total young male population.

In August 1967, I was hired to spend the 1967–68 school year starting an African-American youth center in a small ghetto in Philadelphia. The site was an expensive new wing added on to an old historic Quaker Meeting House. For my living quarters, the civil rights pioneers Wally and Juanita Nelson provided the third floor of their house in one of Philadelphia's other small-sized ghettos, Powelton Village.

At the youth center, things got dicey sometimes because that was the year Black Power hit Philadelphia, or anyway reached our small ghetto of East Frankford. My minimum-wage salary of $1.40 an hour was paid through the YWCA, which also made its nearby West Frankford neighborhood headquarters available for any resources or work stations that I needed for the making of announcement fliers, press releases, meeting minutes, etc.

We had after-school children's clubs run by female college students who were majoring in education. We had a wonderful Saturday children's party featuring the professional children's party-giver and puppeteer Pipp Bauman. We had junior-high-school aged clubs run by our own in-house gang The Brothers Incorporated, which consisted of male high-school students and dropouts. We even had a special branch of the state employment office. We held a few high-school aged dances, but neighbors complained about the late-night noise.

Martin Luther King gave a high-profile speech at a Philadelphia junior high school that fall of 1967. When he was murdered in April 1968, the Brothers and I held a somber public demonstration on our local main street, Frankford Avenue, a street which divided blacks to its east from whites to its west. Dr. King's murder didn't lead to any rioting in Philadelphia, but as we vigiled on Frankford Avenue we could see pillars of smoke far to the south that were rising from riot fires in Wilmington, Delaware.

Right about then Chuck Berry came through Philadelphia on tour. I should have tracked him down and invited him to visit the youth center. The media could have been invited to stop by and meet him, gaining the youth center some good publicity. Chuck and I just couldn't have let on that we already knew each other, since that had been in prison. Back when we were in prison, I didn't know he was famous. I just knew he owned two St. Louis nightclubs and was a chess whiz.

I did arrange for my landlord, the civil-rights pioneer Wally Nelson, to meet the Brothers. Wally told them some of the inside story of the civil rights movement—such as why Martin Luther King was chosen to lead the Montgomery Bus Boycott. When Rosa Parks was arrested in Montgomery, Wally and some other civil rights leaders remembered Montgomery was where their old friend Coretta Scott now lived. Back when Coretta had attended Antioch College in Ohio (class of 1951) she had become involved with a tiny group called Peacemakers, which Wally and Juanita Nelson co-founded in 1948. Among other activities, Coretta helped Wally and Juanita gather supplies to transport to sharecroppers in Haywood and Fayette counties in Tennessee. She also became Bob and Marj Swann's babysitter. Wally didn't yet know Coretta's husband, the young preacher she had married in 1953. But he figured that anyone who Coretta would consent to marry must be all right.

As the bus boycott started in Montgomery in December 1955, civil-rights work was new to Coretta's young preacher husband, so Wally Nelson and Bayard Rustin stayed on in Montgomery for a few weeks to troubleshoot—and then it almost all went *smash* because young Dr. King angrily accused them of fabricating what he allegedly said at the bus boycott's mass meetings in his church. Fortunately, one or two of those meetings had been tape-recorded, so Wally and Bayard played the tapes to Dr. King and he finally had to admit that exalted claims for the power of love and nonviolence had indeed come out of his own mouth.

(Later in rural Appalachia, I learned about "preaching in the Spirit" and found out preachers can barely remember anything they say while doing it. So Dr. King's inability to remember his famous first civil rights speeches apparently means he started his civil-rights ministry inspired.)

By when the 1967–68 school year ended, I realized that urban community organizing was *not* my calling and I happily turned the youth center over to a new director who was African American. By that point I felt the Tetons calling, so I returned that summer of 1968 for a long-postponed fifth summer in Jackson Hole. My last summer there had been 1959, before summers 1960 and '61 in Yosemite Valley.

By 1968 Jackson Hole was no longer the same. Its airport had been enlarged to accommodate jet airplanes and Jackson Hole was being gentrified by and for people who arrived and departed in jets.

Then one morning "out of nowhere" I woke up with a conviction that

America was going to need millions of small farms. I was camping then in northern Jackson Hole on the shore of Leigh Lake across from its Mystic Isle, but I hurried down the valley to the Murie Ranch, where I knew my conservationist friend Mardy Murie would have a spare typewriter. She urged me to take a conservation-movement job but I declined.

I sat there at the Murie ranch typing a long article on America's future need for millions of small farms and sent the article to one of the largest "underground" newspapers, the *Los Angeles Free Press*, which published it. Suddenly I was very, very ready for Appalachia but I barely even knew it existed as a distinct region. Despite my foreshortened Appalachian Trail hike back in spring 1960, I knew almost nothing about Appalachia. There, a model already existed for the millions of small farms that I suddenly felt future Americans were going to need, but I didn't realize it. I hadn't yet seen Appalachia at close quarters.

CHAPTER 4

From Woodstock to West Virginia

The Woodstock Festival wasn't my type of event but my cousin Lois Salstrom insisted. She's the daughter of my woodworking/businessman Uncle Phil. At Kent State University in Ohio where she attended college, and *to* where she falsely told her parents she had to return early (several weeks *before* the fall 1969 classes started) Lois rendezvoused with her fellow-student boyfriend, who had a car. They came and picked me up in Philadelphia (so she says) and we headed north toward the festival. After hours of inching along the last ten miles, we finally arrived as the infamous *rain* let loose.

My memory of who played music is sketchy. Crosby, Stills, and Nash seemed to play a long time. Arlo Guthrie resisted pleas from the audience to perform his twenty-minute masterpiece "Alice's Restaurant" in favor of something about Moses and the Israelites wandering in the wilderness, just as whimsical as "Alice's Restaurant" but lacking Arlo's own quirky troubles with the powers that be.

Saturday around mid-afternoon the rain slowed to a drizzle and I was walking to fetch something from the car when the loud speakers said someone named Yogi Bhajan would next lead kundalini yoga exercises on stage. That sounded like a blessed reduction of decibels so I found a big wet clump of grass to sit down on (the alternative was mud). It turned out I liked Yogi Bhajan's exercises and continued doing them afterwards. My cousin Lois and her boyfriend ended up in the Woodstock feature film. They're the young couple walking through the right half of the split screen 18.15 minutes into the film, with Lois wearing a sea-green shirt. Myself, I ended up doing kundalini yoga.

Usually every fall I would live with some friends in Derry, New Hampshire in a cold unheated summer cabin on Derry Pond (a large *lake*) and pick apples up the road at Apple Hill Farm, earning enough money to last the entire next year. But in fall 1969 Apple Hill Farm had Jamaican apple pickers and didn't need us. Instead, I visited my Uncle David Salstrom near Lock Haven, Pennsylvania—my communal and pacifist Quaker uncle from Celo Community in the North Carolina mountains who had gone back to school at Berea College in Kentucky. Now in 1969 he was teaching education at Lock Haven State College in north-central Pennsylvania.

He lived at the foot of a mountain and I did my kundalini yoga where the mountain came down to his back yard and a tangle of snapdragons or hollyhocks grew up against his stucco garage. One afternoon I noticed a thin little man, neither old nor young, slightly under four feet tall and wearing green clothes with a pointed green hat on his head. He was examining the flowers and was transparent. He immediately realized I could see him. Turning his head, he shot me a sharp look that started suspicious and ended certain. Then he turned his head away and over the next few seconds gradually faded into thin air—he must have amped up his frequency. If I knew any more about this transparent little man in green clothes, I'd be glad to tell you. Or you can try kundalini yoga for yourself but that's not advisable without expert instruction.

Personally I suspect transparent "little people" are related to, if not identical with, the imaginary playmates of children. My daughter (who comes along later) reveled until she was five or six years old with some mysterious beings she called "my friends who live in the woods," and she would have continued playing with them longer if I hadn't foolishly asked her whether they were real. Her face went blank as she grappled with that question, which I then knew I should not have asked.

Eve Ananda's cousin and summer playmate Seoka was also still an only child. She lived with her parents on a remote wooded ridgetop in Lincoln County, West Virginia, and she too had at least one imaginary playmate until she was five years old, a playmate she called Dodie. I suspect imaginary playmates and transparent "little people" are related, if not identical. If you consider such people unreal, that's fine.

As Christmas neared, I bade my uncle "Merry Christmas" and hitched rides west to Rock Island, Illinois for the annual family festivities there.

Then, skimping on funds due to missing apple work that fall, I decided to spend the rest of that winter doing kundalini yoga on the Pacific Ocean beaches of far southern Mexico—an idiotic plan, but my friend Lawrence Goldsmith of Heathcote Mill (in rural Maryland) had spent the previous winter living on those beaches free of charge with no problem. He gave me detailed directions.

It didn't work. I didn't get anywhere near the beaches, only to Oaxaca, where I was followed around. Apparently I looked suspicious—my beard perhaps? or my lack of Spanish? or my destination of Salina Cruz on the south coast? Walking though the open-air Central Market, a sweet little old lady hissed "Yankee go home" right after I passed her fruit stand. Oaxaca's bus station clerk sternly told me to return to the U.S. and then he made sure I missed the one-a-day bus to Salina Cruz by not announcing it. So I gave up and bought a ticket for Santa Fe, New Mexico.

Back in the U.S. from that Mexican fiasco, I headed for Arroyo Hondo in northern New Mexico where my Seattle friend Paul Berner reportedly lived at New Buffalo Commune near the Rio Grande River. At New Buffalo they told me my friend had moved north to Colorado and reportedly lived as a hermit in a cave on Greenhorn Mountain above Libre Commune on the north edge of Huerfano Valley.

But a different friend *was* at Arroyo Hondo, an energetic peace movement friend in her early 50's named Elaine Mikels. She was starting a dairy-goat farm on the arroyo's north rim and asked me to stay and help her get the place going. I told her I'd return later, and finally I did return six months later and stayed there eight months learning about her ten dairy goats and growing to love them (all except the billy-goat, who was still juvenile but already obstreperous). And growing also to love raw goat's milk and the goat cheese, cottage cheese, and yogurt we made and sold. We also made goat's milk ice cream but promptly ate it all.

Before that eight-month stint with dairy goats and chickens (over 100 pesky chickens since we sold eggs too), I hitchhiked north to Huerfano Valley in Colorado to locate Libre Commune and find out what my old Seattle friend thought he was doing living in a cave. The last five miles to Libre was a dirt road climbing up through rolling hills of dry grass. Mountain bluebirds fluttered in small dry trees along both sides of the road. Libre Commune sat nestled between two ridges at the foot of Greenhorn Mountain, and sure enough my friend was indeed at his cave a short way up the mountain. He told me he had just spent a terrifying spell in the throes of *sammadi* (awareness of oneness with the universe) and then told me "the other cave is vacant, so you can live there if you want." Its prior occupant, Nanao Sakaki, had recently departed south to New Mexico.

The other cave, in fact, *looked* far south—it overlooked Libre's bright silver geodesic domes and the entire upper Huerfano Valley, with the Sangre de Cristo Mountains beyond, and beyond the first row of the Sangres rose 14,344-foot Blanca Peak. On the cave's floor, Nanao had left three wool blankets folded on a deerskin for whoever lived there next. I had a sleeping bag with me as well, thankfully. At dusk, a fussy Canyon Wren informed me I was trespassing.

In World War Two, Nanao Sakaki had commanded a radar station in far southern Japan. On the morning of August 9, 1945, his radar tracked several American B-29 bombers approaching Japan. Nanao knew what had happened to Hiroshima three days before, so he suspected what one of those B-29s was probably carrying. He tried to have some of Japan's few remaining fighter planes attack the B-29s, but failed.

After Nagasaki was destroyed that morning, Nanao in frustration wanted to become a hermit, but first he worked for six years to save money. Then in the early 1950s he went to a remote part of Japan's northern island of Hokkaido and lived as a hermit.

In 1966, Nanao somewhat reemerged by publishing a book of poems. Thereby he crossed paths with the Zen-minded American poet Gary Snyder, who convinced him he could be a hermit in America and maybe do some good. Nanao left Japan for America in 1969 and soon settled at the cave above Libre Commune, but in January 1970 he moved south to New Mexico and I never did meet him.

Meditating at Nanao's cave proved interesting. The high altitude obviously mattered, about 9,200 feet above sea level. My physical awareness would all pull upward until only my head felt anything. Every few seconds a pulse of light would start behind my forehead and flow out like a receding tunnel. I had read a booklet about "color healing" so I thought of those light pulses as going out to people who needed healing. Concurrently, although my eyes were closed, everyone in the world seemed very far below, down at the bottom of shimmering filaments of light that seemed to be billowing in some sort of breeze. It would all last about fifteen minutes and then whatever energy it ran on would evidently run down, returning my awareness back down to normal.

One day on a whim I climbed Greenhorn Mountain—very unwise since I hadn't told anyone and the snow, although powdery, was often waist deep. (Libre folks said snowfall had been unusually heavy that winter of 1969–70.) I tried to stay on a ridge but nonetheless could have fallen into a snow cave with no way to get out. It was a sharp, clear day, and looking north from Greenhorn's summit (at 12,300 feet) a diamond-shaped mountain was visible about sixty miles north, higher than everything else and gleaming in the sun. It must have been Pikes Peak.

My month at Nanao's cave was very good for me. All the meditation seemed somehow to end my post-prison emotional dissociation. I left on March 1, 1970 and left the blankets on the deerskin where Nanao had left them before. That spring I spent walking along the northern California coast and then started hitchhiking east. While I was en route, on May 4th, four students were killed at Kent State University and nine wounded, almost but not quite adding my cousin Lois Salstrom among the victims (my Woodstock Festival cousin).

When I reached Kent a few days later, Lois took me by a circuitous route to within two blocks of the campus Commons shooting knoll. She said National Guardsmen couldn't be eluded any closer so we didn't try. She and about nine other students had dived behind the second car in Taylor Parking Lot at the foot of the knoll, a light-green Chevrolet Nova. She says, "I thought the guard was firing tear gas, but when I realized it was live ammo, I retreated down the hill to the Taylor parking lot and got behind a light green nova. When it got quiet, I stood up to discover the windows of the vehicle had been shattered by bullets. I think I dropped down in shock and looked to my right where I saw Jeff Miller bleeding out."[10]

On the evening of the shooting day, May 4th, Lois's landlady told her that, the night before, she had been at a bar in Kent and a guardsman who was also at the bar told her that the next day there would be shootings, as indeed it turned out there were.

In hopes some Kent State students would want to march on foot to Washington, DC, I put out word I was willing to do the advance work for

10. Lois Salstrom Chertow, email to author, May 24, 2020.

Kent State shooting, showing the VW beetle convertible and then the
Chevrolet Nova in Taylor Parking Lot. The girl in the black-and-white
striped shirt looks like Lois Salstrom. Courtesy of Kent State
University Libraries, Special Collections and Archives.

them, but so far as I could discover, no one wanted to march to Washington, DC. Not right away, at least. Everyone seemed hunkered down and virtually in hiding. The spirit of the 1960s seemed over and done with. (Actually, it wasn't quite over yet. It just felt that way to me in Kent after the shootings.)

The '60s had whisked me around-the-block politically, but in the process I think I lost something. Not hope, since I hadn't felt very hopeful to start with, but I still thought that certain steps—a *lot* of steps actually—might help the U.S. pull itself together. By 1970, however, the big 1960s movements had lost interest in "steps." They were demanding big changes and fast. Personally, I believed in taking steps (still do). The only big political change the United States could make *quickly* would be to fascism. That seemed obvious then and it still seems obvious. The last thing the U.S. needs is a "revolutionary moment" of constitutional gridlock or any other kind of gridlock.

Personally, I had been focused on non-protest "alternatives" rather than protests for five years by then—ever since attending, back in August 1965, the first large "coalition" demonstration against the Vietnam War. It was called the Assembly of Unrepresented People. ("Coalition" meant that the peace movement leaders who organized the protests invited the Far Left to attend them and to do more or less whatever they wanted to do during the protests.)

We protestors had gathered in Washington, DC on August 6th, 1965, and marched up the Mall to the U.S. Capitol grounds, where the protest quickly turned disastrous—with Far Left youngsters in the back of the crowd yelling obscene insults at the police up front, and the police up front responding with billy-club knocks to the heads of pacifists upfront who were committing civil disobedience in a nonviolent sit-down. I was incredulous that the organizers of the protest (Dave Dellinger and Staughton Lynd) acted as though everything was hunky-dory. *It was not.*

What I saw and heard at that first large coalition event was a turning point in my life. Joan Baez had foreseen what was coming and she and her Institute for the Study of Nonviolence group distanced themselves from the march up the Mall. Instead, later on the same day, they held a disciplined nonviolent civil disobedience sit-down in front of the White House and got arrested.

I argued as hard as I could against the majority of the peace movement's new coalition with the Far Left, and particularly against the coalition's policy of allowing protestors to "do their own thing." But my arguments were futile because several months earlier (in February 1965) the U.S. had started bombing North Vietnam daily, and in March 1965 President Johnson had suddenly started sending large numbers of U.S. troops (soon including Moe Armstrong) into South Vietnam. Therefore the peace movement's top leaders wanted to just as quickly multiply the number of antiwar demonstrators. They wanted to rapidly multiply the crowd sizes at antiwar demonstrations.

One idea for strengthening the *nonviolent* movement was to try placing American "voluntary peace hostages" in North Vietnam to help rebuild a U.S.-bombed hospital there, and then to organize nonviolent vigils in the U.S. to increase public awareness of those American "voluntary peace hostages" in North Vietnam. My older colleague Bob Swann of Voluntown Peace Farm agreed and, at his request, the Yale historian Staughton Lynd conveyed our offer to North Vietnam when he went to Hanoi at Christmastime 1965 with the young activist Tom Hayden and the aging communist scholar Herbert Aptheker.

In Hanoi, Staughton Lynd set forth our offer to North Vietnam's premier, Pham Van Dong, telling Pham that a group of American pacifists wanted to come to North Vietnam as voluntary peace hostages and help rebuild the U.S.-bombed hospital. In reply, Pham told Staughton Lynd that the DRV (North Vietnam) was turning down *all* foreign offers of on-site assistance of any kind because allowing in foreigners would turn the Vietnam War into a re-run of the Spanish Civil War of the late 1930s—into an international ideological struggle rather than what it actually was—a big country beating up a small country. Pham said he had just turned down a team of twelve Italian doctors who were all communists. He said the DRV had reluctantly accepted 4,000 Chinese railroad-repair workers because his country literally couldn't keep going without them, but that the only way the DRV could stay free of Chinese political control was by turning down *all* other offers of on-site help so that China couldn't force any more Chinese help on them. So right then and there, the idea for American voluntary peace hostages in North Vietnam reached a dead end.

Since I wasn't organizing for the new coalition between pacifists and the Far Left, and since voluntary peace hostages weren't going to be allowed into North Vietnam, I began looking closer at newly emerging non-protest "alternatives." Besides ideas for nonviolent peacekeeping those included community land trusts as alternative land holding, yurts as alternative housing, low-budget farming, rural apprenticeships, economic sharing plans, micro lending, and supplemental local currencies (supplemental to the U.S. dollar).

Those were just a small fraction of the "alternatives" that kept popping up in the 1960s but those were the ones I personally explored most, often following the lead of Bob Swann. For instance, Bob Swann invented community land trusts in the mid-1960s and then grew involved in micro-financing as a logical companion of such land trusts. Back then micro-lending was in its infancy and was still called "supervised agricultural credit."[11]

---

11. In winter 1965–66, Bob Swann and I both started collaborating with Ralph Borsodi, who thirty years earlier had founded the School of Living. The best account of our ambitious micro-finance plan is in Loren Gatch, "Dr. Borsodi's Constant," *Paper Money* magazine, Sept.–Oct. 2013, pp. 339–345. Crucial to the plan was India's J.P. Narayan since it entailed making thousands of small crop loans in Gramdan (cooperative movement) villages in rural India, using Borsodi's inflation-proof Constant currency to make the loans. That plan fell through. Later, in fall 1972, I was The Constant's comptroller when Dr. Borsodi began issuing Constants through a bank in Exeter, New Hampshire. Still later, after Bob Swann and Susan Witt founded the E.F. Schumacher Society in 1980, they issued a different supplemental currency called "BerkShares" that circulated in the Great Barrington, Massachusetts area.

As for Community Land Trusts, in the late 1960s they were still few and they were almost all rural, whereas now they're numerous and are mostly urban. Yurts too are numerous now, but they've *stayed* almost all rural. Although, I did help Bill Coperthwaite build an urban yurt in the backyard of a Harvard School of Education building. That yurt was a "demo" for his PhD, and no one was supposed to live in it. Bill's main PhD project was to teach Lapp crafts to natives of northern Alaska. He spent several months in Lapland learning Lapp craft skills and gathering tools, supplies, and finished samples. Then he packed those into a compact unit weighing 600 pounds, transportable by bush planes and dog-sleds, and traveled around northern Alaska's native settlements teaching the Lapp crafts. He told me Inuit women especially loved to copy the neck broaches that Lapp women wove with pewter wire. Later the Santa Fe Folk Art Museum talked Bill out of his 600-pound Lapp crafts unit, and I assume it's still there.

As for "rural apprenticeships," those were still decades shy of today's online Workaway and WWOOF listings with their thousands of hands-on-learning offers from small organic farms. WWOOF stands for World Wide Opportunities on Organic Farms, and that kind of "rural apprenticeship" is an alternative that now seems crucial to help Americans "build a new society in the shell of the old," to quote Dorothy Day again.

Which is all why Appalachia hit me right between the eyes when fate landed me in rural West Virginia a few years later, because Appalachia already had most of those alternatives deeply embedded in its rural traditions. Not yurts of course but log cabins, which even more than yurts are embedded in neighborly solidarity. Only one or two days are needed to lift and corner-lock the log walls of a cabin or barn, but that day or two requires *many* arms lifting. Likewise it takes just one day but many arms to tighten and clamp the woven steel-wire cable (the "tension cable") around the girth of a yurt. How that's done is described and illustrated in the 2015 book *A Man Apart* about America's yurt-building pioneer Bill Coperthwaite.[12]

In other words, when I landed in rural Appalachia in 1971, I didn't see it as a backwater that was lagging behind the rest of the country. I saw it

12. See Peter Forbes and Helen Whybrow, *A Man Apart* (2015), pp. 160–61 including the photo there of tightening a yurt's tension cable.

Tightening a yurt's "tension cable" in 1974. Bill Coperthwaite is
on the right, the first puller in line. Once the cable is pulled tight,
it is clamped in place. Courtesy of Peter Forbes.

as a beautiful bouquet of alternatives *to* the rest of the country. Two decades later in a book titled *Appalachia's Path to Dependency: Rethinking a Region's Economic History* (1994), I set forth the logic and good sense of rural Appalachia's traditional way of life.

It's a way of life *localized*—which movement groups call "decentralist." Movement groups talk of community land trusts and of "commons governance." Well, rural Appalachia once was (and much of it still is) a crazy-quilt of overlapping "commons" under informal local understandings. But yes, as everyone knows, the last 140 years have seen a lot of Appalachia become depleted or worse. Much of it has been placed off-limits to local hunters and foragers while it's used for unsustainable resource extraction like strip-mining to feed industries located elsewhere, devastating the land and leaving highly acidic what's still there.

But to continue—movement groups talk about micro-lending and alternative local currencies. Well, kin and neighborhood *networking* is the heart and soul of rural Appalachia's traditional economy. It's a crazy-quilt of overlapping local mini-systems of lending and borrowing and time-lapse bartering that still saturates much of rural Appalachia. It could also be called "voluntary reciprocity" and it usually comes with ample leeway after someone does you a favor before you are expected to do them a return favor—or maybe you can do their cousin a favor and it counts the same, assuming they happen to owe their cousin a favor, or are willing to have their cousin owe them a favor.

Such time-lapse trading of favors back and forth with kin and neighbors still saturates many people's lives in rural Appalachia. The poorer people are, the more they tend to network. And the poorer they are, the more likely it is that their contributions will consist of labor, whereas better-off households are more likely to lend equipment or to contribute supplies. Historical studies of such networking say that more of its benefits flow downward toward its poorer participants than flow upward toward its better-off participants. The historian David F. Weiman says such "communal arrangements effectively transferred wealth to those at the lower end of the [wealth] distribution."[13]

As for *net* benefits, net benefits tend to be received by everyone involved. In other words, almost everyone who networks gains more from it than they lose to it. Why? Because it isn't a zero-sum system like the money system. But (you may say) if it's an economic system, how can it *not* be zero-sum? It's not zero-sum because a household's day-by-day economic life is more about having things *when* they're needed than it is about having things *for* when they're needed. It's mostly about timing, in other words—whereas having things *for* when you need them, or having money for when you need things, *is* zero-sum if you don't share what you have. Networking entails sharing *whatever, whenever,* with *whoever*—sharing *whatever* you have *whenever* someone you know needs it, *whoever* they may be. Asset-duplication is thereby drastically reduced. When you yourself need to use something, one of your neighbors or kinfolk can probably provide it.

City dwellers of course usually find cash more convenient than trading workdays back and forth with their neighbors, and more convenient than bartering and borrowing tools and consumables back and forth. But cash isn't convenient if you don't have any, and if, in order to get any you'd have to leave your land and family to go work somewhere for wages.

All this affected not only ordinary people in rural Appalachia but also affected local businesses and professional services. A great deal of rural Appalachia's business was conducted on a barter "in-kind" basis well into the 20th century—heavily so through the 1950s in the case of Lincoln County, West Virginia. (Less so since the mid-1960s when President Lyndon Johnson started his Great Society welfare outlays.)

What about all the extraction of coal, timber, etc. in some rural areas?

---

13. David F. Weiman, "Families, Farms, and Rural Society in Preindustrial America," *Research in Economic History,* supplement 5, part B (1989), p. 259.

Surely *those* businesses couldn't operate "in kind"? But actually they could and did. Wages were about two-thirds of their operating expenses and they used to pay a large part of their wages in company scrips. Appalachia's resource-exporting companies were shipping out trainloads of coal and lumber and getting back shipments of food, clothes, etc. to sell in their company stores to their employees in exchange for their own company scrip that they themselves had paid out as wages *to* their employees. So in effect, Appalachian coal and lumber companies were often paying miners and lumbermen for their labor in food, clothes, and other merchandise rather than in money. Thus the barter economy wasn't just a grassroots phenomenon in Appalachia's past. It was common as well in the region's rural industries.

And then of course there's nonviolence, which is a full-fledged alternative in its own right. India's Mahatma Gandhi showed that nonviolent protests *and* nonviolent alternatives (which Gandhi called "constructive programme") could both lead to positive changes without hurting people. Granted, you might get hurt yourself, but that was a risk you'd be taking voluntarily because you cared about an issue.

I've never personally received credible death threats. Going back-to-the-land in rural West Virginia didn't necessarily rule out death threats, however, as my younger brother John found out when he co-organized a group against mountaintop-removal coal mining that was planned to start next door to my first parcel of land there, which by then (in 1988) had been he and his family's home for fourteen years. He calls the contention about the planned mountaintop removal "very intense," which is an understatement. The most nerve-wracking spell was the first few months in winter and spring 1988. Soon afterwards, I was there for summer 1988 and the tension that summer about strip mining brought back my memories of the '60s.

We won't completely reach that tense summer until Chapter 16. A lot happened first that made the outcome of 1988's strip-mining controversy very important to many of the newcomers, including me. Granted, I was a *former* newcomer by then, since I had moved away. But even if you stay in Lincoln County the rest of your life, you're *still* a newcomer. A "native" is someone who was born there, or at least was raised there.

CHAPTER 5

Getting My Feet Wet

E ntering West Virginia in summer 1971 was my entire lifetime's eeriest experience. It was about an hour after dark. I walked from the state of Ohio into West Virginia across a high bridge above the Ohio River. The bridge stood a few miles upstream from Gallipolis, Ohio and emptied out near downtown Point Pleasant, West Virginia. The sky overhead seemed lurid green and the air felt eerie. I vaguely recall that as I crossed the bridge, something very large was flying to the left of the bridge near the West Virginia shoreline, something like a bird but far larger than any bird could be. I remember thinking "that's bigger than even a condor." I recall it landing ten or twenty feet above the surface of the river at an opening in the wall of a long-abandoned factory or warehouse, about fifty yards up-river (left) of the West Virginia end of the bridge I was on. Then it immediately disappeared into a dark recess.

Much later I learned that an Ohio River bridge had collapsed right about there several years before, killing forty-six victims, which didn't just shock local people but spooked them because it happened after a year of very credible "Mothman" sightings, including several Mothman sightings near the ill-fated "Silver Bridge" just a few days before it collapsed.

Reports of Mothman sightings had begun in November 1966, a year before the bridge collapsed. The Mothman was described as brownish, shaped like a man six-and-a-half to seven feet tall, with large wings that folded down on its back, and with large reflective red eyes. Sightings were reported by teenagers, teachers, police, housewives, and pilots, among others. After several sightings were reported over the Ohio River at Point Pleasant in the first half of December 1967, the "Silver Bridge" located there collapsed during the evening rush-hour of Friday, December 15th, killing forty-six victims.

Afterwards, reports of Mothman sightings in the area continued. They were still occurring when I crossed into West Virginia there in summer 1971.

None of this did I know, mind you, until decades later when the *West Virginia Encyclopedia* asked me to write an entry about "state mysteries." That wasn't my field, and what I wrote was never published, but that was when I first learned any details about the Mothman and the bridge collapse. Still later, Richard Gere's 2002 film "The Mothman Prophecies" told the story but added some fiction by inventing phone messages directly from the Mothman.

Since the year 2002 when the film premiered, Point Pleasant has tried to capitalize on the Mothman—or maybe just tried to control a lingering case of the creeps?—by holding an annual weekend "Mothman Festival" every September. But for me the eeriness of that summer night I crossed the Ohio River into West Virginia is still vivid.

I hitched rides on southbound but had lost my bearings. So I purposefully called to mind my two previous Appalachian friends to help steady myself. The first was a young man from eastern Kentucky who shared my job at the Chicago steel mill after I quit college. He and his family were new to Chicago and he alone among my co-workers wasn't hoping to escape from our cold, dirty, dangerous job of working with 10,000-pound steel billets underneath a huge magnetic crane. The Kentucky youth and I helped the crane operator rotate the five-ton billets for "scarfing" (to close their surface air bubbles) and then helped the crane operator move the scarfed billets to the storage end of our huge open-air shed.

The young Kentuckian was simply glad his earnings were helping his family. He had no escape hopes like all my other co-workers did. The job of "scarfing" to close the billets' surface air bubbles was done by hand with seven-foot blow torches. One of the scarfers was a family man newly arrived from the country of Jordan. He told me he was ardently job-hunting because there surely must be some better way he could support his family in Chicago. A handsome Hispanic scarfer in his late 20's had been a gas-station attendant but couldn't save any money pumping gas. Now he hoped to save enough money by scarfing steel to buy himself a gas-station franchise.

A short African American man shared my own job. He had been stuck in it for years. Beyond the call of duty, he kept our hand-warming fire burning in a 55-gallon barrel and he also kept the work flowing smoothly, which the scarfers appreciated because they were paid as piece-workers. He told me he had given up on finding a better job but that he always hoped for strikes in summertime. In the summers, he said, the daytime temperature in our open-air shed often exceeded 115 degrees.

One of the operators of the magnetic crane that we all worked underneath was almost 70. He had been raised on a farm and was putting off his retirement, trying to save enough money to buy a small place in the country where he could do a little hobby-farming after he retired.

But the young man from eastern Kentucky told me was he didn't care where he worked or for how long. He said he was happy to be helping his family and that's all he wanted.

My *other* previous Appalachian friend was one of my fellow federal prisoners at Springfield, Missouri. He too came from eastern Kentucky, from Hazard in Perry County. As a young man in the 1930s he'd been a coal miner there. He could tell a story for all it was worth, regaling me endlessly with details about eastern Kentucky's 1930s mine wars, including who exactly ambushed which busload of "scab" strikebreakers, who exactly set off explosions at which coal tipples on which nights and carried out other sabotage. It may have all been true. I've long since forgotten the details he reeled off.

So I was *slightly* informed about Appalachia, and of course had personally spent a month in spring 1960 hiking through some of it. Now in summer 1971 as I hitched rides south through West Virginia my destination was Lincoln County, southeast of Huntington, where Tony and Sue Norris my friends from Heathcote Mill in Maryland had recently relocated and invited me to "come on down" for a visit.

I arrived in pouring rain, which continued pouring the entire twenty-four hours of my visit. Mud was everywhere, mostly out-of-doors but that's where we usually were too, out in the pouring rain because things couldn't wait. Gasoline had to be siphoned out of the old beat-up car that wouldn't run and poured into the old beat-up car that *might* run. (Ever siphon gas?) Then Henry Mandel, fresh from Heathcote Mill, tried to race his new four-wheel-drive jeep through a slanting soupy-mud dip in Sand Gap Ridge Road and instead skidded fifty feet down into the woods. A neighbor's little horse named Bob, totally blind, managed to pull the mud-coated jeep back up on the road—that strong little horse plus a "come-along" (a winch) which we ratcheted simultaneously. *All* the roads were mud, incidentally. Nothing was paved for miles in any direction.

The jeep was rescued thanks a wiry neighbor named Chester Ray Elkins, owner-operator of both Bob the small blind horse and the "come-along" (winch). So Henry Mandel thereby owed Chester Ray Elkins some sort of return favor. No hurry at all, just someday when it's convenient for everyone concerned. And it is not *mentioned,* either then or later, by the person who you owe. That person won't go near it—won't even mention *any*one owing *any*body *any*thing, or anyone being owed anything by anybody. It's simply understood between you and the person you owe, and it's totally voluntary. But keep it in mind. It's what keeps the mud from taking over completely. It's the nuts and bolts and winches of the local economic system.

After my drenched West Virginia initiation (not to mention the ee-rieness of just entering the state) it might seem odd that I moved there. But land was cheap and I wanted to buy some land. I didn't think of it as settling down but simply as owning some land. The previous fall, win-ter, and spring I'd been in northern New Mexico helping Elaine Mikels handle dairy goats (and over 100 pesky chickens) at her organic farm on the north rim of Arroyo Hondo twelve miles north of Taos. Meanwhile I was scouting around for land. But northern New Mexico's land prices were out-of-sight, and the price of the water rights (which were separate) sometimes exceeded the price of the land.

In fact, the price of land and water rights in northern New Mexico was probably climbing then, what with an influx of hippies arriving from the San Francisco area. Even some Haight-Ashbury "hip merchants" packed up their posters, pipes, and pre-faded blue jeans and moved to Santa Fe or Taos, pursuing their clientele. I had spent two spells in Haight-Ashbury myself, the first by accident in spring and summer 1967, the so-called Summer of Love, when I was there with the Free Cities Plan for a Viet-nam War compromise.

On that occasion, walking up Haight Street, the visiting photographer Diane Arbus told me, "These aren't actually freaks, Paul, they're imita-tors." She wouldn't even take hippies' pictures or return phone calls from an editor at *Newsweek*. But now in New Mexico, hippies lives were turning quite real. Some Hispanic youth reacted violently to the hippie "invasion" and a few of the newcomers had been murdered, including one of my California friends. His case was quickly solved and his parents then came to New Mexico and met with the mothers of some of their son's killers. His parents refused to support any felony charges (not to mention murder charges) against the Hispanic youths who had killed their son, which surely helped.

Looking for land also took me back to southern Colorado's Huerfano Valley, where I had spent February 1970 living in Nanao Sakaki's cave on Greenhorn Mountain. After my eight-month New Mexican dairy-goat apprenticeship, I went back north to Huerfano Valley in spring 1972 as a non-hermit, and found the prices of land and water rights out-of-sight there too, despite Huerfano Valley's hippie influx not being full-tilt yet (soon it would be).

So that spring of 1972 I returned to West Virginia, to central Lincoln County, and put out word I was looking for land, which soon led to my buying "12 acres more or less" for $400 from an elderly widow named Hazel Adkins who I never did meet in person. Most of the land parcel was covered by pine and white-oak trees. White oak is good for making log buildings. Pine is too, and weighs invitingly less. The twelve acres lay mostly along the top of Sand Gap Ridge just one mile south of my friends who had relocated from Heathcote Mill in Maryland. In other words, it lay a mile south along Sand Gap Ridge's dirt road from the head of Little Laurel Hollow, which was where Chester Ray Elkins lived whose blind horse, winch, and know-how had proved so timely in the pouring rain the previous summer.

The land transaction between myself and the elderly widow Hazel Adkins was handled from beginning to end by a former Logan County underground coal miner named Woodrow Mosley who lived in retirement a mile on further west along the top of Sand Gap Ridge. Woodrow and his wife Beatrice and one of their grandsons lived beside the ridgetop's dirt road right before it steeply descends west to the Guyandotte River near the small town of Branchland. Their little house held framed color portraits of Jesus, Franklin Delano Roosevelt, and John F. Kennedy in the living room, which come wintertime would be stifling hot because its coal-burning stove heated the whole house—a common set-up thereabouts, including the same framed color portraits on the living room wall, sometimes joined by the man with bushy eyebrows, John L. Lewis of the United Mine Workers.

Owning land energized me. I borrowed a chain saw and before long had cut down enough straight oak and pine trees to build a cabin. I removed all their bark with a borrowed drawknife and propped them all up a foot off the ground so they'd season over the winter. Then I went off to pick apples in Derry, New Hampshire (my annual money-making custom). From there the School of Living founder Ralph Borsodi hired me as comptroller to help him launch his alternative currency, The Constant, out of a second-floor office in downtown Exeter, New Hampshire. That took a few months.

So I didn't return to Lincoln County, West Virginia until January 1973 and then came yet another tangent. I was living in Tony and Sue Norris's smokehouse near the head of Little Laurel Hollow. (More about Tony and Sue Norris comes later.) My fellow newcomer Charley Bates asked me to co-buy with him a beautiful farm that had been deserted for several decades. It included a log cabin eighty years old and a log "pole barn," and it lay three miles east along McComas Ridge via dirt roads that almost no one ever traveled except, at night, fox hunters did. They had a roadside shack where they would lay listening to their fox hounds yelping and howling down in the hollows—yelps of joy and howls of despair as the hounds found and lost and re-found the scent of a fox.

What I then co-bought with my friend Charley Bates was an unbelievably beautiful old farm on two high but almost level benches near the top of McComas Ridge. (A "bench," in typography, is any fairly long and fairly level section of the side of a hill.) Since the farm sloped east, it received the warming early-morning sunlight and the cooling late-afternoon shade. Listed on its deed as "29 acres more or less," it was actually fifty-six acres. The price was relatively high, $5,000, but only $1,000 was required as a down payment, and then at least $1,000 annually during the next four years. So I sold the Sand Gap Ridge twelve acres to my younger brother John for its customary $400, and hitchhiked out to my Uncle Phil Salstrom's wood-carving business in northern Illinois to earn money for this more expensive new land.

The ex-miner who lived a mile further out Sand Gap Ridge, Woodrow Mosley, befriended my younger brother just as he had befriended me.

(Not that Woodrow ever told either of us where he was digging up valuable ginseng roots nearby. He told us he *was* but he never told either of us *where* he was.)

Later, during the tense Lincoln County strip-mining controversy in 1988, Woodrow saved my brother's sizable self-built house and maybe saved his life. (I say "maybe saved his life" because he's stubborn.) A troop of angry young men from the town of Branchland came up the road on foot one day to beat him up and burn down his house. They presumably wanted strip-mining jobs to become available close to home. My brother received a phone call from Woodrow that they were coming and sent his daughter with his infant son into hiding off the premises. But then, as the angry young men passed Woodrow's house on their way to my brother's, Woodrow went out and confronted them. He told them he knew exactly who each and every one of them was, which in fact Woodrow did know because for many years he had been the part-time janitor at Branchland School.

No longer anonymous, the young men turned around and headed back down the road toward Branchland.

My brother John and his group Home Place, Inc. won that protracted strip-mining struggle, thereby saving from mountaintop removal the adjacent ridge and probably a lot more of central Lincoln County. (Once the headwaters are strip-mined, the land downstream becomes contaminated and often floods, lowering what it costs strip-mining companies to buy it up so they can strip-mine there too.)

It was touch-and-go but ended as an environmental victory despite public statements by the strip-mine developer, a woman named Sandra Perry from Indianapolis, claiming my brother was in contact with Russia via two-way short-wave radio equipment he allegedly had in the turret of his self-built *dacha*. Actually he *didn't* have a short-wave radio, not even for reception, but if he had needed one to hear Cincinnati Reds baseball broadcasts, he would have had one.[14]

---

14. The full story is in *The Soviet Union and Lincoln County USA* (2014) by Julian Martin. It's also in "Green Civic Republicanism and Environmental Action in Lincoln County, West Virginia, 1974–1990" by Jinny Turman, *Journal of Southern History*, November 2016, pp. 855–900. The phrase "green civic republicanism," incidentally, has nothing to do with the Republican Party.

According to a knowledgeable estimate made by the newcomer Pete Shew, by the mid-1970s at least 400 young newcomers had moved into Lincoln County. The first was a photographer from the Chicago area named Ric McDowell. Ric had worked somewhere in Appalachia for the War on Poverty and then decided to stay in the region. In 1968 he began living on a farm about one mile up a short hollow from Lower Mud River Road (paved). Early on, Ric McDowell became involved against strip-mining and in 1973 he co-founded a group named Save Our Mountains, Inc. The group soon went statewide and became West Virginia's most active anti-stripping organization. That was due particularly to Ric McDowell's hard work along with Betty Jones, Nancy White, Anne Farewell, Bill Ragette, Joe and Marian Footen and many others, some of whom (like Ric himself) lived in Lower Mud River Valley a few miles downstream (in other words *north*) from the county seat, the town of Hamlin. Once in summer 1974, Ric recruited a few dozen of us to march through Charleston with placards protesting strip-mining, and then to stay and vigil all night in front of West Virginia's state capitol building next to a newly-erected statue, "Abe Lincoln Walks at Midnight."

A year after Ric McDowell arrived in 1968, another veteran of the region's War on Poverty, Chuck Smith, started a Catholic Worker Farm in 1969 in a different hollow a mile or two from Ric McDowell's place. Early on, the Catholic Workers who came and lived in that vicinity held a public demonstration against the Vietnam War. They held it at the county seat (the town of Hamlin) in a public park bordering Mud River. The young men in the demonstration were tossed into Mud River for their alleged lack of patriotism.

The Ric McDowell/Catholic Worker neighborhood of Lincoln County lay about twelve miles north (downstream) along Mud River from where I personally settled in the center of the county. Halfway between those two locations was the county seat town of Hamlin.

Most of the young newcomers who had already moved and were still moving into my own central Lincoln County locality were ones who I had known at Heathcote Mill, which was (and still is) a back-to-the-land center nestled in a small green valley forty miles north of Baltimore—a little valley barely inside Maryland, almost in Pennsylvania, just one mile south of the Mason-Dixon line.

The back-to-the-land organization named the School of Living, which Ralph Borsodi had started in 1934 during the Great Depression,

Heathcote Mill's valley in Maryland, looking downstream (south)
with the Mill itself on right. Courtesy of Sue Norris.

Ralph Borsodi (*left*) and Mildred Loomis (*right*) at Heathcote Mill in 1969.
Courtesy of Sue Norris.

purchased Heathcote Mill in 1965 and turned it into a new back-to-the-
land center. They made it an outreach and conference center but also a
site for rural apprenticeships. I spent a lot of time there off and on in the
late '60s and early '70s, helping out with this and that and occasionally
tree-trimming in Baltimore's northern suburbs to make some money.

Heathcote *really* got crowded when weekend music festivals were added to everything else going on. No wonder Heathcote's young staff members started moving to central Lincoln County, West Virginia and trying to find and buy *their own private place*.

But how "private" that actually turned out to be had a lot to do with the networking lifestyle of the people who already lived there—the Lincoln County natives.

CHAPTER 6

The Natives

I n the early 1970s, the mental world of most Lincoln County natives included a lot about their own personal and family support system, their "network." And beyond that, they could reel off many other people they were related to, and exactly how. "Oh her—on my Mom's side she's my niece and on my Dad's side she's my second cousin."

Most of the natives also cared about *religion* and *churches*. The author Lenore McComas Coberly tells me that in the county seat, Hamlin, most people's social activities revolved around the churches. In *rural* Lincoln County, however, many churches had no social activities at all, just religious activities—except that many of the rural churches did hold an annual all-day "homecoming" pot-luck early in the fall.

Their other big events were religious revivals, which usually came about every five years and lasted a few days to a few weeks. Every night during a revival there'd be a service with visiting preachers as well as the church's own pastor (officiating). On average, revivals would run about a week, but "however long it takes" was the basic idea, as the ex-storekeeper Raymond Black told me as he looked me straight in the eye like I was a prime candidate.

Maybe that helps explain why the rural churches weren't necessarily popular. As *between* religion and churches in rural Lincoln County, most people ranked religion way above churches. Few if any of the natives in our vicinity were non-believers, but many of them felt they could do just fine *without* any churches, usually. And sometimes emphatically! One sunny summer afternoon in 1973 I was strolling up Little Laurel Hollow's dirt road when a man suddenly emerged from the doorway of his small house and started walking beside me. He snapped open his switchblade knife and pretended to sharpen it while bitterly denouncing "church folks."

It was personal. He clearly assumed I had something to do with his teenage son being baptized in Mud River where it flows past Myra Methodist Church. Actually I had nothing to do with it, but kept that fact to myself so he wouldn't think he'd intimidated me. Granted, I did attend Myra Methodist Church and had just become a member, which turned out to entail being baptized by immersion in Mud River one Sunday morning after church. They were United Methodists so I had assumed they were mainstream, but it turned out they agreed with Baptists that infant baptism doesn't count. The teenage son of the disgruntled father was likewise baptized in the river that same Sunday morning after church, but I barely knew him. Summer Bible School had converted him and I had nothing to do with it.

Rejecting infant baptism wasn't the only way those United Methodists acted Baptist. Usually I was the only adult male at the Wednesday evening prayer service, so they'd designate me to pick a passage of scripture and read it from the lectern. Not from the pulpit, mind you, since I wasn't a minister. Several of the women usually present were better versed in the Bible, but since they weren't men they disqualified themselves from even choosing which Bible passage I should read.

Various other doctrines likewise mattered greatly to Myra Methodist attendees, but which ones were crucially important differed from person to person, even inside families.

Methodist *preaching* did differ from Baptist preaching. Methodist preaching was tame by comparison. The rural Baptist churches were all various types of independent Baptist, none were Southern Baptist. "Preaching in the Spirit" was their ideal—alas not always achieved (*received?*). Preaching that the preacher and his congregation *hoped* would turn Spirit-led was the rural Baptist norm. As for the sermon themes, those didn't differ much among the rural churches whether Methodist or Baptist. And all the rural ministers regardless of their affiliation seemed to agree on the proper social order, and on their own role in maintaining it.

Which I saw in practice sometimes, even during church services. One Sunday morning when I visited a different church (not Myra's), a fairly young local married woman was called by name to the altar to repent of adultery, although the "A" word wasn't mentioned. When summoned by name, she went to the altar and repented. I sympathized with her and went to the altar too, but no one else. Apparently it wasn't customary to join a "sinner" at the altar.

Then the preacher called her husband to the altar and asked him to forgive her, which he did. They went on to a lifelong and happy marriage. On Sunday afternoons, that young woman had often given me a ride as I walked over McComas Ridge to the Guyandotte Valley for Sunday evening Freewill Baptist services in the town of Midkiff. I wondered *why* she was driving "over the hill" on Sunday afternoons, but if I ever asked her, she didn't tell me the truth. (If she had, I would have remembered.) After her alter call, I had to hope someone else would stop and give me a lift because *her* trips "over the hill" were over.

Such church-based discipline, and the area's local community discipline generally, was effective because people were so dependent on each other economically. By contrast, if somebody has plenty of money they could ignore community values (within reason) but then they would have to rely on their own *self*-discipline. No one in the Myra area had much money except possibly old Raymond Black the retired storekeeper, but his wealth was mainly in land rather than money because his major debtors tended to pay him their accumulated store debts in land titles (deeds). If they hadn't owned any land as unspoken collateral, Raymond probably wouldn't have let them run up a high debt at the store.

Although few if any of central Lincoln County's natives were non-believers, only a minority were church members—either at Myra Methodist or any other church—because church members were held morally accountable for their behavior, first and foremost by their fellow members but by everyone else in the vicinity as well. In fact, if church members weren't incredibly saintly, some of the local non-church members considered them hypocrites and didn't mind saying so. (Probably not to their face, but saying so to me.)

Just as a side note, such moral accountability as part of church membership isn't practiced in most of the rest of the U.S., particularly in most urban churches. Granted that what is *considered* moral in puritanical rural Appalachia differs from what is considered moral in mainstream urban America, but most mainstream urban churches don't seem to make *any* moral accountability a condition of church membership. Just saying.

As for everyone else's moral accountability in Lincoln County, not just that of church members, most of the natives felt more lenient toward their fellow natives than they felt toward us newcomers. If any newcomer was totally rejected by their neighbors, one traditional option was arson. It would be carried out when no one was at home so no one would be physically endangered. Arson goes far beyond the Amish practice of simply "shunning" someone who's unwanted, but of course the Amish are pacifists.

In our part of Lincoln County, I know of only one case of arson clearly motivated by total rejection. And that arson wasn't aimed against the newcomer himself (a young social worker from Huntington) but against a friend of his who he allowed to stay at his house. His friend, while there alone, went bonkers on drugs and someone driving on Upper Mud River Road happened to look across Mud River and notice his strange behavior, and notified the state police. A state policeman arrived, took him into custody, and started driving him to Huntington. But from the back seat of the police car, the young man wrapped one of his handcuffed arms around the neck of the state policeman—who was probably just driving him to a hospital (prior to that surprise attack anyway). Several days later, the newcomer's small house where his friend had "lost it" on drugs became a pile of ashes.

By summer 1973 when that occurred, a couple hundred of us newcomers had already moved into various parts of Lincoln County. Gradually I began seeing where we fit (or didn't fit) into Lincoln County's long history. On one hand, most of the older natives did want to have young people around. Lincoln County's economy was flat as a pancake. Forty percent of the county's residents with full-time jobs worked for the county itself, and those job-holders were chosen by local politicians. Older people's children and grandchildren had mostly departed for the city of Huntington forty miles away or for points beyond.

We newcomers did not come to Lincoln County looking for jobs. We came looking for land to buy, or came because of friends who had already moved there and invited us to come and visit. If jobs had been available, then Lincoln County was *not* where we newcomers would have looked for land, because the availability of jobs would have raised the price of land. (Of course, the price of land did rise because of our buying it. Later someone wrote an irate Letter-to-the-Editor of the county's weekly newspaper saying we newcomers had raised the average price of Lincoln County land 16 percent during the 1970s.)

But even though most of Lincoln County's oldsters did want young-sters around, they had concerns about *us*. We didn't look, talk, or act like their own children and grandchildren. Besides which, drugs were a big concern for many of the natives, particularly for those who had children or grandchildren or nephews or nieces still living in the county. But they rarely told us that explicitly until an evangelist for marijuana moved into our part of Lincoln County and attracted a lot of bad publicity. He wasn't burned out by arson, but he probably would have been if he hadn't had a nice wife and quite a few young children, and if he hadn't lived near the head of Little Laurel Hollow surrounded by other newcomers.

I think the last time a threat like us had happened in rural Lincoln County was seventy years earlier, back in the early 1900's when coal min-ing suddenly boomed in the next county to the south, Logan County. In that case, the threat hadn't come from marijuana but from money. After the Chesapeake & Ohio railroad (C&O) reached Logan County in 1905, some of the young men from Lincoln County were drawn south over the ridges to the new coal-mining jobs in Logan County. Or, if they lived on the Guyandotte River side of Lincoln County (the west side) and had the price of a ticket, they could simply hop on a C&O passenger train and *ride* up to Logan ("up" was south because the Guyandotte River flowed north like Mud River flowed).

The author Lenore McComas Coberly, now aged 96, spent her child-hood summers with relatives in Big Ugly Hollow in southern Lincoln County and she once told me that before World War Two "up on Ugly . . . people simply were not going to go over the mountain and into the mines. It was almost unthinkable. And when people did, their families grieved almost as if they were dead or gone to prison. I'm not sure whether they *blamed* them or just felt sorry for them. But those who went into the mines were no longer part of the community. People were afraid mining would draw their sons to the greater income."[15]

Well, you may say, wasn't it the same when Lincoln County's native young people went away to Huntington? Or went farther away to Cin-cinnati or Columbus? No, it wasn't fully the same because that move

15. Paul Salstrom, "Big Ugly Creek, West Virginia: Interview with Writer Lenore McComas Coberly," *Appalachian Journal*, Spring-Summer 2004, pp. 381–382 for this quotation. The full interview is on pp. 368–387. More details appear in Lenore's book *Sarah's Girls: A Chronicle of Big Ugly Creek* (2006).

Lincoln County native writer Lenore McComas
Coberly in 2014 at age 89, with her great-
granddaughter Meridian Benforado. Courtesy
of Lenore McComas Coberly.

probably didn't change their culture. They still networked with each other, and often still networked with their kin and friends back home. They stayed culturally homogenous with Lincoln County.

Coal mining brought with it a different culture—not just a "working culture" but a working-*class* culture—and that tended, over time, to cause greater change than caused by working in Huntington and coming home every weekend, or working in Cincinnati and coming home every few weekends. Antagonism on the basis of "class" was alien to rural Appalachia's traditional way of life. That's one reason (along with company-financed terrorism) why Appalachian miners took so long to unionize.

Native miners were waiting for the coal bosses to reciprocate the favors they did for them, favors far over and above "the call of duty." By the time the miners finally gave up waiting for the bosses to return their favors, they were mad and their class antagonism often went deep.

To Lincoln County's native farmers, we young newcomers must have seemed mad at someone too. We were against a lot of things. Going back to the land was very different from growing up on the land and simply staying put where you grew up. We back-to-the-landers were idea-prone, bookish. Our focus wasn't local, not yet anyway. We were interested in ideas not just about self-sufficiency but about what was starting to be called "the human scale" (rather than the mass scale) in all aspects of life. We were more interested in local*ism* than we were in the local*ity* where we were now living—at first anyway—and more interested in ideas about appropriate technology, face-to-face relationships, local democracy among equals—more interested in those *ideas* than we were in their daily occurrence all around us in the county.

At night by our kerosene lamps we were reading *Living the Good Life* by Scott and Helen Nearing, *Five Acres and Independence* by Maurice G. Kains, *Diet for a Small Planet* by Frances Moore Lappé, and *Stalking the Wild Asparagus* by Euell Gibbons. We also passed around a dog-eared copy of *Night Comes to the Cumberlands* (1963) by Harry Caudill. Caudill didn't call anything "alternative" but he sure wrote colorfully about rural Appalachia's culture.

I did know one Lincoln County native who subscribed to *Organic Gardening* magazine, but he was an exception. His interests were worldwide and he was especially well-informed on feats of engineering all over the world, past ones as well as present-day.

His name was Ray Elkins, almost the same name as Chester Ray Elkins who owned the blind horse Bob and the "come-along" winch, and who lived at the head of Little Laurel Hollow. *That* Ray Elkins was often called by his full name "Chester Ray Elkins" to distinguish him from *this* Ray Elkins, who was often called "Mud River Ray Elkins."

Elkins wasn't a very common last name in Lincoln County, but at least twenty other last names *were* very common. About one-tenth of the county's natives were named Adkins. Smiths came next in numbers, and then about three percent of the natives were named Hager. There were also scores named Baker, Bias, Black, Brumfield, Chapman, Cremeans,

Dingess, Farley, Flowers, Fry, Lovejoy, Lucas, McComas, Midkiff, Mullins, Pauley, Plumley, Sias, Spurlock, Stowers, Triplett, Vance, White, Workman, and Wysong.

And quite a few named Yeager, including Lenore McComas Coberly's childhood friend Chuck Yeager—always called "Charles" in Lincoln County, never called Chuck even after he broke the sound barrier as Chuck. Chuck Yeager was born in Sandlick Hollow, about a mile up that hollow in back of the store/post office at the tiny hamlet of Myra. The small one-and-a-half story log house where he was born in February 1923 was in poor condition but was still being used as a barn. It leaned about 15 degrees and was propped up to keep it from collapsing into the road. Sometimes I spent the night there after Miriam and I bought the hilltop above it toward the northwest—which is the high Plum Knobs land that Chapter 9 will be about.

So Lincoln County was extremely homogenous. It had lost plenty of out-migrants since it was formed in 1867 and named for the martyred president, but it had seen comparatively few in-migrants since then except for 1900–1910. One of Lincoln County's main exports since at least the 1920s had been young people, but the county's population had kept rising anyway because of natural increase in the form of large families. The county experienced a major oil and (especially) natural-gas boom in the early 1900s and that boom did draw quite a few in-migrants. In fact, the county's population grew by 5,000 people from 1900 to 1910. But those in-migrants came mostly from nearby counties. They weren't culturally alien like we 1970s back-to-the-land in-migrants were.

One surprise for me about rural Lincoln Countians was their individuality. They were distinctly different from the "lonely crowd" of conformists who were trying to keep up with the Joneses out in mainstream America. They were individualized and individualistic, like rural New Englanders. And I think their individuality had roots in their homogeneity with each other—in their daily dealing with the same practical problems as almost everyone else they knew, and their frequent up-dates with each other about those problems. Not only did their daily experiences resemble all their neighbors' daily experiences, but their daily activities often occurred in each other's company because they often traded workdays back and forth. They truly knew each other and *had* to know each other because they depended on each other economically.

Mind you, their economic dependence didn't *seem* dependent to them-selves—because they could always switch who they depended on. If need be, they could quit networking with someone and start networking with someone else. They didn't depend on networking with any specific per-son or persons, but they did depend on networking with *someone,* and that made them homogenous with everyone else who networked.

And their homogeneity in turn made their differences (their individu-ality) socially welcomed. Live-and-let-live feelings were pervasive and in-dividual differences weren't just accepted but welcomed. They took pride, for instance, in Lincoln County's perpetually wandering preacher and eagerly shared their stories of meeting up with him, to which I added my own encounter because he had walked past my first place on Sand Gap Ridge Road one summer afternoon in 1972. Standing out in the dirt road, he had preached at me most of an hour and then said he had to hurry on. "I must preach at Ranger tonight," he said—which was physically impos-sible unless he could get there by magic carpet. People told me he was completely insane, yet everyone respected him.

Besides fostering homogeneity and individuality, rural Lincoln Coun-tians' economic dependence on each other bred solidarity—a solidarity that was directly opposite to individual*ism.* In my own experience, rural New Englanders tend to show both individual*ity* and individual*ism,* but rural Appalachians tend to have individuality *without* individual*ism.* In-stead of individual*ism* they have solidarity—they have each other's back.

In February 1972, Buffalo Creek Valley in Logan County (just south of Lincoln County) was devasted by a massive flood of Pittston Company coal slurry that killed 125 of the valley's 5,200 people and left 4,000 of the survivors homeless. Within just three days of the flood, before na-tional relief could start arriving, central Lincoln County people delivered a truckload of blankets and winter coats to the survivors there—only to discover so many blankets and coats were already there from other nearby counties that the flood survivors were burning them in bonfires to keep warm—which my friend Charley Bates saw with his own eyes when he helped deliver the truckload from central Lincoln County.

In 1958, a statistically weighed survey of almost 1,500 Appalachians had been conducted to find out "household attitudes." The survey found that 85 percent of the rural population who were surveyed lived in the vicinity of relatives. When both rural and urban Appalachian residents were asked "Do you and your relatives call on each other for help?" the responses were 95 percent "yes." When they were asked "Do you think a person has an obligation to help relatives even though he does not feel real close to them?" the responses were 83 percent "yes." And when asked "If you were in trouble, would you be more likely to turn to your close friends or to your relatives for help?" the responses were 67 percent "to relatives" and 26 percent "to close friends."[16]

Thanks to the solidarity within families and localities, a family hit by sickness or any other affliction was never expected to reciprocate the favors that it received while stricken. The local networking system would absorb those favors collectively. And like everything else about networking, it was all voluntary. Those who helped stricken people did so voluntarily. Nothing was "assigned" although some things were *expected*. For example, able-bodied offspring were expected to look after their own elderly parents if and when the parents grew decrepit. Or at least to arrange for someone else to look after them. So the caretaking of decrepit elderly people was not automatically shared out among a neighborhood or even among *all* the relatives of those elders. Which I think was because the need to caretake decrepit elders was *predictable*, whereas diseases and injuries were *un*predictable.

That was also apparently how Lincoln Countians saw the Great Depression of the 1930s—unpredictable and thus calling for all-inclusive solidarity. Many of the county's farm families lost their draft animals to the drought of 1930–31, and as the drought relented in 1932, a group of well-off farmers in Upper Mud River Valley who owned tractors created a free-of-charge plowing service in their neighborhoods.

And when the New Deal started in spring 1933, Lincoln County's solidarity displayed itself county-wide. To the irritation of New Deal higher-ups, the "relief" (welfare) staff in the county felt that since the Depression afflicted everyone, the whole county should share in the relief funds they were handing out. As of July that summer, 84 percent of Lincoln County's households were on relief whether they needed relief or not.

Then over the winter of 1933–34, a great many Lincoln Countians acquired federal work-relief jobs at high wages (high by local standards).

16. Thomas R. Ford, editor, *The Southern Appalachian Region: A Survey* (1962), p, 52. For this 1958 survey's logistics and many more details of its findings, see pp. 9–34.

By the time that temporary work-relief ended in spring 1934, its paychecks had disqualified hundreds of the county's households from *non-work relief*. Nonetheless, the county's relief staff promptly put almost all those households back on non-work relief anyway. In Lincoln County, that non-work relief averaged only $9.66 a month per household (plus free vegetable seeds and gardening tools), but the professional New Deal relief official who was in charge of monitoring all this reported to West Virginia's state relief headquarters that hundreds of Lincoln Countians were being "pauperized" by receiving relief funds they didn't qualify for. (Pauperized *pshaw!* The relief staff simply shared the funds with everyone because everyone was affected by the Depression even if it didn't impoverish them. The county's monthly average of $9.66 relief assistance per household, by the way, would now be worth $190 in the year 2020.)

Then when the Works Progress Administration (WPA) began in mid-1935, hundreds of Lincoln Countians again received work-relief jobs—upgrading roads, installing metal-frame bridges, constructing schools and other public buildings, etc.—again at high wages (high by local standards) just like the 1933–34 winter work-relief wages had been high.

The WPA's work-relief jobs continued more than five years in the late 1930s and might have led to some subsequent poverty for families who didn't leave their land when the WPA ended—families who stayed put in Lincoln County rather than leaving to find war-time jobs during World War Two. In 1973 the storekeeper-postmaster at Myra, Ray Gene Black, told me "It was the WPA that started farming on its downhill path all around here. The WPA paid farmers to work on the roads, and work on this and that, till they started counting on that money and neglecting their land."[17]

But don't assume that the New Deal's "excessive" outlay of relief funds in subsistence-farming areas like Lincoln County was simply a mistake that the federal government made through ignorance of local facts. It wasn't a mistake. It was integral to the New Deal's overall recovery plan—at least that's what New Deal officials indicated to West Virginia's Democratic governor when he went to Washington, DC in mid-summer 1933. The governor came back from Washington and told West Virginians that "there must be placed within the reach of the people of the rural

17. Ray Gene Black to the author at the Myra store, verbally, June 1973.

sections of our country purchasing power before this problem [the Depression] will be solved, and that is the situation with which the Federal Government is wrestling."[18]

The purchasing power that the New Deal's WPA work-relief put into the hands of Lincoln Country farmers did indeed, yes, help to revive the major U.S. commodity markets—*which was the main goal of the New Deal*—but when that work-relief ended in 1941, many of those farmers faced a choice between staying put in Lincoln County and risking impoverishment, or else leaving the county to do war-related work elsewhere.

But the reason why impoverishment threatened some of the farm families who stayed behind in Lincoln County wasn't only because of why the storekeeper told me. Because whether or *not* the farmers employed by the WPA had neglected their farms, the simple fact that so many of their neighbors left to do war-time work tended to impoverish those who stayed behind. Losing neighbors shrinks your opportunities for trading favors back and forth. By reducing your networking it increases your need for money.

Rural Lincoln Countians did leave the county in droves to find war-time jobs. A native named Jack Roy told a Lincoln County public meeting in 1988, "People, I was raised in this country during the Depression. . . . In 1940 me and my brother bought an old truck—the war broke out—we moved people out of Lincoln County, out of these hills, by the truckloads—to Logan [County] to the mines, to Cabell County [Huntington] to industry."[19]

And of course many of those Lincoln Countians who moved away went farther than just Logan County to the south or Huntington to the northwest. Some didn't move farther away immediately but did so later. The 1950s brought a wave of coal-mining mechanization, and the census of 1960 revealed that the net out-migration from Appalachia as an overall

18. H. G. Kump (governor of W.Va.), "Address to a Regional Meeting of County Boards of Education," Charleston, W.Va., July 21, 1933. In H.G. Kump, *State Papers and Public Addresses*, Charleston, WV (no date), p. 170.

19. Jack Roy, at West Virginia Department of Energy Public Hearing, Lincoln County, June 28, 1988; Oral History of Appalachia Collection, Marshall University Library, Huntington, W.Va.

region during the twenty years from 1940 to 1960 was 1.7 million people. That's how many more people moved out of Appalachia than moved into Appalachia during the 1940s and 1950s—31.43 percent of Appalachia's 1940 population of 5,408, 856.[20]

During the Depression decade of the 1930's, Appalachia's in-migration had almost exceeded its out-migration, because many people were moving back to their home farms and home neighborhoods as a way to survive. The population of Appalachia's basically rural counties increased almost 15 percent in the 1930s.[21]

Specifically in Lincoln County, which is officially all rural, the population rose by 4,000 people during the 1930s, about a 20 percent increase. But then during the next thirty years, from 1940 to 1970, Lincoln County's population *fell* by almost the same amount, 4,000 people, and as usual the county particularly lost young people. That's at least partly why we young newcomers who arrived in the early 1970's were welcomed by most of Lincoln County's natives.

20. Thomas R. Ford, ed., *The Southern Appalachian Region: A Survey* (1962), pp. 43, 58–60 (tables). That book's definition of Appalachia as encompassing 190 counties is the definition which I have always used in my own research.

21. *The Southern Appalachian Region: A Survey*, edited by Thomas R. Ford (1962), p. 43.

CHAPTER 7

We Newcomers

Turning now to we newcomers who suddenly showed up un-announced and started buying land and inviting our friends to "come on down"—several differences between us and the natives jump out. For one thing, their lives were *place-based* lives and our lives weren't, at least not when we first arrived. Typically we were third- or fourth- or fifth-generation urbanities. Often we were second-generation *sub*urbanites. In almost all our cases, our birth families' ties to farm life had long since withered away.

Even though I personally didn't move to central Lincoln County until spring 1972, I do know exactly how the newcomer influx started there two years earlier in the spring of 1970. Really, it had started several *decades* earlier in the hills of Czechoslovakia with a peasant girl named Anna who was growing up in a small Czech farm village. Anna told me that one of her childhood playmates was a gypsy boy named Karel Triska whose family owned a touring circus. While still young, Karel left their village to become a tightrope walker, but as a young man he came back to visit. To Anna's surprise he asked her to marry him—on condition she become a tightrope walker. She thought "what the heck" and said she'd try it. She told me that "after a few months it wasn't so bad" and that within a few years she was riding on her husband Karel's shoulders as he pedaled a unicycle across the high wire, and on her own shoulders rode their successive children, several of whom I knew in Lincoln County later, including Anna's second-oldest son Matej Triska, an incredible high-wire performer. Matej maintained a less-than-tight practice rope stretched across his back yard in Little Laurel Hollow.

In the 1970s, Matej and the other Triska youngsters lived with or near their mother Anna in Little Laurel Hollow but they were also still spending months at a time with their father Karel Triska and his high-wire troupe.[22]

Back in Czechoslovakia, Anna's husband Karel had inherited the family circus. About 1950 he moved the high-wire act to France and then on to America as "The Triska Troupe." Later in the 1950s, Karel and Anna's marriage dissolved and Anna found herself in Florida with her five small children and living from hand to mouth. One winter she met a divorced man from Lincoln County, West Virginia who had brought his own five small children south because he liked Florida's winter fishing. She thought "what the heck" and married him. And when spring arrived they bundled their combined ten children into his car and drove north to his home in rural Lincoln County. They planted a large garden and eked out a precarious livelihood.

To support such a large family, Henry (his name was Henry Baker) would purchase rundown farms, often simply by paying the sheriff the meagre back taxes. He and Anna and their children would fix the rundown house enough to live in it and then they'd cut down all the accessible timber that was of saw-log quality and sell it to sawmills. When the accessible good timber was all cut and sold, they would sell that farm or just abandon it and buy another rundown farm with good timber, moving around Lincoln County from one rundown farm to another.

As fate would have it, one spring day in 1970 Henry Baker happened to be at the Myra store—Black Brothers General Merchandise store, located on Upper Mud River Road (paved) in central Lincoln County. Just inside the store on the right-hand side was Myra's post office, a tiny "office" behind a service window. Myra consisted of that store/post office, plus the substantial farmhouse and enormous old barn of the storekeeper-postmaster and his wife, Raymond and Frieda Black, located about eighty yards behind the store up Sandlick Hollow. There was one other house, plus the small Methodist church. I guess you could also count the rickety

---

22. The Triska Troupe's history has never been compiled, but some fragments can be read, and one photo seen, by going online to "IT's Triska." Karel and Anna's second-oldest son Matej Triska is the high-wire acrobat pictured at that online site. Several short films of Triska Troupe performances in France can be viewed online by typing in: "Triska Troupe High Wire Acrobats."

old metal-frame bridge that crossed Mud River there. Drivers had to cross it at a crawl but you couldn't quite call them Myra residents. Transients maybe. Rumor said a troll lived underneath the old bridge but I never saw him so I'm not counting him.

The store/post office is now a private residence, and today's sleek new bridge over Mud River wouldn't even make cars slow down except the road curves 90 degrees there. But Myra can still be found on most West Virginia maps. After all, Chuck Yeager was born just a mile behind Myra up Sandlick Hollow.

In Myra's store that day in spring 1970, Henry Baker overheard a young man with a wispy beard ask Raymond Black the storekeeper if any land thereabouts was for sale. The young man wasn't very well dressed but Henry wasn't either, and Henry figured the young man must have some money or he wouldn't ask about land so bluntly. So Henry drew the young man aside and told him he knew of a place that just *might* be for sale "if the price was right."

The price for "93 acres more or less," very recently timbered, turned out to be merely $2,700, and the place turned out to be Henry and Anna's current residence, located on Chaney Fork off Little Laurel Hollow, about three miles from Myra (or two miles by walking a short-cut). The place came with a four-room log cabin and a small pole barn suitable for air-curing a small crop of burley tobacco. When surveyed immediately afterward, its platted size was 140 acres. (Acreage estimates in Appalachia are low because the size of a land parcel usually helps determine its property-tax bill.)

Later, we newcomers learned that Henry was allowed by the local neighborhood to sell that farm to our friend Lawrence Goldsmith (of Heathcote Mill in Maryland) because, by local tradition, strangers and suspicious characters were allowed to live in Little Laurel Hollow. In fact, a couple years earlier, allowing in strangers may have been the reason why Henry Baker himself was allowed to buy the farm he was now selling to Lawrence Goldsmith. Henry was from Ranger Ridge, located within Lincoln County but far to the south, and west beyond the Guyandotte River.

Having sold their de-timbered farm, Henry and Anna and their blended family moved up near the head of Little Laurel Hollow to a much smaller farm not far below Chester Ray Elkins' place at the very head of

Little Laurel. Henry and Anna's new farm was barely large enough for a potato patch, chicken coop, pig stye, moonshine still, and a five-acre hillside field of corn and pole beans, with those two crops planted right together so the bean vines would climb the cornstalks and no bean poles had to be pounded into the ground. You can't do that with *bush* beans of course since they won't climb, but planting *pole* beans and corn together makes sense if you harvest everything by hand. Which of course is easy if you have ten kids who'd better obey you "or else."

Besides "switching" children's backsides, Henry's many other skills included moonshining and his product was superb. His moonshine still's corn mash went to feed the pigs. And Henry truly loved Anna's corn pone, johnnycake, grits, and hominy, not to mention her fried chicken with bulging red-stripped green beans steam-fried with bacon strips and onions and chunks of red potatoes fresh from the potato patch.

Lawrence Goldsmith had come to Lincoln County from Heathcote Mill in Maryland, and he promptly put an article about Lincoln County's low land prices in *Green Revolution,* the monthly tabloid that Heathcote published. Meanwhile, that year of 1970 saw the birth of *Mother Earth News* magazine. Its editor saw Lawrence's article in *Green Revolution* and promptly printed a shorter version of it in *Mother Earth News.*[23] *Mother Earth News's* editor also trumpeted Lincoln County's low land prices in radio ads that he was using to boost *Mother Earth's* magazine-rack over-the-counter sales in its native southern Ohio.

A minor land-hunting stampede then ensued from southern Ohio to Lincoln County, which happened to include Charley Bates, the future co-buyer in early 1973 of my (and his) beautiful old farm on two high hillside benches of lush meadow near the top of McComas Ridge. Charley had moved to central Lincoln County before I did. By then, in fact, besides helping to gather supplies for Buffalo Creek flood survivors, he had built Lincoln County's first yurt and was living in it.

The leading scholar of Lincoln County, West Virginia's back-to-the-land influx (Professor Jinny Turman) calls we newcomers "alter-natives" because we practiced alternatives. Personally, I called us "neonatives" because that's what John Alexander Williams called us in his well-known book *Appalachia: A History* (2002). I liked the label "neonatives" because

23. Lawrence Goldsmith, "How to Buy Land," *Mother Earth News,* May-June 1970.

most of my fellow newcomers seemed to be trying to blend-into-the-woodwork and act just like the natives. They even acquired some of Appalachia's accent and diction, often on purpose if you ask me.

But a Lincoln County native named Lenore McComas Coberly, who writes books and short stories from a Lincoln County viewpoint, has revealed just how controversial we newcomers actually were. From her perspective and that of her Lincoln County friends and relatives, we didn't blend in at all, particularly at first. We were glaringly different.[24]

Reactions on the part of local natives to we newcomers ran the full gamut from total rejection to total acceptance. Total acceptance was shown by Henry and Anna Baker, who were themselves still newcomers to the central part of Lincoln County. Henry and Anna were also atypical by being parents of a blended family, Anna's half of which came from her previous life married to Karel Triska and performing high-wire acrobatics with him and their five children. As more and more newcomers surrounded Henry and Anna in upper Little Laurel Hollow, Henry and Anna's ability to network grew by leaps and bounds. Their many transient years on successive rundown farms, doing too much hard timber work for too little income, were now over because of all their new networking opportunities with we newcomers. The arrival of Lawrence and Joanie Goldsmith in Chaney Fork of Little Laurel Hollow proved to be just the beginning!

More newcomers arrived only gradually, however. Pete and Marjie Shew moved down from Heathcote Mill in early summer 1971 and bought a stretch of McComas Ridge from Lawrence and Joanie. They spent their first winter in a small lean-to, with a continuous campfire facing the open end. Then Charley Bates arrived from Ohio and, like Pete and Marjie, he acquired some McComas Ridge acreage from Lawrence and Joanie Goldsmith.

But first, the Goldsmiths spent almost a year (1970–71) pretty much on their own. To make money in summer 1970, they grew a huge plot of organic tomatoes, toiling away all summer. "We mulched with sawdust from a local [saw]mill," Joanie says. "So much work bringing it in and

24. For example, see Lenore's story "The Fellowship at Wysong's Clearing" in Lenore McComas Coberly, *The Handywoman Stories* (2002), pp. 81–91. Lenore also put that story in her co-authored book *Writers Have No Age*, 2nd edition (2005).

spreading it. But we didn't have to hoe because of the mulch. . . . It looked like an acre of tomato plants growing out of sand." (Word to the wise here: Sawdust is acidic. Tomato plants *like* a somewhat acidic soil, but most plants don't. Both white and sweet potatoes, for instance, prefer a somewhat *alkaline* soil. Full details for all common garden vegetables can be found online by typing-in "soil acidity.")

The Goldsmiths had pre-arranged to sell a vanload of their tomatoes to a health food store in Washington, DC. So they had a friend named Bob caretake their three Toggenburg goats, including their billy-goat Shiva who was known for his huge horns. And then, says Joanie, "We drove overnight in our van full of tomatoes. [But] the store that was to buy them was closed for a vacation so we spent an entire day hustling to many stores to sell organic tomatoes. All done by phone from some city commune we had been steered to. [Organic was not yet] a popular concept at the time. It was a fiasco. We made almost no money but *c'est la vie*. Life went on and thereafter we had lovely gardens and bartered our produce." Which wasn't actually that saga's end since Lawrence and Joanie arrived home to find their caretaker Bob trapped by billy-goat Shiva in a corner of the barn where Shiva had kept Bob under guard all night. Not long afterwards, Joanie says, "we ate Shiva."[25]

The newcomers who I personally knew best were the Goldsmiths and others who arrived from Heathcote Mill, the back-to-the-land center in Maryland. They had enjoyed their Heathcote lives and they genuinely liked each other (nowadays they hold Heathcote reunions) but Heathcote wasn't exactly home to them. In all but name it was a rural commune—which may sound bleak but it wasn't bleak at all. In fact, it *could* have become a nice cozy home if it hadn't become a rural drop-in center located just thirty-five short freeway miles north of metropolitan Baltimore.

For most of its resident young people, Heathcote was where they spent a few carefree years in between their birth-family and college years (at least *some* college in most of their cases) and what they were now doing.

Heathcote Mill was where they temporized two or three years in-between two longer phases of their lives. And after their communal experience at Heathcote, almost none of them wanted to create a commune as they entered adulthood in central Lincoln County, even though

25. Joanie Goldsmith, emails to author, June 20, 2020.

An elderly Mildred Loomis surrounded by Heathcote's young staff
on the millhouse steps in 1970, including the author seen at the top
of the photo in the doorway. Many of the young people in this photo
moved on to Lincoln County, W.Va., by 1972. Photo by Pete Shew.

communal living might have reduced the economic challenges they
faced in their new surroundings—challenges which some of them, sadly,
failed to solve.

Newcomer Tony Norris says that over fifty of Lincoln County's 1970s
newcomers had some connection to Heathcote Mill. But sadly, Tony
Norris (and his wife Sue) failed to solve Lincoln County's economic challenges. They were a charismatic young couple with two infant boys who
had lived at Heathcote Mill for almost two years. On a spring 1971 visit
to some of his friends in Brooklyn, New York, Tony met a young woman
named Nancy Greenberg and her three-year old daughter Jennifer. Tony
urged Nancy to visit Heathcote, which she did. There, Nancy heard about
Lawrence and Joanie Goldsmith and their four-year old daughter Alice.
So Nancy and her daughter Jennifer proceeded on to Lincoln County and
visited the Goldsmiths at the farm they had bought the previous summer
(1970) from Henry and Anna Baker.

Right then, an old frame house in Little Laurel Hollow became available to rent for $25 a month and Nancy snapped it up. It was just one story high but spacious. Nancy called it "Possum House" but I don't recall any possum stories about it.

Nancy lost no time inviting Tony and Sue Norris to move on down from Heathcote Mill to share "Possum House" with her, and Tony and Sue promptly did so. That all happened by mid-summer 1971, and Tony and Sue's charisma immediately made Possum House the focal point of the Little Laurel Hollow newcomers' social lives. Although possum-less (to my knowledge) the house did come with the ghost of an itinerate horse-and-wagon peddler someone had murdered on the premises about 1910. Tony told me that for the first two weeks, he saw the murdered peddler's ghost floating around at night, but something about the ghost's new co-habitants must have spooked him. He disappeared.

It was Tony and Sue Norris who invited me to visit that same summer of 1971, and their charisma drew many other Heathcoters to likewise "come on down" to visit. Many of them stayed, or (like me) left but came back. Tony was a fine musician and so were some of the other newcomers from Heathcote. Soon native musicians were stopping by for the evening jam sessions on Tony and Sue's front porch. One of the regulars was a local constable who brought along his ukulele. A moonshine jug often made the rounds but the constable seemed to consider it no big deal— maybe because it hadn't been bought or sold? It was Henry Baker's world-class moonshine made right next door up the hollow.

Tony Norris hailed from rural central Texas and had some farming background. He taught me how to harness a horse and plow behind it on foot, "gee" telling the horse to turn right and "haw" to turn left. Loosening and shaking the reins telling the horse to walk forward and pulling on the reins telling it to stop. I had plowed before with tractors (in the Missouri prison and in Tunbridge, Vermont) but I had never steered a draft animal before. Knowing how to do so would soon prove handy on the beautiful McComas Ridge farm with the blind horse Bob.

Tony and Sue Norris were searching for more land than just the quarter-acre garden of the de-haunted Possum House, but they couldn't afford to *buy* anyplace. And they had the two infant boys to look after. In spring 1973 they moved south five miles (as the crow flies) to spacious

Nancy Greenberg's daughter
Jennifer with Barigoat, her
Toggenburg nanny, summer 1972.
Photo by Fawn Yacker.

Furnetts Hollow and one other young couple followed them to that vicinity, but in late 1974 that all fell through and they had no place to live.[26]

It all fell through for Tony and Sue because the abandoned Furnetts farmstead they moved to was "tied-up" in a family heirship, and not all the heirs wanted Tony and Sue to live there because some of them worried Tony and Sue would pay the land's delinquent property taxes and then would claim ownership. (Let's skip why the property taxes were delinquent. Appalachian feuds are supposed to be *between* families, not inside them.)

26. "Furnetts" is *not* a local name. It probably isn't a name anywhere. It started as "Van Atters," the name of the hollow's first settlers. On old maps the hollow is labeled "Van Atters" but on recent maps it's labeled "Furnetts"—because that's how Lincoln County people pronounce it. Van Atters' double "tt" is still there and so is its "er" sound, but they've switched places with each other. And what about the new opening "F"? Lincoln County's German settlers must have turned the Dutch "Van" into the German "Von" (which is pronounced "Fon") and then Scotch-Irish settlers must have turned the "Fon" into "Furn," which conveniently uses the "er" sound and lets the "tts" end the name. Anyway, Van Atters became Furnetts.

Almon Lewis showing Lincoln County newcomers Tony Norris (*left*) and
Pete Shew (*right*) how to butcher a hog. Courtesy of Sue Norris.

Our friend Almon Lewis, being one of the many heirs, had invited
Tony and Sue to live at the Furnetts heirship because none of his fellow
heirs explicitly objected. Then complaints started. Almon took me to
the town of West Hamlin to talk to some of his fellow heirs and vouch
for Tony and Sue. Those fellow heirs wouldn't tell Almon "no" but they
wouldn't tell him "yes" either. "It all depends on (so-and-so)," they would
say, "but that depends on (such and such)." Round and round it went.

Then I negotiated elsewhere in West Hamlin for the *other* prime site
in Furnetts Hollow, an open park-like area a mile further up the hollow
where Furnetts Creek forked. The land there was solely owned by the
well-off owner-operator of a gas station at the south edge of West Hamlin. That land at the Forks lacked any buildings—not a problem, however,
since Tony and Sue could have stayed where they were while Tony built
a cabin at the Forks. The owner of the Forks land was well-off thanks to
his gas station and he told me that if he did sell the land to Tony and Sue,
he would accept gradual payment from them. But alas, he finally decided
he wanted to keep it as a place to hunt.

Then a nice large bottomland meadow became available, Burns Creek.

It ran parallel to Mud River and almost alongside it. But its price was $4,000 "cash on the barrel head," so *it* was out of reach.

Tony and Sue's departure in winter 1974–75 to Sue's family in South Dakota was a blow to us all. There Tony found work at a slaughterhouse. (Now he's a very successful cowboy musician and master-of-ceremonies in Flagstaff, Arizona, and most of he and Sue's sizable family live close by them.)

Tony and Sue weren't the only newcomers who departed for financial reasons, but most of our financial departures were temporary, not permanent like Tony and Sue's departure was. We had come to central Lincoln County hoping we could more or less isolate ourselves, not just from the on-going three-ring-circus at Heathcote Mill but from society overall. How? By living off the land. For most of us, however, things turned out differently. Yes, in Lincoln County we could isolate ourselves from outside, mainstream society. But we couldn't isolate ourselves from *local* society, from receiving and giving local favors, because we weren't independently wealthy. And back then in the 1970s, remember, it wasn't yet possible to perform paid jobs "remotely" by computer. So we were soon deeper and deeper in local give-and-take, at first mostly with each other and almost from the beginning with Henry and Anna Baker's large blended family, then gradually with more and more other natives as well.

Lincoln County often turned out to be our lifetime's main location, as in my younger brother John's case, but usually it didn't, as in my own case. If you hadn't grown up on a farm, you had to find out or figure out an awful lot. Finding-out was easier than figuring-out, and we were blessed with willing mentors—particularly Henry and Anna Baker near the head of Little Laurel Hollow and Almon and Glenna Lewis who lived near the downstream end of Little Laurel and a couple hundred yards up a spacious side hollow, Horse Fork.

Almon Lewis was a World War II veteran and a retiree from the C&O railroad. Like Henry Baker (a non-retired moonshiner) Almon was a born teacher. Almon and Henry both had a knack for using things in ways that the things weren't made to be used. But if you asked both of them anything at the same time they'd start contradicting each other. They each had a streak of the *prima donna!* They were both log-construction experts, so they were both invited to almost every log-raising. But exactly *how* should the end of each unique log be notched to fit snugly

Log-raising at a large cabin under construction in
Chaney Fork of Little Laurel Hollow in 1976.
Photo by Jan Salstrom.

with the unique log that it overlapped? Don't ask that within earshot of *both* Henry and Almon if you're in a hurry! The solution we found was to put Henry in charge of notching at two corners and Almon in charge of notching at the other two corners.

By contrast, their wives Anna Baker and Glenna Lewis always agreed with each other. Together they would deftly help the hostess-of-the-day (the woman-of-the-house being raised) prepare a feast for everyone to eat after the logs were all raised. A log-raising usually took one long day, but it could take a second day for a multi-room cabin or a sizable barn.

My part in log-raisings and plowing and bean-picking and log-splitting (log-splitting to sell mine posts at underground mines in Wayne County), and also controlled pasture-making burn-offs (and how to stop them!) all came in handy several years later, in 1975, when Heathcote Mill's benevolent matriarch and de facto head of the School of Living, Mildred Loomis, unexpectedly appointed me editor of the School of Living's monthly publication, *Green Revolution*.

It then also proved invaluable that one of Lincoln County's newcomers named Larry Lack had moved back to Heathcote Mill, where he applied his organizing skill to gathering lots of raw material to print in the pages of *Green Revolution*—raw material I couldn't have pulled into the magazine any other way since I wasn't on-site at Heathcote where "alternative" projects and workshops and speakers were virtually continuous. Larry Lack also organized Heathcote's address-label brigade and zip-code sorting "bee" so *Green Revolution's* 900 subscribers would receive their copies as fast as possible. Every month I sent 1,000 copies of the magazine to Baltimore by Greyhound bus parcel-express, and the team at Heathcote drove down to Baltimore and picked them up and did all the rest, with Larry Lack coordinating it all.

Probably Larry Lack also suggested the title "Rural Apprenticeships' for our back-section of each month's *Green Revolution* devoted to descriptions from small organic farms of what they would teach the people who came to live at their farm for a few weeks or months. Those self-descriptions also set forth what each small organic farm would expect from its apprentices in return—namely work, since the idea was to learn by doing. *Green Revolution's* ever-growing monthly section on "Rural Apprenticeships" was probably its chief contribution to future posterity, since back then in the mid-1970s there wasn't yet any other national listing of U.S. "rural apprenticeships" in print on a regular basis by that name or any other name—none that we knew of anyway. Our *Green Revolution* way of listing rural apprenticeships is still today how they're listed (online of course) by "Workaway" and by "World Wide Opportunities on Organic Farms" (WWOOF).

But *Green Revolution* magazine was part of an editing-and-printing phase of my life that didn't start until spring 1975. We won't get there until Chapter 10. First come two beautiful Lincoln County places each with its own chapter.

CHAPTER 8

The Beautiful Farm

Most of us newcomers came to rural Appalachia willing and anxious to learn. But how to even get started? No "rural apprenticeships" by that name or any other name were being formally offered anywhere nearby. Our apprenticeships were all informal.

When I moved to the beautiful McComas Ridge farm in spring 1973, I was the first person to live there in about thirty years. I was alone, which suited me just fine. No electricity, no phone, no neighbors, *nice*. I sold the Sand Gap Ridge land to my younger brother John who had accidentally on purpose followed me to West Virginia.

John settled down on that more-or-less twelve acres, built a cabin from the trees I had cut down and debarked and seasoned. Soon he became a carpenter and married a fellow newcomer named Jan LaVoy who was an apprentice midwife. Later they built the ridgetop *dacha* with its turret of ill repute—site of my brother's alleged Russian-communist short-wave radio connection during the 1988–1990 strip-mining controversy that we'll reach again in Chapter 16. Unlike myself, John has stayed put in Lincoln County—despite the telephoned death threats he received during that tense strip-mining controversy in 1988–1990. He and his wife Jan have a daughter Seoka and son Matthew who grew up there on Sand Gap Ridge but are now long since out on their own in Vermont and North Carolina respectively. It was Seoka who, until she was five years old, had an imaginary playmate who she called Dodie.

Lest this sound like smooth sailing for my younger brother John, he actually had a hard time starting as a carpenter in Lincoln County because he was chronically short of money. His start-up investment was

John Salstrom with Charley Bates (full beard)
building John's first cabin on Sand Gap Ridge.
Courtesy of John Salstrom.

John and Jan Salstrom's cabin on Sand Gap Ridge
in winter snow. Courtesy of John Salstrom.

Seoka Salstrom, age 8, bottle-feeding a lamb in
front of her living room heating stove in 1986.
Photo by Elaine Stalzer.

to buy some used tools at a flea market. Using those, he dismantled old
barns and houses in exchange for their wood. Sometimes he needed the
help of work crews and he recruited those by swapping workdays with
the individuals who he wanted to have on his crews. This was accepted by
his crew members so long as John himself intended to personally return
the favor to them. Early on, John built three or four fairly large pole barns
for the air-curing of burley tobacco. Those required less outlay of money
for wood than regular barns required, but later he also built three or four
fairly large regular barns, one of which I worked on with him.

One summer my brother organized work crews to help a young couple
who were newcomers build a small but high-quality frame house on the
next land parcel up from Henry and Anna Baker's place near the head of
Little Laurel Hollow. Since that young couple couldn't pay for the work
but were able-bodied, it was they themselves (not my brother) who we expected to eventually re-pay our volunteered hours by doing return favors
for those of us on the work crews. I recall Charlie Ott, a newcomer land-
scape painter, being quite disgruntled—because he felt sure the young
couple wouldn't actually live in the new house we were building for them

free-of-charge, but instead would sell it and move somewhere else, and thus they wouldn't be able to return very many of our house-building favors.

And sure enough, that's what happened.

Almost all of the networking among us newcomers was very localized. I do recall some of the natives telling me about favors their family members gave or received locally during World War Two as reciprocation for favors they themselves gave or received while they lived and worked far away in cities like Cincinnati and Columbus, Ohio.[27]

I could help do favors for people like the young newcomer couple who said they "needed" a new house because I hadn't moved very far away, only three miles east along McComas Ridge to the beautiful two-bench farm—a farm which still occupies a special place in my heart. I moved there in late spring 1973. The cabin had seen eighty years but remained in sound condition, although the mud chinks between its logs had all dried up and had mostly fallen out. And although its massive "sill log" under its front wall had rotted in half directly underneath the front door. It took a borrowed railroad jack to lift the front of the cabin off its corner-stones—only one cabin corner at a time because my co-owner Charley Bates managed to borrow only one railroad jack for that job. Besides ourselves, several additional helpers were needed to pull out the two halves of the rotted sill log, one at a time, and to put a brand-new sill log in place one corner at a time. (Back trouble, anyone?)

The cabin faced south and about twenty-five feet in front of it stood an old apple tree, probably eighty years old like the cabin itself. It no longer

27. I didn't make written notes when Lincoln County natives told me about such long-distance networking during World War Two. But for Wayne County, which borders Lincoln County on the west, such long-distance networking of favors exchanged hundreds of miles apart is documented in John Lozier and Ronald Althouse, "Social Enforcement of Behavior Toward Elders in an Appalachian Mountain Settlement," *The Gerontologist,* February 1974, p. 79. The full article is recommended reading, pp. 69–80. *Mainly* what Lozier and Althouse document is local help given to retirees who returned to their local roots from careers elsewhere and were *then* rewarded decades *after* they did favors in faraway cities for members of other local families—favors such as housing them and finding them jobs. Lozier and Althouse say that a retiree who returned to his roots in rural Appalachia could often "negotiate an environment for his elder years with a combination of cash and a specialized coin whose exchange value is limited to the local system" (p. 79).

produced any apples. Beyond it, at the far end of the large front yard stood a sizable pole barn that was high and airy. A "pole barn" is a log barn (logs laid horizontally, just like cabin logs) and this one, like hundreds of others in Lincoln County, had never been chinked because it was built to hang burley tobacco in so the tobacco would air-cure. Burley tobacco was Lincoln County's leading cash crop from the 1910s until the 1990s, and old pole barns are still numerous in the county. But all of the county's tobacco producers were small-scale, and the selling of their tobacco was only profitable thanks to a large tobacco market warehouse in Huntington where they could have their tobacco auctioned off to tobacco companies. Then in the 1990s, tobacco companies quit buying tobacco from small producers and Huntington's tobacco warehouse soon closed its doors in 1997. (Today, in all of Lincoln County, only one farm still grows tobacco to sell commercially.)

In the other direction, behind the cabin toward the north, lay the two long grassy meadow benches, undulating back for a sixth of a mile before they climbed up into the woods toward a road-less gap—a gap I would sometimes use as a shortcut to reach the farm via Almon and Glenna Lewis's Little Laurel side-hollow. Each of those two long grassy benches was nearly level, particularly the lower one, and each of them averaged thirty or forty yards wide. The blind retired mine pony Bob could usually be found on the upper bench. Bob was very dark brown and was either a small stout horse or a large pony. He was totally blind from spending many years underground. (To pull coal carts, many of the smaller underground mines still used draft horses or mules or ponies, or combinations thereof if the height of their coal seams varied. Often they used underground stalls for their draft animals rather than bringing them up to the surface after each day's work. Years spent entirely underground would turn the creatures blind.)

Bob was the same blind horse that back in 1971, in pouring rain, pulled Henry Mandel's new jeep back up onto Sand Gap Ridge Road. Later, my land-buying partner Charley Bates paid Chester Ray Elkins $50 for Bob and led him over to our new McComas Ridge farm to graze on the verdant fescue-grass meadows of the two long benches. If the meadows weren't grazed, they would gradually revert back to woods. The previous owner, Halleck Adkins, had kept several beef cattle there, but Halleck moved those cattle elsewhere after Charley and I bought the farm from him.

In the barn I found an old horse collar and harness and bit, along with an old plow and singletree. Blind Bob still knew "gee" (right) from "haw" (left) when I harnessed him up with those to plow the garden. If no mares were visiting, Bob was gentle enough to put visiting children on his bare back. They would grab his mane and then kick his sides to giddy him up, and very slowly he'd oblige. Charley Bates had acquired a new galvanized garbage can and put a large bag of dry field corn inside it, so every day or two I'd invert the lid of the garbage can and rattle some of the dry corn in it, and Bob would come slowly down off the upper meadow and enjoy himself eating corn.

Twenty-five paces downhill from the cabin's back porch, under tall shade trees, a spring of cold water that never ran dry had been boxed in concrete to make an animal watering trough about six by three feet, and two and a half feet deep. Beside that boxed water-spring grew a spice bush, whose leaves proved convenient a year later when someone, as it turned out, would be cooking meals. Behind the cabin's back porch was a tube well that provided the water for human use. It never ran dry either.

Inside the cabin, the living room was dominated by a large stone fireplace where copperhead snakes liked to coil up and warm themselves when the fire was burning low. They were snaking in through cracks at the base of the rock chimney. I would "shoo" them back out of the fireplace and run outside with an axe in hopes of killing them before they skedaddled. One day when my brother John was visiting, he says I fired Charley's shotgun into the fireplace at a copperhead. I don't remember that, but I do recall he was visiting when I accidentally discovered their nest containing quite a few snakes. It was in a weedy rock pile in front of the barn. Those McComas Ridge copperheads (come to think of it) were the first time I had killed anything but bugs and New Mexican chickens since summer 1961 when I was Sierra Club's lone staff person in Yosemite Valley and two park rangers' wives came running to fetch me. A rattlesnake was loose in our campground. That time was harder, what with a boy about seven years old tugging on my belt. "Don't kill it," he yelled at me, "put it in here!" His "in here" was a flimsy orange crate he planned to keep the rattler in as a pet. "Would *you* want to live in an orange crate?" I asked him but he kept tugging my belt and obtruding his orange crate. The women had given me an axe but they had to add a broom and yank the boy away before I could kill that rattler.

The long grassy benches lay out back, north from the cabin, and its front faced south. Farther south, past the apple tree and across the yard and past the barn, stood more woods and another gap, this one denting McComas Ridge itself. Crossing over that gap from the left (east) was an abandoned dirt road. It came up out of Panther Branch and crossed McComas Ridge Road (also dirt) and then dropped down west into Bluelick Branch, a fork of Sixmile Creek which in turn flowed into the Guyandotte River. That abandoned dirt road showed signs of much past use but right in plain sight on its uphill bank lay a collapsed moonshine still—right next to the road, suggesting lax enforcement of the federal liquor Revenue Act of 1862 (one of those Yankee laws passed during the Civil War).

Later I learned some of that dirt road's past when I interviewed the elderly retired storekeeper Raymond Black of Myra. Raymond told me his father, who everyone called "Uncle Billy Black," had operated a small sawmill in Sixmile Hollow starting about 1930, and that he himself (Raymond) sometimes hauled wagon-loads of lumber from the sawmill, up Sixmile Hollow's Bluelick Branch, and over this gap and then down Panther Branch to Mud River and Myra.

I never thought to ask old Raymond Black if the moonshine still next to the road was in operation and doing business when he was hauling lumber over the gap. But I did learn first-hand in the 1970's that liquor laxity still prevailed, because I attended a large social event where a constable was present in uniform and yet moonshine was openly available. It was a large wedding reception. The father of the bride went to the podium and announced moonshine was available in its one-gallon jugs at the help-yourself refreshment tables. (Paper cups were provided, of course. It was a formal occasion.)

Moonshining and timbering were just two of *many* ways to make a living in Lincoln County's by-gone eras. The reason why our new-bought farm's pole barn was so large was because, at one time, the farm's entire lower bench was growing burley tobacco. I don't know the years or the economic specifics of that, but I do know that a few miles to the north in Lower Big Creek Hollow a family named White sold the tobacco off their one-acre-plus tobacco plot for $666.66 one year and for only $35 another year. Both times were during the 1915–1925 era and the White family made both sales at the large tobacco market warehouse in Huntington on 26th Street between 1st and 2nd Avenues. For a few years back then, Lincoln County even had its own smaller tobacco market warehouse located in the railroad town of West Hamlin.

My six months in 1973 on the beautiful McComas Ridge farm were not another "hermit" spell like my February 1970 at Nanao's cave on Greenhorn Mountain in Colorado. I did join Myra Methodist Church, remember, and one weekday per week I'd saunter down to Myra to get mail and buy some food. (Myra's store was closed on Sundays, of course, so I couldn't combine Sunday church with shopping.)

Along the way, I'd often stop and visit my friend Ray Elkins (Mud River Ray Elkins) who was usually in his workshop inside his barn on Mud River Road. Ray loved to discuss famous feats of engineering all over the world, but we also had a lot else to talk about. So I'd look for him as I strolled down Mud River Road toward the Myra store/post office.

Back in October 1809, an uncle of one of Ray's grandfathers had been a "second" in the duel that killed Meriwether Lewis. It happened at an inn along the Natchez Trace in Tennessee. Ray said that Meriwether Lewis provoked the duel and didn't even seem to know the other duelist beforehand. The other duelist survived unhurt, and immediately after shooting Meriwether Lewis dead, he and the duel's two seconds departed quickly and separately to avoid any possible consequences since Meriwether Lewis was governor of Louisiana Territory and a friend of Thomas Jefferson.

Not all historians believe Meriwether Lewis died in a duel. Some historians think he simply committed suicide at the Natchez Trace inn— but Ray Elkins and his family knew the facts from their long-gone relative who seconded. They just didn't know whether he seconded for Meriwether Lewis or for the man Lewis provoked and was killed by.

Besides that, right there in Ray's barn was an enormous home-made loom constructed from un-sawn wood. The loom was large enough to make blankets and was extremely old. Ray said some of his forbears had brought it hereabouts by wagon from Tazewell County, Virginia around 1800. The loom looked like it might have *already* been old by then. Ray wanted to give it away free to a museum, to any museum, so I telephoned the West Virginia Division of Archives and History (in Charleston) about it. I phoned them three times, in fact, and each time they set a day and time when they said they'd come and look at it but they never showed up.

Most interesting of all to me was that Ray had recently retired from four decades of walking along the natural-gas pipelines in the surrounding hills for Columbia Gas Company. His job had been to check for natural gas leaking from the pipes and also to write down the numbers on the company's gas-well-production meters. The gas company paid royalties to landowners for the volume of natural gas extracted from the gas wells on their property. So even though Ray was now retired, he knew the topography of central Lincoln County like the back of his hand and would tell me where abandoned farms could be found and who owned them— farms which I'd often then go and examine in person. If I liked them I'd go to the County Courthouse in Hamlin and examine the current deed and any extant deeds "on back," because I was trying to find farms for quite a few newcomers to buy.

In some cases it worked out, especially if the abandoned farm-of-interest wasn't tied up in a joint heirship. My younger brother John liked to come along with me to the Courthouse and he soon became enamored of tracing Lincoln County deeds "on back," which he now does for a living at the Courthouse, where he maintains accurate property lines and ownership data on Lincoln County's property-tax maps.

I had moved to the farm on McComas Ridge in late spring 1973—too late for the peak of spring's songbird migration, but later I was there for it. Only one other place in my life have I heard such a volume of simultaneous birdsong. McComas Ridge is a long north-south ridge rising between the two parallel rivers that both flow north through Lincoln County, Mud River on the east and the larger Guyandotte River on the west. As they flow north through central Lincoln County, the two parallel rivers flow only five or six miles apart as the crow flies. And the long north-south ridge which rises in between the two rivers, McComas Ridge, was obviously still part in the 1970s of a major songbird migration flyway.

Only along the Mississippi River at the height of spring migration have I ever personally heard an equal volume of simultaneous birdsong.

Back in summer 1945, my family had moved to the crest of the Mississippi River bluff at the west end of Davenport, Iowa. Soon thereafter, the Hiroshima and Nagasaki atomic bombs were dropped and then I turned five. For my birthday my parents gave me a chestnut-brown 700-page history of the United States and a light-grey dictionary almost as thick. (They thought I was asking too many questions. They also showed me how to use the two-volume encyclopedia and the large world atlas in our living room.)

One evening the next spring, my dad suggested I get up early the next morning at the crack of dawn and go out our front door and sit on the front steps. I asked him how I could wake up so early. Just tell myself to before I went to sleep, he said. So I told myself to and sure enough woke up at the crack of dawn. I went down the front stairs, out the front door, through the enclosed front porch, out its door, and sat on the front steps overlooking the Mississippi Valley. It was a clear, warm morning. Birdsongs had barely started in the large trees overhead but soon they became a ringing crescendo that didn't slack off for at least ten minutes. Finally they subsided enough for me to hear some individual birds and I went back up to bed.

That stupendous dawn crescendo was equaled by spring's northbound birds on McComas Ridge in the 1970s. Whether it still happens I don't know. I guess I could go online to Google Earth and see where and how much of McComas Ridge on southward has been strip-mined so all the search engines will keep running including Google Earth's, and so my own computer will run as well. But at least, before the ridges are blasted for their coal, the trees are "harvested" to make paper pulp, so we do get our million copies of *Hillbilly Elegy* cut-rate. (Yes I'm being sarcastic! But I'll mention J.D. Vance's *non*-Appalachian, south-west Ohio rust-belt memoir *Hillbilly Elegy* only one more time, below in Chapter 18.)

As it turned out, the beautiful farm on McComas Ridge with its lush woods and grassy meadows and old blind Bob didn't mark the end of my own migrations. I rarely saw the farm's co-owner Charley Bates since he was out in the world earning money to pay off our farm's purchase price as soon as possible. And I did spend one more long spring, summer, and fall on McComas Ridge in 1974, accompanied by a young woman named Miriam Ralston and in sight of getting married. (I met Miriam at a used-book and imported-tea store I co-owned a few months in Davenport, Iowa in winter 1973–74.)

After that year's idyll on McComas Ridge, things turned urban for Miriam and I the next three years as we became printers and editors in the city of Huntington, West Virginia. But before recounting that transition and where it led us, there's one more beautiful place to tell you of, the high Plum Knobs land—which was *not* a farm, alas, and still isn't a farm.

CHAPTER 9

The High Plum Knobs Land

T he idyllic spring, summer, and fall of 1974 that Miriam and I spent on McComas Ridge sped by all too fast. We would have spent the winter there too but my co-owner Charley Bates would not agree to our chinking of the cabin. Plenty of good clay was available right there to chink with.

In fact, the very best time *to* chink a log building is fairly late in the fall when the weather is both damp and chilly but before any nights drop much below freezing. Don't let anyone tell you different. Chinking done in the fall lasts longest because the damp clay you pack between the logs will dry *slowly* all winter and thus it won't crack and loosen like it would if it dried fast. Slapping the clay in between the logs by hand works best (rather than using a trowel) because your hands can get the clay farther into the crevices. Granted, it isn't pleasant having half-frozen hands hour after hour, so borrow a pair of insulated rubber or plastic gloves from someone.

Charley Bates was still away earning money, enough money to buy out my half of the farm ownership if I were willing to sell it, and meanwhile winter was approaching with the cabin still un-chinked. Christmas 1974 almost arrived before Miriam and I finally left the farm and moved to the city of Huntington.

That winter the blind old pony Bob seemed to do perfectly well on his own, even with snow on the ground. He knew where the barn was, and where its stall was, and presumably he spent cold nights there in the stall. Every two or three weeks I'd hike up to the farm and rattle some dry corn in the metal lid of the garbage can, and Bob would show up about twenty minutes later and enjoy a regular meal.

But out of the blue, just *before* Miriam and I moved to Huntington, we were told of a larger and higher piece of land for sale. It sounded just as beautiful as the farm on McComas Ridge but it had no cabin or any other building. We were told it did have a never-failing water spring at the top of its high eight-acre pasture. The rest of the land was all a wooded basin draining down toward Mud River. On the U.S. Geological Survey topographic map, I could tell that the hilltop pasture stood as high as any other land in the vicinity—except that immediately to its north the rocky Plum Knobs rose another 200 feet higher in elevation, to 1,252 feet above sea level. Those Knobs were the highest points for at least fifteen miles in any direction. It turned out all seven of Lincoln's surrounding counties could be seen on a clear day from Plum Knobs' double summit, and also turned out that delicious little wild plums were plentiful on the way up their sides. The Knobs were not part of the land for sale, but they were uninhabited and were never visited by whoever did own them.

Naturally Miriam and I wanted to see the place before we agreed to buy it. It would take a five-mile hike to get there—a downhill half-mile east to get off McComas Ridge, then two more miles east down Panther Branch Hollow's dirt road to Mud River, across the swinging footbridge there, then north down Mud River Road a mile to Myra, and then without much of a path, a steep mile-plus up the hill that rises immediately to the northeast behind Myra Methodist Church, up to that hill's very top. And there it would be.

Late fall is prime hiking time. The day we went was crisp but not cold and the sky was clear blue. Brown and yellow leaves covered the ground including the paths. Next to the paths we noticed green leaves pushing their way out from under the dead leaves. "Christmas ferns" a foot long and "ground pine" were both pushing out from under the fallen leaves and veering south toward the sun. We also passed patches of wintergreen. Wintergreen's delicious red waxy berries appear only in early summer (and get 'em before the critters do) but the waxy green leaves taste just like the berries and we pulled off some leaves to chew on.

Finally there, we found out the hilltop pasture and particularly its long "outer ridge" enjoyed spectacular views. The outer ridge hovered more than four hundred feet of altitude above Mud River Valley. From its outermost point we could see for many miles up, down, and across the wide valley. On the outer ridge itself were countless persimmon trees and their delicious juicy fruit *hadn't* all been eaten by critters. From along the outer ridge's lengthy north edge, the forested basin dropped down sharply. Somewhere down there pawpaw trees probably grew but I never looked for them. I had been violently sick that fall after over-indulging in Miriam's pawpaw pie.

Grass and flowers averaged above our waists in the eight-acre pasture, with the highest grass near its center—except where about eight deer had been bedding down and matting everything flat. Near the pasture's lower edge in the direction of Myra, we found wild strawberry patches hidden down in the grass. Most of the field was flat but its lower edges drooped a bit and its upper edge rose. And at its upper edge, we discovered that the spring of water would need major chopping away of brush and a general cleaning.

That's where we decided to build a cabin, there at the pasture's highest edge where it started to steepen and then ended in a grove of pine trees—nice and close to the water spring and overlooking not just the field but far beyond it. Even from that height, still two hundred feet of altitude below the Plum Knobs' double summit, we could see toward the southwest at least twenty-five miles, which meant we were seeing distant ridges in "Bloody Mingo" County.

We had heard about Mingo County because of the 1800's Hatfield-McCoy feud, and the Matewan Massacre of 1920, and then as the goal of the 1921 Miners March that fought an army of anti-union forces along the top of Blair Mountain in Logan County.

Little did I know that nine months later I'd be printing 100,000 copies of leaflets for roving pickets to use in shutting down most of the underground coal mines east of the Mississippi River. Or that I'd be putting a brand-new photo of a gnarled old miner with a sign scrawled "Remember Blair Mt." on the cover of *Green Revolution* magazine. That was ahead come summers 1975 and 1976 during runaway wildcat strikes by coal miners demanding back their traditional right to go on strike if their mine wasn't safe to work in.

We bought the new land immediately, then accepted Charley Bates' buy-out of my equity in the McComas Ridge farm, and then moved to the city of Huntington before we froze to death. The new land cost $4,000 for "59 ¾ acres more or less," actually about 90 acres judging by the U.S. Geological Survey topographic map, although we never had the land

Coal miner with placard "Remember Blair Mt. . ." at
August 1975 wildcat-strike demonstration. Cover of
Green Revolution magazine for March 1976. Courtesy
of the School of Living. Photographer unknown.

surveyed. The buy-out money from Charley Bates covered only about
one-third of the $4,000 needed for the new land, so naturally we had to
work full-time jobs in Huntington. That aside, moving to town always
seemed much more complicated than moving to the country. But we
managed.

Come spring 1975, we even managed to get a small covered trailer-
wagon up to the top of the new land's high field. The trailer-wagon's canvas cover folded down its sides and that's how we usually kept it, with the
canvas folded down but the mosquito netting up. We had managed with

someone's jeep to pull the trailer-wagon there to the top of the field via a dirt road that the natural-gas company maintained. (*The* natural gas company in Lincoln County meant Columbia Gas Company.) The dirt road took us there the back way. Starting out north-eastward from Myra store, an unpaved public road first meandered up Sandlick Hollow (often right in its creek-bed) past Spec and Ginny McComas's place; then just past Chuck Yeager's leaning birthplace (now gone) it climbed to the ridge above the head of Sandlick Hollow. There the public dirt road turned right but the gas company's private dirt road turned left and followed the north rim of Sandlick Hollow around to the southern foot of Plum Knobs. At that point, we quit the road by turning left (south) because by going just a hundred yards under a fragrant grove of pines carpeted with pine needles we reached the northeast corner of our new land. And another hundred yards under more pine trees brought us to the top of our eight-acre field next to the spring of water.

We made a campsite there, including a dug and rock-circled camp-fire for cooking, and we cleaned out the water spring enough to pail clear water from it. Then I cut down about forty straight medium-sized white-oak and pine trees and trimmed them for use as cabin logs. We left their bark on—which was *not* best practice but no one thereabouts had a drawknife and we were in a hurry. With a neighbor's horse the logs were pulled to the cabin site, and in the course of a neighborly workday we hoisted and "set" (interlocked at the four corners) the log walls of a cabin fifteen feet square. Then we put floor joists into place using lumber-yard 2 × 6's, and we also brought up enough 2 × 4's to use as rafters.

But then, lacking money enough to buy floor boards and roof boards, not to mention a roll of asphalt roofing to cover the roof boards with, I grew obsessed with clearing the pasture of multi-flora rose bushes. I don't know *why* I attacked those plants. We had no animals in need of forage. Bob the blind horse was owned by Charley Bates, and even if Miriam and I had owned Bob, he was best left where he was on the McComas Ridge farm with its lush meadows. We planned to get some dairy goats later on, but the pasture's big nasty multi-flora rose bushes wouldn't have bothered goats one bit. (But no, they wouldn't have *eaten* them. That's wishful thinking.)

Multi-flora rose bushes are bad, bad plants that as late as the 1960s the U.S. Department of Agriculture was still urging farmers to plant—only in fencerows, of course, and supposedly they alone could *be* fencerows thanks to their sharp thorns. But alas, since birds like to eat rosehips, the seeds of multi-flora rose were planted everywhere with bird poop as their start-up fertilizer. And multi-flora's vicious thorns could make it worse than kudzu. (Not that kudzu had yet reached West Virginia by then in the 1970s, just saying.)

Most of my knowledge of our new land came from the people we bought it from. They were heirs of an enterprising farmer and gas-well driller named Jason Pridemore. Logically, our hilltop field was the upper pasture of a Mud River Valley farm that Jason Pridemore gave to his son Danny Pridemore. But for some reason (into which we didn't pry) Danny was only one-fourth owner of the high field and the basin full of woods. They were owned jointly by *four* heirs of Jason Pridemore (or by *their* heirs in two of the four cases).

In West Virginia, in order to sell heirship land, all of the heirs have to agree to the sale—with the result that a great deal of West Virginia's land is tied up in heirships. In this case, fortunately, there were only four heirs (not counting *their* heirs) and they all agreed to sell the land to Miriam and I for $4,000. Danny Pridemore himself had died fairly young, and it was his widow Anna Lee Pridemore who handled the land transaction with us, helped out by a Hamlin lawyer.

Another one of the four Jason Pridemore heirs of the land Miriam and I had bought was my close friend Edith Pridemore Edwards. She too, like her brother Danny, had inherited a large Mud River Valley farm from their father Jason Pridemore, and she still lived there with her husband Hallie Edwards. She liked to feed me lunch when I passed their farm in order to cross Mud River on their swinging footbridge near the mouth of Panther Branch. Panther Branch is the watershed which the beautiful McComas Ridge farm lay at the head of. (Incidentally, in this part of Appalachia, the "n" and "t" in "Panther" are almost silent but not quite, and the "h" is totally silent. So "Panther" is pronounced halfway between "Painer" and "Painter.")

As for the Plum Knobs themselves, although of unknown ownership (unknown to me) those Knobs were well known as a landmark because in the 1920s they became the favorite destination of a "barnstorming" pilot who would visit this part of Lincoln County to sell rides in his airplane, charging $5 for adults and $3 for children. The barnstormer would fly his passengers to the airspace above Plum Knobs, which rise as fairly bare rock near the center of Lincoln County. The barnstormer would circle the Knobs so his passengers could scrutinize this central part of the county laid out below like an immense bumpy quilt.

I wish someone had taken an aerial photo back then of the eight-acre hilltop south of the Knobs that we had just bought. I like to visualize how things used to be. Edith Pridemore Edwards' husband Hallie Edwards told me he used to grow wheat on the hilltop in the late 1940s and early 1950s. After that, the Danny Pridemore cattle had it available for grazing until 1974 when Miriam and I bought it, but the cattle hadn't kept the grass very short. A lot of it was rough-stemmed grass that reached well above our waists, as did many of the flowers.

Mostly, of course, I wasn't thinking about that hilltop's history but of what it could become—a first-rate *dairy-goat farm*.

CHAPTER 10

Appalachian Movement Press

In spring 1975, Miriam and I were living in Huntington but we were up on our new hilltop land for weeks at a time, camping in the small netting-covered trailer-camper. Things were getting done up there, including the cabin-raising. But then fate intervened when a new opportunity suddenly appeared and was too good to pass up. We "temporarily" set aside our homesteading plans and became printers and editors at Appalachian Movement Press just across the C&O railroad tracks from downtown Huntington, West Virginia.

Huntington is a city you've probably heard about in the "news." Ten years ago Huntington was pilloried by America's mainstream media for having the highest rate of obesity and the worst overall health statistics of any city in the United States. Some media outlets insinuated that Huntington's poor health was caused by its rural mentality. But the poet Tom W. Gibbs told us in the 1970s that Ashland Oil Company was polluting Huntington's air by discharging tons of oil-refining waste two or three times every week from its smokestacks, always in the middle of the night. Ashland Oil had been doing that for years, Tom Gibbs told us. (Maybe it still does so today?).

In 1998 Ashland Oil Company (quote) "agreed to spend $32.5 million to settle U.S. government allegations that its refineries in Minnesota, Ohio, and Kentucky illegally discharged pollutants and failed to report violations."[28]

---

28. Source: "Ashland Settles Pollution Claims," *Oil and Gas Journal*, Oct. 12, 1988; accessed 6/26/2019 at: www.ogj.com. Five years prior, some of the pollution emitted by Ashland Oil Company from Catlettsburg had already been settled out of court.

The Kentucky toxic discharges were the ones Tom W. Gibbs told us were being released in the middle of the night two or three times a week from Ashland Oil's smokestacks in Catlettsburg, Kentucky at the western edge of Greater Huntington—from where the prevailing west wind carried those toxins over Huntington. Tom W. Gibbs lived on a hill in West Huntington and those toxic releases in the middle of the night would immobilize him with asthma attacks.

Even though Ashland Oil settled out of court by paying many millions of dollars in 1993, and then settled more suits in 1998 by paying $32.5 million (which was a pittance for a company of its size) that doesn't necessarily mean the company quit releasing toxins into the wind blowing toward Huntington. The mainstream media's attack on Huntington's good name didn't mention what might well be *the main reason* for the city's health problems. Mainstream media often overlook abuses committed by major corporations.

In spring 1975, still unaware of Ashland Oil Company's brazen pollution of Huntington's air, Miriam and I were living in Huntington but were usually camping up on our new land and getting things done there. Then one day in Huntington, a young man named Tom Woodruff changed our lives by offering me the job of managing Appalachian Movement Press. We set aside our homesteading plans "temporarily" and became printers and editors.

Appalachian Movement Press had been founded in 1969 by several students active in Marshall University's chapter of the Students for a Democratic Society (SDS), including Tom Woodruff and Danie Stewart. Its first location was a storefront facing 8th Avenue at the corner of 16th Street, just south across the C&O railroad tracks from Marshall University. First thing, the Press started printing a monthly newsletter aimed at Marshall University's SDS members and other local radicals.

Meanwhile, however, SDS at its *national* level was committing hara-kiri by letting the terrorist "Weathermen" gain control over it. As awareness

---

See "Ashland settles emissions' lawsuits," Feb. 22, 1993, UPI Archives. Polluters like to settle lawsuits out-of-court so that they won't be required to quit polluting. When a case goes to trial, and the polluter loses, the court's judge or judges can prohibit the polluter from continuing to pollute—but *can't* do so if the case is settled out-of-court.

of that extremism reached Huntington, the new Press's monthly newsletter lost many of its readers. So the Press discontinued the newsletter and instead started publishing short booklets about the region's labor history.

Much later we learned (small world) that back in 1969, the poet Tom W. Gibbs had lived briefly with Tom Woodruff and Danie Stewart in an apartment on 16th Street while Tom Woodruff and Danie Stewart and some others were starting Appalachian Movement Press in the nearby store-front. The Press stayed there several years and then moved one mile west along 8th Avenue to its longer (and final) location at 745 7th Street, again on the 8th Avenue side (the south side) of the C&O railroad tracks that run east and west through Huntington between 7th Avenue and 8th Avenue, paralleling the Ohio River but almost a mile south of it. At its new location, the Press was no longer across the railroad tracks from Marshall University but was across the railroad tracks from downtown Huntington. 745 7th Street remained the Press's home until it eventually closed its doors in 1979 and donated all its equipment to Don and Connie West's Appalachian South Folklife Center near Pipestem, West Virginia in Summers County.

Meanwhile, throughout its ten-year existence, the Press was usually humming with activity. It had to do commercial job-printing to pay its bills, but its whole purpose was to print on behalf of the movement. The Press issued its own distinctive line of original booklets under its own imprint and logo. (Its logo was an old-fashioned miner's pick.)

Many of the Press's own first-time publications were authored by the poet-activist Don West. Don was a legendary Appalachian labor organizer from north Georgia and a good poet. In 1965 he and his wife Connie had established the Appalachian South Folklife Center near the town of Pipestem, West Virginia in Summers County, and had immediately started hosting annual folk-music festivals there. In the early 1970s Appalachian Movement Press published many vibrant new booklets authored by Don West, including some about Appalachian abolitionists of the early and mid-1800s. The Press also published quite a few new booklets by other authors.

And the Press re-printed labor journalism from the past, such as reports written in the midst of the Paint Creek-Cabin Creek coal strike of 1912–13, and the mine wars of the 1930s. (In March 2021, West Virginia

University Press published a heavily-illustrated book by Shaun Slifer setting forth the full history of Appalachian Movement Press.)[29]

The Press moved to its 745 7th Street location in 1974, and also that year Tom Woodruff and Danie Stewart became full-time labor organizers in western West Virginia and eastern Kentucky for "1199," the National Hospital Workers Union based in New York City. So just like Miriam and I doing *our* two things simultaneously (in Huntington and up on the hilltop land), Tom Woodruff and Danie Stewart were likewise doing two things at once. They were keeping Appalachian Movement Press in business part-time while working full time to organize blue-collar hospital workers into local chapters of the National Hospital Workers Union. (The union's full history is told in John Hennen's book *A Union for Appalachian Healthcare Workers.*)

In spring 1975 Tom Woodruff and I crossed paths in Huntington and he hired me to manage the Press and keep it going. Tom Woodruff thinks fast but also logically. (These past few decades he has helped lead one of the world's largest unions, Service Employees International Union—SEIU—which numbers about two million members worldwide.) Tom kept ultimate control over the Press in his own hands but hired me to manage it. He handed me keys to the front door and added my name to his as the account's two check-signers. He also showed me how to withhold and mail in the Social Security wage-tax. And he taught me how all the equipment worked except for the A.B. Dick offset press (which I learned to operate later from Miriam, who learned at a high-school night class). I started managing the Press immediately and hired Miriam to work there too. And immediately came a crisis.

Just before our arrival, the offset-press operator Charlie Berry had heard from a group of Vietnam veterans in Morgantown, West Virginia who had a 250-page book about their experiences in Vietnam (including photos) ready to be printed. Charlie Berry had agreed that Appalachian Movement Press would take the raw copy, not yet typeset or laid-out, and turn it into several hundred copies of a square-backed 250-page paperback book (including numerous black & white photographs) for $1,000.

---

29. See Shaun Slifer, *So Much to Be Angry About: Appalachian Movement Press and Radical DIY Publishing, 1969–1979* (Morgantown: West Virginia University Press, (2021). Also see Miriam Ralston, "The Birth of *MAW: A Magazine of Appalachian Women*," *Goldenseal* magazine (Spring 2021), pp. 58–61.

When Charlie told me he had committed the Press to such a large printing job for a paltry $1,000, I couldn't believe my ears, but it was a done deal. The raw copy might arrive any day and I resigned myself to typeset it and lay it out.

I forget if the photos arrived first or everything arrived all at once, but many of the photos showed soldiers posing next to topless waitresses at Saigon and Da Nang nightspots. Miriam refused to countenance those photos being printed at the Press even though we wouldn't be the book's publisher. So I wrote the Vietnam veterans in Morgantown that we wouldn't print those photos and suggested they substitute some others. They wrote back saying they planned to come to Huntington and totally trash our premises unless we printed what they had sent us. I wrote them back that I had spent almost three years in prison for refusing to be drafted. They replied somewhat friendlier and also said they had located a press in Morgantown that was willing to print the book for $1,000 if they made it photo-ready first.

I wrote them back my sincere congratulations for finding a good deal there—because $1,000 was a low price for printing such a substantial book even from photo-ready copy. Apparently they had no idea what it took to typeset and lay out a book in order to make it photo-ready. (Computer programs like Publisher and Photoshop were still far in the future.)

Overall, my business strategy at the Press was to keep everything simple and cheap by doing business whenever possible "in kind" rather than by using money. That's what I had grown used to in Lincoln County. The offset-press operators and other employees (as needed) did have to be paid wages, but Miriam and I *didn't* have to be paid wages.

Why not? Well, again unexpectedly out-of-the-blue right about then, I was appointed editor of *Green Revolution*, the back-to-the-land monthly of the School of Living, based at Heathcote Mill in Maryland. It was totally coincidental. The benevolent matriarch Mildred Loomis and the rest of the School of Living had no idea I had started managing a print shop. As a result of that coincidence, Miriam and I didn't have to be paid by the Press, and we didn't even have to be paid by the School of Living for editing its magazine. Every month the School of Living sent Appalachian Movement Press a hefty $500 check for producing 1,000 copies of its magazine at the Press. Back then in 1975, $500 was still a lot of money. Today it would be worth $2,400. And offset paper (now called "copy paper") was far cheaper in the mid-1970s than it is now, even allowing for inflation.

Technically, Miriam and I were unpaid employees of the Press, sort of serfs. If serfdom was still legal in West Virginia in the 1970s, then we were legal. West Virginia had begun as western *Virginia* and when it split off as a separate state in 1863 it kept many of Virginia's laws. Maybe it kept indentured servitude? In our particular case it was benign since Miriam and I ran the shop we were serfs of. I used the Press's checks to pay our meagre living expenses. Our bondage to the Press even included one perk: an Employees' YWCA Membership Plan. Huntington's YWCA was just a few blocks away and after our long workdays I liked to relax in its sauna and Miriam loved to swim.

Nevertheless, keeping the Press going wasn't easy. That same year of 1975 saw Minuteman Press start opening franchised print shops which used new instant plate-makers invented by the 3M Company. PIP Printing had started franchising print shops as early as 1968, but the new 1970s plate-makers are what led to the mass franchising that was blanketing the U.S. with print shops. Being franchises, those print shops could finance the expensive new instant plate-makers. We at Appalachian Movement Press were losing our commercial job-printing customers right and left because we couldn't afford to buy a $12,000 plate-maker. Our old-fashioned darkroom negatives and arc-lamp plate-burning entailed several more steps, and lots more supplies, than the new franchise print shops had to deal with.

In their turn, the franchise print shops still had to perform two steps more than *their own* competitors, which were the new photocopying machines. The print shops had to make plastic plates and strap them on their offset presses and then run off the paper copies of whatever it was, whereas photocopiers could simply make final paper copies directly from paper lay-out sheets, which was cheaper below about 150 final paper copies.

So Appalachian Movement Press was losing the bread-and-butter job-printing that it needed in order to survive—or, as things actually turned out, that the Press *would have* needed if Miriam and I hadn't come along with our two successive magazines, first *Green Revolution* and then *MAW: A Magazine of Appalachian Women*. And if *Mountain Call* magazine hadn't also shown up at our doorstep, coming all the way from "Bloody Mingo" County.

In the case of *MAW Magazine,* Miriam invented it. But first came our year and a half of editing and printing *Green Revolution* for the School of Living. As for *Mountain Call*, the third movement magazine that helped the Press survive, it was edited and laid out at Kermit Knob near the town of Kermit in Mingo County by two young twins named John and Michael Fanning. John was a writer and Michael a photographer. Their third editor, a young man named Greg Caranante, was the one who usually brought their photo-ready copy to our premises at 745 7th Street in Huntington.

We received *Mountain Call* already typeset and laid out, ready to have the negatives shot and developed. Then the metal plates were burned, and those plates were strapped on our offset press and the multiple paper copies were run off. After that, doing the rest required no special skill—collating the magazine pages, folding the magazines, "saddle-stitching" each copy on our saddle stapler, and locking down about twenty copies of the magazine at a time into our large, sharp-bladed paper-cutter to trim three of the magazines' four edges. (*Not* trimming the folded and stapled edge—let's not daydream at the paper cutter!).

Then, alas, *Mountain Call* magazine went broke. It fell victim to West Virginia politics. Its major source of funding was the Robert F. Kennedy Foundation, which unofficially supported the fall 1976 Democratic Party candidate for governor of West Virginia, John D. (Jay) Rockefeller IV. The young editors of *Mountain Call* supported Jay Rockefeller too, at *first*. Back in the mid-1960s Rockefeller had been a VISTA volunteer in heavily strip-mined Boone County, and starting in 1970, influenced by his time with VISTA but also influenced by his political calculations, Rockefeller came out totally and adamantly against strip-mining.

When he first ran for governor in 1972 he made strip-mining his main theme. In one campaign speech he said:

Government has turned its back on the many West Virginians who have borne out of their own property and out of their own pocketbooks the destructive impact of stripping. We hear that our Governor once wept as he flew over the strip mine devastation of this state. Now it's the people who weep. They weep because of the devastation of our mountains, because of the disaster of giant high walls, acid-laden benches, and bare, precipitous out-slopes, which support no vegetation at all but erode thousands of tons of mud and rocks into

A strip mine near the town of Keith in Boone County, W.Va., about 1969.
Courtesy of West Virginia State Archives, Si Galperin Jr. Collection.

streams and rivers below. Strip-mining must be abolished because
of those who have given most to the cause—West Virginians who
have suffered actual destruction to their homes; those who have put
up with flooding, mud slides, cracked foundations, destruction of
neighborhoods, decreases in property values, the loss of fishing and
hunting, and the beauty of the hills.[30]

Jay Rockefeller's strong stance against strip mining helped him win the
Democratic Party nomination for governor in 1972, but then he lost the
general election to the incumbent Republican governor, Arch Moore, who
was *for* strip-mining—despite weeping when he saw it from an airplane.

Come 1976, Jay Rockefeller again got the Democratic nomination for
governor. He kept quiet about strip mining until after the primary election, and many of his fellow Democrats assumed he was still against it.

30. Jay Rockefeller, 1972 speech at Morris Harvey College in Charleston, W.Va.,
quoted in Shirley Stewart Burns, *Bringing Down the Mountains* (2007), p. 200.

Then in the fall 1976 general election campaign he came out totally *in favor* of strip-mining. And that got him elected governor.

Mountain Call magazine's young editors were upset that Jay Rockefeller had switched his stance on strip-mining and they weren't discrete about their feelings. The magazine soon lost its funding from the Robert F. Kennedy Foundation and gradually went broke—sad because it had been an uncensored and independent voice in Mingo County. (Its local town of Kermit later became one of West Virginia's record-setters for opioid drug abuse. Maybe if *Mountain Call* had survived, it could have helped prevent that.)

Down the line of dominos, *Mountain Call's* demise made it harder to keep Appalachian Movement Press in business. Right about then the Press also lost its hefty monthly checks for producing *Green Revolution* magazine, because the aging Mildred Loomis retired from active leadership of the School of Living and her successors thought they could edit and produce *Green Revolution* as well as Miriam and I were doing.

Back in mid-1975 when I had started editing *Green Revolution*, I switched it from an 8-page monthly tabloid on newsprint paper into an offset press magazine of 24 to 36 pages on good offset paper ("copy paper"). Every month the magazine carried at least one how-to-do-it feature on alternative energy, and almost every issue carried a new article on alternative economics by Bob Swann. Plus it always carried descriptions of "Rural Apprenticeship" opportunities that were available all over the U.S.

The School of Living's new leaders thought they could perpetuate *Green Revolution* that way, as a substantial magazine, but it soon went downhill. Within a few years it shrank down to 4-to-8-page quarterly newsletter. (On good paper, I'll admit that. It didn't revert back to newsprint paper.)

So, early in 1977 the income of Appalachian Movement Press sagged for a few months. Around that time, Ric McDowell dropped by the shop and we did some Save Our Mountains printing for him. We also had a visit from the anti-stripmining ex-Congressman Ken Hechler and did some printing for him. And we continued printing the quarterly literary journal of the Soupbean Poets who were based at Antioch College/Appalachia in Beckley, West Virginia. They called their quarterly *What's a Nice Hillbilly Like You . . . ?* Some good poets were in that radical Beckley bunch, including P.J. Laska, Bob Baber, and Pauletta Hansel.

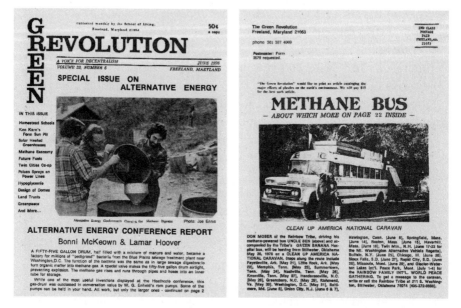

Heathcote's Alternative Energy Conference of spring 1976, *Green Revolution* magazine, June 1976. Courtesy of the School of Living.

Strip mining caused major floods that spring of 1977 in southern West Virginia, and those floods prompted Beth Spence and others to start what they called the Appalachian Alliance. Beth came to Appalachian Movement Press and talked to us about printing things for the Alliance, but I don't recall that leading to any actual print jobs for us. Beth's family owned Logan, West Virginia's daily newspaper, the *Logan Banner,* so printing became possible for her to arrange there. And the Alliance's *big* project was the Appalachian Land Ownership Task Force which produced "Who Owns Appalachia?" in six volumes, state by state, all funded and printed by the federal government's Appalachian Regional Commission (ARC). That happened during a brief spell of ARC idealism which the ARC soon regretted and repudiated. (The coal industry had the ARC in its pocket. Maybe it still does. By building hundreds of miles of new four-lane "corridor" highways through Central Appalachia, the ARC made hundreds of thousands of additional mountain acres profitable to strip mine. Thanks a bunch, ARC!)

Flood in Mingo County in spring 1977. This shows the county
seat, Williamson. Courtesy of Robert Beanblossom.

A door waits to be opened on
the *MAW Magazine*'s first cover.
Courtesy of Miriam Ralston.
Photo by Yvonne Alsip.

Then, however, Appalachian Movement Press bounced back out of its doldrums. Summer 1977 brought the Press new life when Miriam created the emerging Appalachian movement's first women's magazine, *MAW: A Magazine of Appalachian Women*. Miriam felt a magazine was needed where Appalachian women could reach out to each other and express themselves, including artistically. Five-dollar subscription checks poured in all summer in anticipation of the first issue, which was dated September-October 1977 but actually came out in mid-August.

The press run totaled 1,500 copies. At least 500 of those were added after Miriam sent one of the first printed copies to West Virginia's leading newsstand magazine distributor, based in Charleston. The distributor immediately ordered at least 500 copies (I forget the exact number but at least 500) and he came to the Press in person to pick them up. Money! All of *MAW*'s earnings, like all of *Green Revolution*'s earlier earnings, went directly into the Appalachian Movement Press pot. Neither *Green Revolution* nor *MAW* had its own checking account, nor did Miriam and/or I have a checking account.

After *MAW*'s first two issues appeared, the local Associated Press (AP) writer, our friend Strat Douthat, gave *MAW* another boost with a feature story that ran in about fifty newspapers nationwide, accompanied by a photo of Miriam holding her pet white dove while she explained her motives behind *MAW*.

We also started an Appalachian Writers Project to teach writers how to print, but financially that merely broke even. Several famous writers have been printers beforehand (such as Benjamin Franklin) but few printers have been writers beforehand. So we created an Appalachian Writers Project to teach Appalachian writers how to print. Only poetry was eligible. Under our guidance, the poet would typeset his or her own poetry chapbook, then lay it out on the light table, and then—well, then he or she would be spared those old-fashioned steps our print shop still performed. Only the final step remained for the poet-printer, learning to run the offset press well enough to print his or her own chapbook. Three credible poetry manuscripts were submitted, but only one of them seemed to me ready to see print—*No Willows for the Zen Cowboy* by Tom W. Gibbs of West Huntington. (That's how Miriam and I came to know Tom W. Gibbs and to learn from him about Ashland Oil Company secretly polluting Huntington's air year after year.) Tom Gibbs' chapbook appeared and sold well. Later another publisher, Sullen Art Press, re-printed it.

By the time Miriam and I joined the Press in late spring 1975, its two main founders had been working for about a year full-time as the regional organizers of the National Hospital Workers Union, so of course the Press served as that union's main printer in our region. And labor mili-tancy was in the air, especially in eastern Kentucky because of a long and bitter strike underway at Brookside coal mine in Harlan County, where Brookside's 180 coal miners wanted their mine unionized. Brookside was a "captive" mine, owned by a subsidiary of Duke Power Company, and thus it wasn't covered by the United Mine Workers' labor contracts with the Bituminous Coal Operators Association. The strike there started in 1973 and went on and on, escalating into violence. (The Academy Award winning 1977 documentary film "Harlan County USA" tells the story.)

The militancy of the Brookside miners inspired thousands of other workers in Kentucky and beyond. As of 1975, the U.S. minimum wage was a paltry $2.10 an hour (worth $9.95 now in 2020) and it was common in Appalachia for non-professional workers to be paid only that minimum wage, if even that much. Early on, Tom Woodruff and Danie Stewart helped out a five-and-a-half month strike at Doctors' Memorial Hospital in Welch, West Virginia. Welch is the county seat of McDowell County, one of southern West Virginia's major coal counties. After five-and-a-half months, the strike there was finally beaten when the hospital sim-ply closed down rather than pay its non-professional staff a few pennies above the federal minimum wage of $2.10 an hour. The hospital's 140 blue-collar workers thereby lost their jobs along with the rest of the staff. (Seven years later, in the early 1980s, I visited Welch and went by Doc-tors' Memorial Hospital. Its building was still there, closed and forlorn-looking. And much later, in 2014, McDowell County ranked second among all 3,142 counties in the United States in its number of drug-overdose deaths per capita.)

Other hard-fought hospital-workers' strikes occurred in Pikeville and Prestonsburg, Kentucky, and in Charleston and Huntington, West Vir-ginia. In Huntington, we at the Press had a ring-side seat, and Miriam had *MAW Magazine #3* give the strike prominent coverage. Cabell-Huntington Hospital's first union contract had been signed in 1975 to run for two years. That contract granted only a 6 percent pay increase

(3 percent a year), which was less than the official U.S. inflation rate as of then. Simultaneously, in order to discredit the union, the hospital administrators gave the hospital's *supervisory* staff a 30 percent pay raise and an additional week each year of paid vacation.

Come the fall of 1977, as the date neared for the 1975 labor contract to expire, Cabell-Huntington Hospital's administrators offered their blue-collar workers a mere 4 percent wage increase to be spread over the next two years—which was less than one-fourth of the official U.S. inflation rate as of then. The members of the hospital-workers' union who worked at Cabell-Huntington Hospital voted to *reject* that wage offer. Many of them were making only $2.51 an hour (before deductions). One woman who had worked there eighteen years was making only $3.05 an hour (before deductions).

Huntington's powers-that-be then started pouring abuse on the unionized hospital workers. Huntington's daily newspaper reported that Cabell-Huntington Hospital planned to raise all of its charges by 17 percent the very next day after its old contract with the union expired. The hospital also hired a professional strike-breaker for a salary of $400 a day. The union members responded by voting to go on strike the very day the old contract expired, and they started picketing the hospital immediately at dawn that morning.

At 6:00 A.M., Huntington's chief of police showed up in front of the hospital and began harassing the picketing strikers. He singled out one woman who he physically abused and then had arrested. Another picketing woman was hit by a strike-breaker's car. One of the men picketing was beaten up by a doctor, fracturing his ribs and requiring stitches on his face.

Meanwhile, the hospital went to court. It got a court injunction declaring the strike illegal and ordering all the strikers back to work. But the strikers then voted unanimously to *stay* on strike, and the court meekly withdrew its injunction. Huntington's other unions fully supported the strike, but the city police continued harassing the picketers in front of the hospital.

After a week and a half of stand-off, the hospital's trustees secretly started meeting behind closed doors, and after another week and a half they offered the workers an immediate 8 percent raise—a victory for

Striking hospital workers picketing in front of Cabell-Huntington Hospital
in fall 1977. Courtesy of Miriam Ralston. Photo by Carlene Barber.

the workers, especially because the hospital gave them the right to allocate the 8 percent raise themselves. They could thereby help their fellow workers who had the greatest needs to eat a little better and stay a little warmer (it was late fall with winter around the corner).

But *would* the hospital workers really allocate higher raises to those with the greatest needs? Yes, they would and did. Many of them were first-generation city dwellers with one foot still back home in the countryside. They used the hospital's raise to look after each other, just as they would have done with any windfall back home. In fact, in rural areas, helping kin and neighbors was what many recipients of federal black-lung compensation were then doing. The black-lung victim Gobel Greenhill who lived in central Lincoln County wasn't unique when he used his large federal compensation checks to buy each of his four children a new pick-up truck. (We'll reach the black-lung story in the next chapter.)

We at Appalachian Movement Press were elated by the success of the three-week hospital workers' strike in Huntington. And Tom Woodruff was ebullient. After the hospital officials offered the 8 percent raise, Tom said such nice things about those officials that I couldn't believe my ears. I chalked it up to his growing political savvy. After all, Tom had recommended to the union members that they *should* accept the hospital's 8 percent raise offer, and that was what the union members did.

CHAPTER 11

We Print for the Wildcatters

But a year earlier, back in fall 1976, I had been very disappointed by Tom Woodruff's growing political savvy when he extolled the president of the United Mine Workers, Arnold Miller, even though Miller was disastrously inept at negotiating union labor contracts. Even earlier, in fall 1975, Tom Woodruff had refused to let Appalachian Movement Press publish a well-written and objective forty-five page report on the 1975 wildcat coal miners' strike written by the movement journalist Les Levidow. Tom Woodruff prohibited our publishing that excellent booklet simply because its subject matter was a *wildcat* strike—in other words, a strike not authorized by the union which the strikers were members of, in this case the United Mine Workers. I did print two sections of Les Levidow's excellent booklet in *Green Revolution* magazine (in the February and March 1976 issues), but most of it has never been published.

Back in 1974 things had been different at the Press. Tom Woodruff and Danie Stewart had printed thousands of copies of a leaflet titled "Contract Stinks" condemning the 1974 labor contract that Arnold Miller, as president of the United Mine Workers, had just negotiated with the Bituminous Coal Operators Association. The "Contract Stinks" leaflet criticized Arnold Miller's failure to even maintain the status quo between the United Mine Workers and the coal operators—despite the coal boom that was underway because of 1973's Middle East oil embargo and the skyrocketing of oil prices.

And a year later, in summer 1975, Tom Woodruff didn't object to the Press doing the same thing, printing that summer what became a total of 100,000 copies of three anti-Arnold Miller leaflets—this time to foment a wildcat strike by 80,000 coal miners. But we printed those leaflets anonymously.

Another year later, in summer 1976 when another massive wildcat strike by coal miners broke out—by then Tom Woodruff must have *totally* committed himself to union leaders' solidarity with each other. I recall him smoking cigars by then and I couldn't believe my ears when he praised Arnold Miller for the very same thing that the leaflets he himself had printed in 1974 criticized Arnold Miller, namely the mine-safety grievance procedure that Arnold Miller had foolishly agreed to in the UMW's 1974 labor contract with the Bituminous Coal Operators Association. Tom Woodruff did, however, allow Appalachian Movement Press to again print tens of thousands of leaflets for the wildcat strikers of 1976—first 80,000 copies and then another 60,000. The name of our Press was again not mentioned on the leaflets, of course.

Arnold Miller of West Virginia had been elected as president of the UMW in late 1972 as a reform candidate nominated by the Miners for Democracy. Miller replaced Tony Boyle, who was later convicted of murder. Back in 1969 Boyle had paid $20,000 of UMW money to have his leading UMW opponent murdered. But he wasn't finally convicted for that murder until 1974.

Tony Boyle had been hand-picked by John L. Lewis in 1963 to become president of the UMW. Soon, however, more and more coal miners disliked Boyle became he kept evading the issue of black-lung disease, which causes a slow and frustrating death from suffocation caused by coal dust coating the inside of one's lungs and inhibiting the transfer of oxygen to blood cells. (Gobel Greenhill, the black-lung victim in Lincoln County who bought new pick-up trucks for all his children, told me that he didn't want anyone to lay hands on him for healing, because if he got better he might have to go through black lung all over again. He'd rather just die than take that chance, he told me.)

For decades the federal government had ignored evidence that black-lung disease was caused by coal dust. The government wouldn't even recommend that coal miners wear air-filter masks. Finally in 1969 under pressure from much of the medical profession as well as coal miners and their families and widows, the federal government finally admitted that black lung was caused by coal dust, and Congress then voted substantial federal compensation to black-lung victims.

That 1969 black-lung victory, however, was followed by the fraudulent reelection of Tony Boyle as UMW president and then by the murder of Boyle's leading opponent, Jock Yablonski. In 1972 the U.S. Labor Department voided Boyle's 1969 reelection because of voting fraud, and ordered that a special election must be held. Arnold Miller soon emerged as the leading candidate to oppose Boyle in that special election for the UMW presidency. Miller had long been an effective organizer for black-lung compensation payments.

Black lung was coal miners' biggest issue, but Arnold Miller's successful UMW election campaign also called for the union's rank-and-file members to have the right to veto (and thereby to make void) any labor contract negotiated by the UMW's leaders. The next UMW national convention turned that into official UMW policy, and Arnold Miller was in favor of it. At that time he was still the rank-and-file personified.

So a year and a half later in 1974, what Arnold Miller negotiated with the Bituminous Coal Operators Association was called a "tentative" three-year national labor contract, and it was then put to a vote by the UMW's full membership. Some of the miners were alarmed to discover that the new contract omitted their traditional right to go on strike immediately against any mine with unsafe working conditions. Instead, the 1974 contract created an elaborate new grievance procedure. Under it, even if a safety or health violation was life-threatening, miners no longer had the right to quit working or to exit their mine before their shift ended. Or the right to go on strike against any health or safety violation. Instead, the new labor contract created five new levels of grievance arbitration.

Most UMW members still trusted Arnold Miller and voted to approve the 1974 labor contract, but some radical miners in West Virginia got together and started a "Right to Strike Committee." That Committee wrote the leaflet titled "Contract Stinks" and Appalachian Movement Press printed thousands of copies of it for them.

Coal miners had been losing faith in their union ever since Tony Boyle became its president in 1963. Because of Boyle's indifference to black-lung disease, it required a wildcat strike by 40,000 West Virginia miners in 1969 to get that year's federal Health and Safety Act passed. When the reformer Arnold Miller replaced Boyle in 1972 as the UMW's president, miners' faith in their union was renewed, but then came Arnold Miller's agreement in 1974 to the ridiculous new health and safety grievance procedure with its five levels of appeals.

The eye-opener that the UMW's rank-and-file miners were not going to take that lying down was the wildcat strike of summer 1975, idling eighty thousand miners in the eastern U.S. for several weeks. That hot summer evaporated what was left of the top-down control by the president of the United Mine Workers over the union's rank-and-file members—the top-down control that the legendary John L. Lewis had achieved in the 1920s and had enforced until he retired in 1960.

Miriam and I started working at Appalachian Movement Press in late spring 1975. Then came the Vietnam veterans' book of memoirs and photos which we refused to print because of its photos of topless Vietnamese waitresses. Then we put out the first of what eventually became our sixteen monthly issues of *Green Revolution* magazine. And then (although we didn't know it yet) on August 1, 1975 a local grievance arose, and a walk-out began, at an Amherst Coal Company mine at the little town of Lundale along Buffalo Creek in Logan County, West Virginia (—the same Buffalo Creek which a coal-sludge flood had devastated back in 1972). Four days later, on August 5, 1975 that local Lundale walk-out started to spread, but only a little at first.

Then, as reported by the movement journalist Les Levidow, on August 10, 1975 UMW president Arnold Miller "met at a Charleston [West Virginia] suburb with 700 miners from the UMW's Districts 17 and 29 to discuss complaints about the 1974 labor contract. Miller responded as if the main problem was the failure of the industry and union to empanel a 10-member arbitration committee, a late stage in the [1974] contractual grievance process at which many grievances were piling up. He promised to have a functioning panel within 10 days (by August 20th). Nonetheless, many miners reportedly walked out of the meeting in disgust."[31]

During the next week, the wildcat strike spread in southern West Virginia, and during the week after that it started spreading to other states, first to eastern Kentucky and then tenuously as one-day sympathy strikes in Ohio and Virginia.

31. Les Levidow, "The United Mine Workers in the Coal Strike of 1975," *Green Revolution*, February 1976, pp. 12–13.

And by the middle of that week, by August 19th, the previous summer's "Right to Strike Committee" had come back together and had a strategy. The "Right to Strike Committee" was the group for which Appalachian Movement Press had printed thousands of "Contract Stinks" leaflets in summer 1974. I know the Committee came back together in August 1975—by August 19th to be exact—because late that afternoon the phone rang at the Press. The caller told me he was with the Right to Strike in Beckley, West Virginia and he asked "Are you willing to work late to print 30,000 copies of a leaflet?" I told him "sure, we'll wait here for you and print it tonight."

He and some others arrived a few hours later with the copy, which was not photo-ready. They had titled it "Bulletin #1" and what I read as I typeset was eloquent and militant. They slept out in their car while we printed 30,000 copies. When we finished about 1:00 A.M., I went out and woke them up. They paid in cash—in ones, fives, and tens they said they had collected at a rally earlier that day (well, the previous day by then).

First thing next morning the Press got another phone call, from a woman this time. She identified herself as with the Right to Strike in Charleston. Could we print 20,000 copies for them of the same leaflet? I told her "sure." She said someone would be over in a few hours to pick them up. Strike activists, she said, were working around the clock, driving from mine to mine in pairs to picket the shift changes.

So that was their strategy and it was working. Within a few days, 30,000 of West Virginia's 50,000 coal miners were on strike and it was spreading not just to Kentucky, Virginia, and Ohio, but also to Pennsylvania, Indiana, and Illinois. Within about a week, 40,000 of West Virginia's total 50,000 coal miners were on strike. As far away as Alabama, at least two large "captive" mines owned by U.S. Steel Corporation went on strike. Several hundred roving picketers, maybe 400 maximum, were idling most of eastern America's underground coal production. Soon the railroads announced freight personnel layoffs for lack of coal to haul. A federal court injunction was leveling a fine of $100,000 a day against the national United Mine Workers because tens of thousands of its members were wildcatting. Mining areas were pervaded by a holiday atmosphere.

What amazed me and surely others who weren't native Appalachians was that except for the original strikers at an Amherst Coal Company mine on Buffalo Creek in Logan County, none of those thousands of striking miners had a grievance. Their mine had been picketed and they were on strike, simple as that. Miners had a tradition of never crossing a picket line. And obviously they agreed with the Right to Strike Committee's point—that they should have the right to refuse to work under safety or health hazards. The miners seemed aware that the Right to Strike Committee consisted of radicals, but miners had a history of indifference to the ideology of their organizers and 1975 seemed to be no exception.

As the strike continued, however, it began to dawn on the striking miners that the Right to Strike Committee had no intention of negotiating with the coal operators. Maybe the Committee leaders didn't know how to negotiate? Attendance in West Virginia at the Committee's open-air rallies sharply declined. UMW officials started encouraging miners to go back to work if no picketers were in front of their mine, but not to cross a picket line if one was there. They figured the Right to Strike Committee's roving picketers couldn't picket *every* shift change at *every* mine. UMW president Arnold Miller even said that publicly.

Meanwhile, the Right to Strike Committee leaders seemed as uninterested in good media relations as they were uninterested in negotiations. They started growing defensive and a new sign appeared on the door of their Boone County headquarters located in Madison, West Virginia: "You need a union card to get in. Strike Center. No scabs." By early September, a month after it started, the wildcat strike was starting to collapse even in its West Virginia heartland.

At the time, I wrote in *Green Revolution* magazine that "during the first weeks of the strike, one picket 'line' of two or three activists on a Sunday night was sufficient to keep a mine deserted the rest of the week. [But] once Illinois, Indiana, Ohio and so on were returning to work, it began to take picketing every night to keep many mines shut down. The activists worked harder than ever. We printed 30,000 of a leaflet #2 for them and 20,000 of a leaflet #3."[32]

Those second and third leaflets that we printed for the Right to Strike Committee, just like their first leaflet, lacked any hint whatsoever of any grounds for compromise—of any basis for negotiation. The Committee apparently hoped the coal companies would cave in completely to all of

32. Paul Salstrom, "Editorial," *Green Revolution,* October 1975, p. 2.

its demands. Other miners began to realize they were following people who didn't believe in wringing a few key concessions from the coal operators and then going back to work.

By spreading the strike so far and fast, the Right to Strike Committee had created a strong negotiating position, but when the Committee held out intransigently for all or nothing, what that got for the miners was exactly nothing. Which of course meant worse than nothing.

Members of the Right to Strike Committee soon became *persona non grata* among their fellow miners. And whereas large protests had occurred when the strike's main leader Sam Howze was jailed on August 18th, a couple weeks later when the strike's other two main leaders were jailed, Skip Delano and Bruce Miller, almost no protest came from anyone. By the second week of September, few picketers were still active and some of those who did try to picket at mines were chased away by miners who wanted to work without crossing a picket line.

Yet surprisingly, despite that useless wildcat strike, Appalachian miners tried all over again in summer 1976 with different leadership. The 1976 wildcat strike became just as far-flung as 1975's strike had been but it didn't last as long. It did somewhat rectify the bad taste left by 1975 because this time many local and even district-level (and thus paid) UMW officers risked the ire of Arnold Miller by speaking out as champions of the miners' right to go on strike locally and unofficially against local grievances. At the 1976 UMW national convention held in Cincinnati, those "converted" officials sponsored a successful resolution that the UMW's next contract (due in 1977) with the Bituminous Coal Operators Association should guarantee the right to strike on a local basis over unsettled local grievances.

But predictably, when the next national labor contract negotiations finally occurred in 1977 and '78, Arnold Miller mostly ignored that resolution even though, in summer 1977, he had had to say he favored it to get himself reelected as the UMW's president. Miller was under great stress during the 1977–78 labor contract negotiations so he hired a consulting firm to "advise" the UMW's negotiators, and that led to confusion bordering on chaos. The negotiations between the UMW and the Bituminous Coal Operators Association dragged on and on.

December 6, 1977 saw the old (1974) labor contract expire, so the UMW officially went on strike. But that official UMW national strike in the winter of 1977–78 led to major strategic losses for the funding of miners' health insurance. (It did admittedly gain a 34 percent wage increase, but the next few years of high U.S. inflation obviated that.) Finally in late 1978, Arnold Miller was eased out of the UMW presidency by creating a new honorary position for him as "president emeritus" of the UMW.

But by that time it was no longer the same United Mine Workers. It was no longer the unified and effective union that John L. Lewis had turned it into from 1920 to 1960. Not only its solidarity but also its morale had been undermined, and of course solidarity and morale are related. The UMW's leadership had been bested by the Bituminous Coal Operators Association, aided by federal judges who supported the coal companies against the miners.

CHAPTER 12

Back to Rural West Virginia

I t always seemed so easy to leave town and move to the country! We were delayed only because Miriam was about to have a baby and we didn't know of any home-delivery midwives up the Ohio River in Mason County where we were moving to. Not all the way up-river to the county seat of Point Pleasant, thankfully. Point Pleasant was where the "Mothman" had scared the daylights out of people ten years earlier and where I subsequently got the creeps myself. Our new home was about fifteen miles south (downriver) from Point Pleasant. It was a few miles "inland" from the Ohio River town of Ashton, West Virginia at a four-room one-story white house with a large enclosed front porch, lo-cated on a narrow (but paved) dead-end road alongside a narrow stream called Hunter Branch.

We left behind Appalachian Movement Press in good financial condi-tion thanks to the *MAW Magazine* bonanza it had reaped, but we our-selves were virtually broke. We did have a car at the time, an old blue Renault that would only start if it was rolling forward at least four or five miles an hour. Once it was rolling forward that fast, in gear but with the clutch foot-pedal held down, the motor could be started by popping the clutch (releasing the foot-pedal) with the gear in "low." The rolling start had to be forward because the car wouldn't go in reverse gear. It could roll in reverse but couldn't be driven in reverse, so it couldn't be started in reverse. It was better than hitchhiking, usually.

We considered staying in Huntington, but as soon as we no longer ran Appalachian Movement Press, living expenses became a problem. It was spring 1978. I had a job offer in Huntington but it was to be a bill collec-tor, which I couldn't bring myself to be. My dad had been a bill collector for two years during the Depression and had told us as children some of his unpleasant memories of trying to extract money from people who had no money.

As long as we lived in Huntington, I had a part-time job researching and writing glossaries for a five-volume series entitled *Global History of Philosophy*, whose author John C. Plott taught philosophy at Marshall University. He told me that if I were a student at Marshall he could hire me as a work-study research assistant paid by the university. It also occurred to me that by returning to college I could take out student loans, but in the event I didn't quite have to do that, because it turned out Marshall University offered a fast-track to finish a bachelor's degree.

I did have a part-time sawmill job the entire fifteen months we lived on Hunter Branch. A small sawmill was located half a mile down Hunter Branch from the small white house we rented for $50 a month. The sawmill stood where Hunter Branch flowed into a larger stream, which then flowed three more miles down to the Ohio River. My job was to stack sawed wood where it belonged after it passed through a large circular saw and rolled toward me on a series of metal rolling pins. The crew of the large circular saw was often cutting boards but they also cut many railroad cross-ties from oak logs—standard railroad cross-ties eight and a half feet long and 7 × 9 inches in diameter. To comfortably lift those ties off the rollers and stack them required two persons rather than one, and I usually had help.

The scraps left over after logs were cut were mostly long outer slabs from the logs, with bark on one side and wood on the other, and I could take home all of those I wanted. Since our little house was heated by a wood-burning stove in its living room (what else is new?) the sawmill scraps provided all our firewood. Unfortunately, if I couldn't break them over my knee, I had to saw them down to firewood length by hand with our cross-cut saw. (We didn't have a chain saw or know of one we could borrow long-term.)

The sawmill had been created long ago by the family of Maude Hunter Dyke, an 87-year old woman who lived a hundred yards up the road from us. For many years Maude had managed the sawmill herself. That was after her father was bitten by a rattlesnake at age 85 and never fully recovered.

Maude was a liberated woman from the git-go. Married at age fifteen

Maude Hunter Dyke, summer 1979. Watercolor by Judith A. Brown.
From the 1981 Anchor book *We Didn't Have Much,
But We Sure Had Plenty* by Sherry Thomas.

and a mother when barely sixteen, she had had four children in all, but a little girl was stillborn and her two little boys both died in the influenza epidemic after World War One. Only Maude's first child, Virginia, survived childhood. Virginia was now age 70 and had recently suffered a medium-strong stroke. She lived a few miles away with her husband.

As for Maude herself, she had divorced her own first husband. Later she married a man named Dyke but she said he didn't like to work. So she divorced him too and by now in 1978 she had lived alone for many years in the Hunter family homeplace. She had started the first high school in the vicinity. She was a Democratic Party Committeewoman who had always sided with West Virginia's "agrarian" Democrats, who were against the New Deal. (Because of that, she told us, the New Deal Democrats refused to finance any project she was involved with.)

She was also an active member of local Chapter 150 of the United Daughters of the Confederacy. During the Civil War, this stretch of the east bank of the Ohio River had been Confederate country. It differed from Lincoln County and most of the rest of West Virginia because it held large bottomland plantations along the Ohio River that were worked by slaves. The Confederate cavalry general Albert Gallatin Jenkins had lived on one of those plantations called Green Bottom (of 4,000-plus acres) downriver from the town of Ashton, and Maude was one of the local Confederate Daughters who still saw to the upkeep of Green Bottom's manor house and grounds.

When the Civil War started, Maude's father was 17 and he became a Confederate cavalryman, serving in the 1st Cavalry of the Army of Northern Virginia under Robert E. Lee and J.E.B. Stuart. Maude was her parents' youngest child, born about 1891 when her father was about 50 years old and her mother was about 40.

For many years Maude was a hospital nurse in Huntington but then her mother became incapacitated and Maude moved back home to care for her. Her father still did almost all the farm work and a lot of the gardening until he was 85, when he was bitten by the rattlesnake one day while he and Maude were gardening. Maude saw his hand come up with an immense rattler fastened on it. He shook off the snake and Maude immediately cut open the snakebite and sucked out as much venom as she could, but from that day on her father lost his spunk. He survived only a few more years.

Earlier, when Maude had moved home to care for her mother, she gave up nursing but took up midwifery. For decades she was the "granny woman" of choice for many miles around. If newborns were sickly, she offered to keep them with her awhile and nurse them along. Sometimes she had so many sickly newborns she had to tend them in the drawers of her bedroom bureau chest.

Eventually West Virginia insisted that midwives must obtain a license, and Maude told us she gave it up rather than apply for a license. We should have asked her why. Maude did say that she always delivered babies "free of charge." Perhaps that was prohibited as unfair competition under West Virginia's licensing regulations? Maude told us that if the family of the new mother could eventually reciprocate in some way to

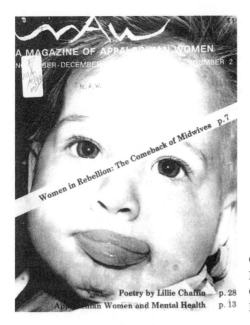

Cover of *MAW Magazine* #2,
November–December 1977.
Courtesy of Miriam Ralston.
Photo by Carlene Barber.

herself or her family, that was fine, but she told us "it didn't really matter one way or the other."

Maude didn't tell us *when* she quit midwifing (we should have asked her) but I suspect it was in the mid-1950s when West Virginia's Department of Health began supervising all lay midwives through public-health nurses. West Virginia didn't finally outlaw lay midwifery completely until 1973—by which time many other states were already re-legalizing lay midwifery in response to the new midwifery movement that my brother John's wife Jan was part of, and which Miriam had featured as the cover story in the second issue of *MAW Magazine* (the November-December 1977 issue).

During the year-plus that we knew Maude, she wasn't very well. Sometimes she stayed in bed past dawn, a self-indulgence she said she never allowed herself before. One early morning she told me she liked to "loll" in bed now and watch the first rays of sunshine creeping down her bedroom wall and reach the chest of drawers she had cared for newborn babies in. She'd just lay there remembering things, she said.

The Hunters were traditional West Virginia farmers and never wanted to be anything else. Their garden and "truck patch" were large but they never sold produce, just gave it away. A lot of their sawmill work they did gratis as well. They were networkers *par excellence*. They did sell their field crops and that brought in enough money to pay their taxes and other cash expenses. But Maude told us their garden and "truck patch" always took priority over working their field crops, because feeding themselves and if need be their kin and neighbors always came first, before earning money.

One day my wife Miriam received mail from a co-editor of *Country Women* magazine and book, Sherry Thomas (a young California sheep farmer), saying she planned to travel around the United States interviewing elderly rural women for a new book. So Miriam wrote Sherry Thomas about Maude and her life story. Sherry wrote back saying she wanted to come and bring along a photographer. Maude agreed to be interviewed, and so it was arranged. Sherry and the photographer camped several days in their two pup tents on our front yard, and Sherry recorded a beautiful interview with Maude. It's Chapter 2 in Sherry's book *We Didn't Have Much, But We Sure Had Plenty: Stories of Rural Women* (1981). The large-format version of the book is best because it includes all the portraits (turned into watercolors) of the women whose interviews Sherry published in the book.

We had moved to Hunter Branch in mid-May 1978, a month after our daughter was born. That summer was just as idyllic for us as our summer 1974 had been on the beautiful McComas Ridge farm. It took three back-and-forths with West Virginia's birth-registry office before Eve Ananda's name was *almost* accurate. After the third back-and-forth, Ananda was no longer "Amanda" so we quit while ahead, missing only the hyphen we had wanted between Eve Ananda's two last names.

Miriam hung bright-colored plastic fish above her crib. Eve Ananda's birth had been hard and she never smiled until we had been out in the country three weeks. Her first smile, however, seemed to come from all of her, a smile of total relaxation. Seven or eight weeks old by then, she seemed to finally be over her hard birth. She was in her crib that day and sunshine poured in through a south window.

Her crib was only for daytime use and we rolled it wherever we were in the house. At night she slept between us. Whenever we were outside, one

Eve Ananda Salstrom Ralston at about age 1, on
Hunter Branch in Mason County, W.Va., spring 1979.
Photo by Miriam Ralston.

or the other of us carried her in front of our body in her frameless orange snuglie. In the evenings, without the snuglie, I would walk her to sleep along our deserted road bordering the stream. Sometimes she'd wake up with a start and eventually I realized that happened whenever I stepped on a bug. So I started experimenting, stepping on bugs on purpose, and sure enough something about it was startling her. So I quit.

Three months after Eve Ananda's birth, Miriam began, gently at first, giving her traditional Indian (Hindu) baby massages as illustrated in *Loving Hands*, the second book by Dr. Frederick Leboyer who had written *Birth Without Violence*.

As fall arrived, it looked like a sparse winter ahead, so we bought a 100-pound bag of excellent Irish potatoes from a local farmer for $10 and stored them cool and dry. We also bought a very large bag of dried pinto beans. And someone told us about a turnip field several miles away where we could gather all the turnips we wanted, which we did every few weeks. That winter we pretty much lived on potatoes boiled with turnips, plus pinto beans and goat's milk. We had a lactating dairy goat who we staked every day in the large field across the stream from us (via a wooden footbridge) where we had garden space as well.

Before leaving Huntington, Miriam had given away free-of-charge *MAW Magazine's* future proprietorship and its mailing list to a group of women from East Tennessee who said they wanted to continue the magazine. They had started a "Council on Appalachian Women." Miriam also sold them the surplus of *MAW's* back issues for 50 cents a copy, half the cover price. But sad to say, that East Tennessee group changed *MAW's* name to something bland and didn't manage to keep the magazine going very long, publishing only two issues.

On the positive side, *MAW's* assistant editor, Huntington native Valerie Staats, went off to college at the University of Iowa and created a *MAW*-like magazine she named *Iowa Woman*, which achieved notable success and probably helped inspire a few other new women's magazines.

Meanwhile, I had registered at Marshall University in Huntington to start finishing college. Dorothy Day considered higher education "the bunk," and I had known plenty of interesting people who didn't have a college degree—but my own personal options seemed to be narrow without one. Dorothy Day had recently come through Huntington and stayed a few days. We borrowed a car and drove her up to Lincoln County's Catholic Worker neighborhood to visit her granddaughter Margaret (Maggie) Hennessy and her long-time co-worker Marge Hughes, plus the other "Workers" who lived in close proximity there. But Dorothy was pushing her limits by still traveling alone on busses around the U.S. at almost age 80, and a few years later she died.

With all the new books coming out recently about her life, it would be nice to ask her some questions, like why she remained such an *orthodox* Catholic even after the liberal Vatican II Council of the early 1960s. Hard as I try, I cannot visualize a Saint Dorothy Day floating up in the heavenly hierarchy of the Roman Catholic Church. But if they *do* canonize her it's her own fault. In fact, she'll feel right at home "upstairs" if any *well-off* Catholics pray to her. She'll zap 'em with pangs of conscience like she used to inflict on all of us in person.

At the University of Chicago in the late 1950s I had earned just twenty-two college credits, so, to graduate from Marshall University, I had to earn 103 more credits. It looked daunting, but Marshall University offered a fast track to a bachelor's degree too good to turn down. If I took at least fifteen credits of Marshall's own college courses, the rest of the credits could be earned by taking exams and submitting "work experience" portfolios. I would then graduate with Marshall University's "Regents B.A. Degree."

So I started taking CLEP tests (the College Level Examination Program tests put out by Educational Testing Service of Princeton, New Jersey). They seemed easy but in order to qualify for credit at Marshall University, the description of each CLEP test I took had to closely match a course description listed in Marshall's official course catalog, so that limited the possibilities. As did my ignorance of subjects beyond the humanities and social sciences. I did pass all the CLEP tests I took but they earned only thirty college credits.

Happily, the director of Marshall University's Regents B.A. Degree program was also chairman of the History Department. He told me I could take the final exams of History courses on a pass/fail basis. So I took ten final exams of History courses and passed all those, adding another thirty credits to my transcript but nowhere near filling it. So I started assembling "work experience" portfolios. Like the CLEP tests, those portfolios had to match courses listed in Marshall University's catalog. That way I garnered thirty more credits, mostly for writing-related and sociology and political-science courses since I still had copies of my unpublished short book on nonviolent peacekeeping, plus countless old memos and leaflets, and numerous feature articles I'd written for the *Catholic Worker, The Distant Drummer* (Philadelphia's late '60s underground weekly), *The Modern Utopian, MANAS, Peace News* (London) and various other periodicals. Plus of course *Green Revolution,* the magazine I'd edited at Appalachian Movement Press.

That put me close. To meet the requirement that fifteen credit hours had to be earned by literally taking courses from Marshall University, I took independent-study "topics" courses rather than classroom ones. I devised those courses on History topics because I had started thinking of graduate school, and getting there might require undergraduate credits in the graduate program's subject. So having already earned thirty History credits by taking final exams, I added fifteen more independent-study History credits.

Spring 1979 arrived and I graduated from Marshall University with its Regents B.A. Degree. No "major" was allowed under that kind of degree, but my transcript now listed forty-five credits with the prefix "HI-" for History. Next question was where to apply for graduate school.

Eve Ananda held by the author in our front yard
on Hunter Branch in Mason County, W.Va.,
summer 1979. Photo by Miriam Ralston.

Marshall University itself seemed the logical choice, but Marshall offered
no teaching assistantships in History. Our choice then fell on Southern
Illinois University (SIU) in Carbondale, Illinois. It was recommended by
a history professor at Marshall University who knew a history professor
at SIU-Carbondale. I liked the fact that Carbondale was a small town
because I figured we could live in the countryside nearby, keep our two
cats, and acquire another goat or two—all of which we did, except our
male cat somehow escaped as soon as we reached Carbondale.

But meanwhile we weren't there yet and it wasn't obvious how to get
all our things to Carbondale. Even if the old blue Renault had still run,
it would have been far too small to load everything into. And it *didn't*
still run. Spring thaw had melted the ice in our driveway and the blue
Renault had rolled backward down the driveway and across the road
and into Hunter Branch, into the stream itself. It could *roll* backward, it
just couldn't be driven backward. And since its emergency brake didn't

Our dairy goat Marcy refused to pull the sled. Then her kid Anaïs
butted Eve Ananda off the sled. Then Marcy (*in front*) blocked Anaïs
(*behind her*) from butting Eve Ananda off the sled again. Winter
1979–80 in southern Illinois. Photo by Miriam Ralston.

work, it did roll backward when the driveway ice melted. (Well, I'd also
forgotten to put the "chock" behind a back wheel.) That soaking in the
stream wouldn't have hurt except the car's motor was in its trunk. The
car wouldn't start even when pushed *more* than five miles an hour. So
how to get even ourselves, not to mention all our stuff, 600 miles west to
Carbondale, Illinois wasn't clear.

The my younger brother John unexpectedly came to our rescue. He
was still a carpenter in Lincoln County (still is, off and on) and he sold
us his first pick-up truck, averring he wanted a newer one. It was an old
faded-blue Ford pick-up. So *voila*, we could move to Carbondale! The
hardest part was saying goodbye to Maude, who we had grown to love. As
a parting gift, Maude gave Eve Ananda a miniature broom to use when
she grew up enough to help Mama.

The Ford pick-up truck did, yes, make it all the way to Carbondale.
Its truck-bed was packed to the gills and it labored climbing the hills on
Interstate-64 across southern Indiana. Soon after we arrived, the old truck
threw some rods and expired. But by then we had found a lovely place in
the country to rent for $75 a month. It was a few miles east of the town
of Anna, twenty miles south of Carbondale. I picked peaches and early
apples nearby for two weeks before school started, earning some money.

Eve Ananda on our side porch in southern Illinois,
already looking purpose-driven. Note goat ears at bottom
of photo. Summer 1980. Photo by Miriam Ralston.

We also found a gentle Nubian dairy goat for sale cheaply, with a
female kid about five months old. I built them a roomy six-by-six foot
shed off to the side of our house and kept it bedded with fresh straw. We
named them Marcy and Anaïs (for Anaïs Nin). Eve Ananda liked to ride
on Marcy's back, much to the chagrin of little Anaïs who claimed first
rights to her mother Marcy's attention.

After the blue pick-up truck expired, I hitchhiked to the university
for a month or two and then we bought a nice old creamy-gray Rambler
sedan. Even the goats liked it (to climb on). Miriam and Eve Ananda
began accompanying me to Carbondale, and soon Miriam was hired to
run an offset press at the university print shop.

For me, a forty-year tussle with academia had begun, but I haven't
regretted it because so much of my teaching, research, and writing has
been about Appalachia.

CHAPTER 13

Starting to Study
Appalachia's History

While working toward a history Master's degree at Southern Illinois University, it didn't occur to me to study Appalachia's regional history. I didn't even know yet that Appalachia had any regional history. I did know it's the backside of seven or eight states and that those states had state histories. And I knew that Appalachia had regional folklore and regional folk music, but I wasn't aware it had any regional history except maybe the labor history we had published booklets about at Appalachian Movement Press. But no one said Appalachia's labor history was somehow different because of where it happened.

The school year was 1979–80. By then, a few scholars like Ronald D. Eller were starting to write that Appalachia had a distinctive regional *rural-industrial* history (including a distinctive rural-industrial *labor* history) but I had no inkling. I wasn't in their loop. The Appalachian Studies Association had started in 1977 at a conference held at Berea College in Kentucky, but I didn't know about that either.

In summer 1980, Miriam and Eve Ananda and I found a nice new home for our goats Marcy and Anaïs and we moved to the Boston area so I could start earning a PhD at Brandeis University. This time we moved by train, with forty-five cardboard boxes packed with our belongings. (The baggage clerk at Carbondale's train station had conniptions.)

At Brandeis University it again didn't enter my head to study Appalachia. I spent several years taking the required graduate courses and meanwhile trying to learn enough German to write a dissertation on the financial diplomacy of Germany's Weimar Republic right before Hitler came to power. That wasn't making much progress because I couldn't get the hang of German.

One day the idea popped into my head to write instead about Appalachia's history. Surely it'd be easier than learning German, so I broached the idea to my dissertation advisor Stephen A. Schuker, who was the world's leading expert on financial diplomacy in the 1920s. To my surprise, he said "sure, why not?" He wanted me to focus on Appalachia during the New Deal era of the 1930s, and to write about *all* of Appalachia, not just about one state and especially not just about one county. In other words, he wanted me to write a "macro" study rather than a "micro" study. Which was fine by me.

Word of my new plan spread among the Brandeis University history faculty and my fellow graduate students, and someone anonymously blessed my mailbox with an announcement of a conference on "Appalachian Frontiers" scheduled to take place a year in the future at two colleges in Virginia's Shenandoah Valley. The announcement invited presentations about the early settlement of Euro-Americans in Appalachia. I figured it wouldn't hurt for my dissertation on the New Deal in Appalachia to have a background chapter on what happened earlier, so I sent in a proposal for the conference.

The conference duly took place in 1985 and worked out very well. Its convener was the Canadian-born geographer Robert D. Mitchell and he invited us to send written versions of our presentations to him at the University of Maryland. Eventually in 1991 a book came out with the title *Appalachian Frontiers*. My essay on "The Agricultural Origins of Economic Dependency" was the book's closing chapter.[33]

By that book's 1991 publication, I had already graduated in 1988 after a total of eight years at Brandeis University, and my dissertation had somehow grown *four* long "background" chapters before it reached the 1930s' New Deal that it was supposed to be about. By 1991, in fact, I had already spent three years trying to turn the dissertation into a publishable book so I could land a long-term college teaching job somewhere in Appalachia.

33. Paul Salstrom, "The Agricultural Origins of Economic Dependency, 1840–1880" in *Appalachian Frontiers*, edited by Robert D. Mitchell, University Press of Kentucky, 1991, pp. 261–283.

A hollow homestead on the cover of *Green Revolution* for November 1976. Courtesy of the School of Living. Date and photographer unknown.

By then too, I had taught for a semester at my alma mater Marshall University in Huntington, and was in the midst of what became five years of teaching American and West Virginia history at West Virginia University (WVU) in Morgantown. Meanwhile, at WVU, I was also taking graduate courses on rural economic development in the Third World.

So my interpretation of Appalachia's history continued to evolve. In fact, it must have been unconsciously evolving ever since 1971 when I first visited Lincoln County in the pouring rain. During the 1970s, both in Lincoln County and then at Appalachian Movement Press in Huntington, I had thought of the two stereotypical images of Appalachia as two separate worlds. The first stereotype was the isolated cabin on a small farm located in idyllic surroundings. I knew that such places did exist, having lived at one on McComas Ridge—although I never came close to achieving self-sufficiency, which is also part of the image. In fact, I had soon realized it is rural *neighborhoods* which can achieve virtual self-sufficiency, not individual homesteads. But let's stick with the stereotypes first.

The other stereotyped image of Appalachia is the complete opposite, the image of haggard, smudged coal miners emerging from the portal of an underground mine. During my PhD research in the 1980s I began seeing that ever since Appalachia's coal mining became large-scale in the 1880s, those two separate images had been merging together into just one economic *system*, a system in which the homestead subsidized the coal mine. More exactly, a system in which the homestead subsidized the coal-mine *owners*, including the financial investors who merely received dividend checks without ever going near a coal mine.

This may sound counter-intuitive. We think of mountain homesteads as the opposite of industry and independent of it. But just because a farm family was rooted in its homestead and in its local networking, that didn't guarantee the family would remain "self-sufficient." The pioneer era's large farms had been subdivided generation after generation down to smaller and smaller farms. A coal-mining job often bridged the economic difference between "not enough" and "enough," enabling tens of thousands of families who lived on "not enough" farms to stay on their farms anyway, at least until the 1940s and '50s.

And like the coal-mine investors who didn't need to go anywhere near a coal mine, many of the coal miners themselves didn't have to live near any coal mine. Their *real* home anyway (their homestead and family) didn't have to be near a coal mine in order for their mining job to subsidize their homestead and family. Subsistence farming combined with wage income kept tens of thousands of farm families on their farms. From their point of view, their mining job was subsidizing their homestead. But at the same time, their homestead was subsidizing their mining job (or, really, was subsidizing the mine owners).

The mine didn't have to be near the miner's homestead. If a farm family's father, or the family's mining son(s) *could* come home every evening from their mining job, that made things all the more convenient. But a coal mine and a homestead could be hundreds of miles away from each other and both still be part of a family's household economy.

Thus, farm families could benefit as well as the mine owners. Mine owners benefited because they didn't have to pay the miner enough to support his whole family. On the other side, wages from the mine job could enable a farm family to pay its property taxes and meet its other cash expenses. The miner's family was partly (and often mainly) supporting itself on its farm, which was presumably still at least semi-viable even if it was small.

Strictly economically, mine owners could usually profit more from that separate-but-linked situation than from any other possible scenario, but it left their workforce unpredictable. They wanted more control over miners, enough control to be sure they would have a large workforce available when a large order arrived for a coal shipment. They wanted to pull miners *and* their families into houses in their private company towns. They wanted the miners' gardens, chickens, pig perhaps or milk cow to be *inside* the coal company's town, not be located somewhere else on land not owned by the coal company. They wanted total control over their employees.[34]

Thus, moving to a coal town was not an Appalachian miner's last resort if he merely moved there himself. Many thousands of miners boarded at coal-town boarding houses and left their family back on the family homestead. But with each successive generation, Appalachian farms were being further sub-divided and their soil was being further depleted. It often did become a last resort to move one's whole family into a coal town, which was especially dire if the family had to sell its homestead in the process, or had to sign it over to a local storekeeper to pay overdue bills. Thereby, the family might have no place it could return to.

To prevent that from happening—to *keep* the ownership of their farm—many a farmer and one or more of his sons went to work in a coal mine. That became common after Appalachia's coal boom got underway in the 1880s. By then, the rest of America no longer held any inviting new frontiers where newcomers could go and established themselves on a piece of good land without needing to bring start-up money along with them. The options for Appalachian people to move anywhere else *rural* had drastically shrunk as the rest of the United States had filled up. Rural Appalachia then began growing crowded with people who didn't want to move to a city.

And sizable families continued being common in rural Appalachia because so much of the homestead work had to be done by hand (or by hoof). The work was subsistence and reciprocity work that miners' families as well as the families of non-miners performed daily. To get all

34. About all this, see "The Captured Garden," chapter 6 in Steven Stoll's book *Ramp Hollow* (2017).

that unpaid work done, miners and non-miners alike kept having large families, and rural Appalachia kept growing more crowded.

With land and resources thus shrinking per person, more and more of the region's families who stayed put in Appalachia mined coal for wages, or mined *more* coal for *more* wages, growing more and more dependent on the unpredictable coal-mining industry. Their livelihood became far less secure than it had been when they relied entirely on their own farming and their network of kin and neighborhood reciprocity. No wonder the farming neighborhoods where miners came from often felt threatened by their return visits. One weekend they might come home flashing a wad of money for their young relatives to envy and another weekend they might come home broke and destitute.

Back in the early 1980s when I started studying rural Appalachia after having participated in it, I found out that Appalachian people were allegedly victimizing *themselves*, self-defeating themselves with "irrational" life decisions. But when I started looking at the agricultural data the government had been gathering every ten years since 1840, I realized the aggregate data made perfect sense as the outcome of separate *rational* decisions made by thousands of farm families generation after generation.

The region's aggregate agricultural data made it obvious that almost every farm family must have, all along, been making *rational* life choices—because in 1840 when the average farm size in Appalachia was still hundreds of acres per farm, the census showed far less land per farm being cultivated for crops or used for pasture than the census showed later on. After the average farm size shrank due to Appalachia's population increase, the census showed a lot more grain per farm being raised to feed the people and livestock both.

Back when land had been plentifully available, plentiful livestock could be raised—or could just be turned loose to "free range" with some sort of ownership brand, usually a distinctive ear-clip. The livestock didn't need grass—they could subsist off the woods. But as the human population grew and the census shows smaller and smaller average farm sizes, the census also shows a lot more grain being raised *per farm*. And a lot more of the livestock's grazing range kept being transformed from woods to pasture, or further transformed to meadow. Pasture and particularly meadow could feed more livestock than woods could feed, and in the case of meadow it could also be turned into hay for higher-quality winter feeding than the woods alone or pasture alone provided.

Thus the aggregate "macro" figures in the census made perfect sense as the outcomes of thousands of separate "micro" decisions that households were continually making, farm by farm, for rational household reasons.

Then too, speaking of clearing away woods to make pasture or meadow (or to cultivate crops), mountain farmers were called "slovenly" if they used slash-and-burn techniques when they cleared the woods. Mainstream public opinion preferred that they strenuously labor to wrest stumps out of the ground (helped by draft animals of course) and thereby make their fields look "proper" right away.

But was it rational or *ir*rational to chop down trees and dig out their stumps if it might wreck your back? Trees could be girded and then simply be left standing in place. Once a tree is girded, it no longer grows leaves, so it no longer blocks out much sunlight. And if you plow between those trees with a light bull-tongue plow rather than with a heavy plow, and if you have a slow-walking ox pull the bull-tongue plow rather than a fast-walking horse or mule, your bull-tongue plow will slither and slide over the tree roots. Eventually the roots will rot and the trees will fall over. In the meantime the girded trees will have dried up while they stood in place, so you can burn them more or less where they fall. When you pile a few of them together and start a fire, they'll keep the fire going because they're so dry. Their ashes will fertilize the soil right where you want the soil fertilized. Is any of that irrational?

I tried to transport myself mentally to each of Appalachia's past decades from the 1730s to the 1930s, trying decade by decade to visualize the economic options that the region's rural people had available. A lot of people were *leaving* Appalachia all along. By the 1830s they had helped to settle the rest of the upland South all the way west to the Ozark mountains, and after that they often went to Texas or the Midwest and helped settle those regions.

But nonetheless Appalachia's own population kept growing quite fast, and thus a lot of internal migration occurred within Appalachia as people moved from the region's more promising sections to its less promising sections. Many people grew marginalized where they were and decided to move somewhere they'd have a better chance to succeed, or at least to hold their own. They moved to places where the typography was less promising but the land and other resources weren't all owned yet by other people, or at least were still cheap to buy or trade for.

I agreed with geographers' sub-division of Appalachia into three sub-regions with three different topographies—the Great Valley, the Blue Ridge, and the Plateau. Then I noticed that starting with the region's first Euro-American settlers about 1730, the overall region's population grew fastest in one *after* the other of those three geographic sub-regions.

In other words, the region's three types of topography were mainly settled one *after* the other, So I called the three sub-regions "Older," "Intermediate," and "Newer" Appalachia.

The first-settled topography and therefore "Older Appalachia" was the fertile, limestone-underlain Great Appalachian Valley that runs southwestward through the heart of the region, which was mainly the direction that Euro-Americans advanced into it, southwestward. It started as the Shenandoah Valley and rest of the Valley of Virginia, then continued as the Valley of East Tennessee and reached well down into northeastern Alabama. That Great Valley separates the Blue Ridge to its *east*—which is widest to the Great Valley's *south*east and which I called "Intermediate Appalachia"—from the Cumberland or Appalachian Plateau which is *west* of the Great Valley, and which I called "Newer Appalachia."

The Cumberland or Appalachian Plateau is a "dissected" (deeply eroded) plateau of thousands of steep, winding hollows separated from each other by thousands of narrow, winding ridges. Eastern Kentucky and western and southern West Virginia make up most of it, but it reaches well down into east-central Tennessee too (just west of the Valley of East Tennessee).

Lincoln County, West Virginia is part of this "Newer" Appalachia, even though most of it isn't quite as rugged and hard to farm as the West Virginia counties south of it, or as southeastern Kentucky's counties like Harlan, Bell, and Perry.

I called "Newer" Appalachia by that name because it was mainly settled after "Older" and "Intermediate" Appalachia were already comfortably filled with settlers. And as it turned out, that's where the coal was located, underneath the rugged and last-settled "Newer" Appalachia—the dissected Plateau with the overall region's worst agricultural prospects because it is a deeply eroded plateau of innumerable steep-sided and narrow-bottomed hollows that twist and turn every-which-way about

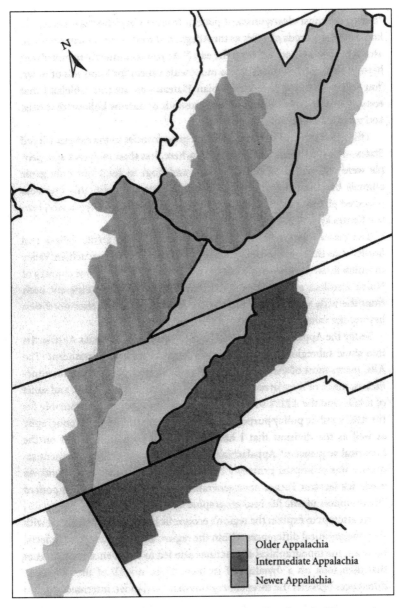

Older Appalachia
Intermediate Appalachia
Newer Appalachia

From *Appalachia in the Making: The Mountain South in the Nineteenth Century*, edited by Altina L. Waller, Dwight B. Billings Jr., and Mary Beth Pudup. Copyright © 1995 by the University of North Carolina Press. Used by permission of the publisher. www.uncpress.org.

400 or 500 feet of altitude below its equally innumerable and equally twisting and turning ridgetops.

I didn't study pre-contact Native Americans, but I studied rural Appalachia's history starting from its earliest white and black settlement. (All along, about ten percent of the region's people have been African Americans, their percentage among the region's people often going up with economic ups and going down with economic downs.) I came to see the rationality of how early settlers lived and made their life choices before I pondered the life choices that their descendants made when rural overcrowding arrived.

By the way, the region's rural over-crowding started in *"Newer* Appalachia," the dissected plateau sub-region, even though that was the last-settled sub-region. The rural over-crowding started there *because* it was the last-settled sub-region. There wasn't any other Appalachian sub-region to move on to. "Newer" Appalachia's rural overcrowding started before the Civil War and made people more accepting of the large-scale capital-intensive coal mining and timber cutting that arrived after the Civil War.

By that same token, however, the life-choice options of that generation—of the *born-*overcrowded generation—included new opportunities. Their young adulthood would have coincided with the 1880s coal boom and steam-powered logging boom, adding new industrial jobs to their options when they made their life choices. They faced tightened living conditions but simultaneously they had new rural-industrial opportunities.

And new mining and lumbering jobs weren't proliferating only in Appalachia. At the same time out West, similar new rural-industrial jobs were multiplying. In fact, after Appalachia's industrial-logging boom peaked in the 1910s, many Appalachian loggers went west and joined the Cascade Mountains' logging boom in Washington State and Oregon, where logging *hadn't* peaked yet. Thereby they kept their lives rural instead of moving to a city.

So when I finally reached my original dissertation topic, the 1930s' New Deal in rural Appalachia, it seemed like just one more added twist. The New Deal added federal economic and social *policy* into the mix that had been created since the 1730s by *laissez-faire*—by *laissez-faire* settlement, then *laissez-faire* over-crowding, then *laissez-faire* rural-sited industrialization, and finally the *laissez-faire* Great Depression.

Thus the interaction of several circumstances—particularly of population expansion, challenging topography, nowhere else attractive to move to, and massive bituminous coal deposits—had laid the foundation for what New Deal policy-makers started to call "stranded populations" in Appalachia. That's what New Deal policy makers called many of "Newer" (Plateau) Appalachia's rural people—"stranded" by the Great Depression's huge cutbacks in both coal mining and lumbering.

Knowing the region's background, its four successive eras of *laissez-faire* economic history, helped me better understand what the *non*-laissez-faire New Deal of the 1930s, the *policy*-driven New Deal, changed in rural Appalachia and what it didn't change.

CHAPTER 14

Appalachia's New Deal

The New Deal was President Franklin Roosevelt's attempt to do three things simultaneously—to provide *relief* from economic distress, to achieve economic *recovery*, and to *reform* what had caused the Depression in the first place. The results were mixed. In Appalachia, the New Deal's short-term results were mainly good. Its medium-term results were mixed, and its long-term results were even more mixed, mainly bad. Particularly good in the short run was that the New Deal ended the survival crisis of the early Depression years and of Appalachia's concurrent 1930–31 drought. The New Deal quickly reduced how many people went to bed hungry and how many children died from the "bloody flux," which was bacillary dysentery.

Most victims of the "bloody flux" were children who ate too many raw weeds too rapidly in springtime. In Bell County, Kentucky, which borders Harlan County on the southwest, at least thirty-five children died of the bloody flux in spring 1931 when agriculture was still drought-stricken and industries kept cutting back as the Depression deepened. Such tragedies were mostly ended by the New Deal—which was all the more welcomed by rural Appalachians because the federal government had *not* helped them during the 1930–31 drought. Even the Red Cross didn't always offer help during the drought.

Likewise, before Roosevelt started the New Deal, both the federal government and West Virginia's state government (both led by Republicans) looked the other way while at least 764 workers fatally contracted silicosis while drilling a three-mile tunnel near Hawks Nest, located about 40 miles southeast of West Virginia's state capital, Charleston. Hawks Nest itself is now a state park overlooking the dam that stops the New River

Hawks Nest Tunnel entrance during the drilling of the tunnel.
Courtesy of West Virginia State Archives.

and creates a reservoir which feeds water into the infamous "Hawks Nest Tunnel." The tunnel was drilled in 1930–31 to divert the New River for three miles underground and downhill, dropping the river 162 feet of altitude and thereby giving it enough momentum to generate electricity at a new power plant built just below the tunnel—enough electricity to make silicon steel, which requires a lot of electricity.

Union Carbide Company realized the tunnel was being drilled through large blocks of 99 percent pure silica. The tunnel's silica cuttings were to be used (and soon were used) to make the silicon steel. To maximize the supply of silica cuttings, the tunnel's diameter was widened twelve extra feet, from 30 feet wide to 42 feet, where it passed through the purest silica.

When the project's managers entered the tunnel to inspect progress, they wore air-filter masks and breathing equipment, but they never supplied either of those to the tunnel workers, who were laboring day after day in a cloud of silica dust. And the managers never told the tunnel

Anonymous graves of some of the hundreds of Hawks Nest Tunnel
workers who died of silicosis. Photo by Lisa Elmaleh, 2016.

workers that the insides of their lungs were likely to bleed them to death,
or at least to respiratory disability and shortened lifespans, because of
the silica dust were breathing. At least 764 of the tunnel workers died
of silicosis within the next five years (by 1936), most of them southern
African-American migrant workers.

On average, workers inside the tunnel lasted four months before they
became too debilitated to keep going. Some local doctors diagnosed their
ailment as pneumonia and some as "tunnelitis." Workers too debilitated
to keep working were evicted from the company housing and usually left
the area, but many of them died before they managed to leave and were
buried in anonymous graves marked by little wooden crosses.

Not just Union Carbide Company and its tunnel-drilling sub-contractor
but also West Virginia's state government tried to hush up the atrocity.
But once Roosevelt Democrats came into national office in 1933, some of
the new federal officials in West Virginia helped to publicized it, and that
helped encourage 300 of the victims or their heirs to go to court seeking

compensation from Union Carbide Company and its tunnel-drilling sub-contractor.

The victims' first court cases were lost, however, which made most of the other victims and heirs willing to settle collectively out of court for a mere pittance ($130,000)—half of which was then taken by their lawyers as fees. But partly thanks to the court cases with their documentation, Hawks Nest Tunnel has gone down in history as America's all-time worst industrial disaster. In truth it was an atrocity, as some New Deal officials helped to show after the fact.

And they didn't let it be forgotten. In 1936 the Labor Committee of the U.S. House of Representatives held hearings about the disaster. The committee concluded that Union Carbide Company and its sub-contractor had shown "grave and inhuman disregard for all consideration for the health, lives, and future of the employees."[35]

Congress then passed a law requiring employers to provide respirators to all of their employees who they assign to work in dusty air, regardless of the source of the dust.

The New Deal's short-term record was likewise good when it came to providing relief (welfare). The national "czar" of relief, Harry Hopkins, famously said "People don't eat in the long run, they eat every day." Hopkins cut corners so millions of people could get adequate food sooner rather than later. Some of the relief came in direct payments and some came as wages for "relief work," which paved or at least pounded gravel into Hamlin's main streets and the roadbeds of Lincoln County's main roads, including Mud River Road, and did likewise on hundreds of roads throughout Appalachia. Other infrastructure that was upgraded or built from scratch included bridges, airports, and public buildings including schools. The new and upgraded infrastructure became the New Deal's main long-term benefit in rural Appalachia.

The New Deal also achieved three major changes with *medium*-term benefits in rural Appalachia. The first of those was the unionization that

35. Quoted in Adelina Lancianese, "Before Black Lung, the Hawks Nest Tunnel Disaster Killed Hundreds," National Public Radio, accessed online on October 2, 2020. Also see Martin Cherniack, MD, *The Hawk's Nest Incident: America's Worst Industrial Disaster* (1989). And see C. Keith Stalnaker, "Hawk's Nest Tunnel," *Professional Safety*, October 2006, pp. 27–33.

protected Appalachian coal miners—except that when the UMW won higher wages for miners, many miners were then replaced by machines. The machines increased coal dust, and that in turn increased the proportion of miners afflicted by black-lung disease. In and of itself, the 1930s unionization of Appalachian coal mining was a long-term benefit, but it didn't cover all the bases. Since it ignored job security and black-lung disease, it ended up being just a *medium*-term benefit.

A second medium-term benefit was the New Deal's system of tobacco "allotments" that protected most of Appalachia's tobacco growers from over-competition. In this case, the benefit was only medium-term because, sixty years later, the large U.S. tobacco companies quit buying tobacco from small producers, which Appalachia's tobacco growers almost all were. (Not to mention the high correlation between tobacco smoking and lung cancer.)

And thirdly, the dams of the Tennessee Valley Authority provided cheap hydro-electricity to farms in the Tennessee Valley. Again, in and of itself, this was a *long*-term benefit. But it gave the TVA financial and public-opinion leverage which, soon after World War Two, the TVA used in order to buy tens of thousands of acres of coal reserves that it then leased out to strip-mining companies, meanwhile building fifty-nine *coal-burning* TVA power plants. The TVA bought cheap strip-mined coal from its land-leasees and burned the coal in its fifty-nine coal-burning power plants so it could sell more and more cheap electricity far and wide, hundreds of miles beyond the Tennessee Valley itself.

So those were three New Deal gains which each later led to losses. In the case of coal mining, when coal miners' wages shot up thanks to the New Deal and to John L. Lewis of the UMW, the coal companies responded by mechanizing more—switching from pick-and-auger mining to coal-cutting machines, and particularly from the shovel-loading of coal carts to machine-loading of conveyer belts, thereby eliminating many miners' jobs and putting more coal dust in the air near the mining face. Miners who operated coal-cutting machines year after year became particularly vulnerable to black-lung disease. Over one-third of them contracted it (including our Lincoln County friend Gobel Greenhill). But the New Deal simply ignored their plight, even though British coal miners by the 1930s were being issued air-filter masks, and by the 1940s were receiving government compensation if they had black-lung disease. In the U.S., the federal government didn't even admit until 1969 that black-lung disease was caused by coal dust.

Two other reforms were championed by the first chairman of the Tennessee Valley Authority (TVA), Arthur E. Morgan, but they never went into effect. They still might help Appalachia if they're ever actually tried. The first of those two was Arthur Morgan's proposal for a supplemental regional currency that would circulate in the TVA area and help compensate for the shortage of dollars. Arthur Morgan and his son Ernest had successfully issued such a currency in 1932 in Yellow Springs, Ohio where Arthur was president of Antioch College. The "Yellow Springs Exchange" currency (as it was called) continued circulating there for several years, adding to the number of local economic transactions taking place.

Late in his life I visited Arthur Morgan in Yellow Springs and he told me his regional-currency idea was one of the main reasons why President Roosevelt eventually fired him in 1938 as chairman of the TVA. He told me that one of the other two TVA directors who he had chosen was an agricultural expert named *Harcourt* Morgan. Harcourt Morgan heard part of a speech that Arthur Morgan delivered on November 9, 1933—a speech partly about the regional-currency idea—and shortly thereafter Harcourt Morgan traveled to Washington, DC and publicly announced that Arthur Morgan wanted to create a separate money system for the Tennessee Valley—rather than telling the public Arthur Morgan's actual proposal, which was to *supplement* the U.S. dollar with an *additional* money system. So Arthur Morgan's credibility had already been undermined by the end of 1933.[36]

Another of Arthur Morgan's attempted reforms was to advance what's now called permaculture by growing more "tree crops" in the Upper Tennessee Valley, such as nut-producing trees, and also mulberry trees

---

36. Arthur Morgan's fullest description of his supplemental regional-currency proposal was his speech at the University of Tennessee in Knoxville that Harcourt Morgan heard part of. Its title is "Group Industries' Problems and their Solution," and Morgan delivered it on November 9, 1933. I reprinted the entire speech as an appendix in my 1988 Brandeis University PhD dissertation. The speech is also available from the TVA Technical Library in Knoxville, Tennessee. As regards Harcourt Morgan's public misrepresentation of Arthur Morgan's proposal, see Arthur E. Morgan, *The Making of the TVA* (1974), p. 58.

(not to breed silkworms but because livestock and humans both love to eat mulberries), and of course persimmon trees and paw-paw trees. Arthur Morgan considered such "tree crops" better suited to hillsides than erosion-causing corn and other cultivated crops, particularly on *steep* hillsides, where he opposed not just cultivated crops but pasture as well. He and the TVA's forestry director Edward C.M. Richards (known as Ned Richards) soon had nurseries underway that were growing several million seedlings of crop-bearing trees.

In October 1934 Arthur Morgan reported that "the raising of tree crops to supply food for hogs, and [non-wood] tree products for sale, is being promoted, and large research and breeding nurseries are already planted. Hickories, pecans, walnuts, Japanese and Chinese chestnuts, Japanese and Chinese persimmons, mulberries, paw-paws, and other tree crops are being developed for land too hilly for plow crops."[37]

Harcourt Morgan, the TVA board's agricultural expert, was a pasture and hay enthusiast known for his "phosphate gospel," and that clearly helped make him an opponent of Arthur Morgan's tree-crop initiative. Harcourt Morgan crusaded for the fertilizing of grass with phosphates and he had the TVA give bags of phosphate fertilizer free-of-charge to farmers throughout the Tennessee Valley. He also convinced the U.S. Department of Agriculture to sell phosphate fertilizer at an artificially low price in the rest of Appalachia. That's one reason why *hay*, rather than corn, soon became (and has remained) the main farm crop grown in the large majority of Appalachia's 190 counties.

So unfortunately, Arthur Morgan's tree-crop initiative, like his supplemental regional currency proposal, was nipped in the bud. The tree crops were voted down and their nurseries were abolished by Arthur Morgan's two co-directors who he himself had chosen to help lead the TVA, Harcourt Morgan and David Lilienthal. And his regional supplemental-currency idea didn't even get as far as the tree crops did.

The New Deal finally straggled to an end while the U.S. was gearing up for World War Two, and that point also marked the end of my PhD

37. Quoted in Arthur E. Morgan, *The Making of the TVA* (1974), p. 62. Also see a muted exposé by the TVA's by-then *former* forestry director Edward C.M. Richards (Ned Richards), "The Future of TVA Forestry," *Journal of Forestry* 36 (1938), pp. 643–652.

Arthur Morgan (*center*) in the 1930s with the other two TVA directors,
Harcourt Morgan (*left*) and David Lilienthal (*right*).
Library of Congress.

dissertation and of the book it led to—which could have been better,
could have been worse, same as this book. By subsequently writing seven
chapters for edited books, and many essays for scholarly journals, I've
been able to fill in some gaps. And writings about Appalachia's distinctive regional history have become far more common by now than they
were thirty-five years ago. Since then, outstanding books about why
Appalachia as a region is historically distinctive have been written by
many authors. I'll refrain from short-listing authors and books here.
Way too many books about Appalachia are too good to omit from even a
"short" list.

CHAPTER 15

"Love My Tender"
(Alternative Economics)

For me, remembering Arthur Morgan includes his alternative economic ideas. I first met him in 1966 when I went to Yellow Springs, Ohio and signed him up to head an honorary committee to welcome the Indian leader J.P. Narayan to the United States on behalf of Dr. Borsodi's Constant currency. In 1967, when I was hired to start an African American youth center in Philadelphia, Morgan sent me a cottage-industry leather-product idea that I should have tried there, but never got around to. It did move my thinking along, and in 1988 in Lincoln County I tried harder but with ideas for wood products.

One well-known institution in Lincoln County is the Lincoln Primary Care Center. Opened in 1975, it's a large health clinic located near Hamlin. During the 1988 Black Gold Inc. strip-mining controversy, I was researching economic alternatives in the county and I asked Jerry Stover, the Primary Care Center's business manager, if he could think of any way the clinic's patients could work off their medical bills by "sweat equity."

Jerry said such an arrangement might be possible to set up at the Demonstration Farm which was run by the state agricultural extension service. He then looked into that possibility, but it didn't prove feasible. The Demonstration Farm was conveniently located on Lower Mud River Road a few miles north of Hamlin. But unfortunately, it didn't generate any profit which could be used to pay the healthcare bills of people who could perform "sweat equity" work there. So people who owned money to Lincoln Primary Care Center could *not* pay off their bills by working at the Demonstration Farm. Jerry Stover told me the Primary Care Center had to buy all its medical supplies from beyond Lincoln County, so it needed dollars from all its patients, not work hours from some of them.

But let's think. The Demonstration Farm included a large "canning" kitchen, professional-grade, which was available for anyone to use. So if the Demonstration Farm had started to charge an in-kind "toll," such as 20 percent of all the blackberries (etc.) that Lincoln Countians (and Putnam Countians to the north) brought there to "can," then that 20 percent toll could have started an economic loop. The Demonstration Farm could have let Primary Care Center patients use its large and immaculate kitchen to turn the Farm's "toll" berries into a line of "Lincoln County Brand" jams and jellies, with the sales income going to the Primary Care Canter to pay down those patients' healthcare bills.

In addition, Primary Care Center patients could have become jam and jelly salespersons, thereby earning a commission which again could have gone to the Primary Care Center to pay down their healthcare bills.

But alas, the Demonstration Farm never started charging any in-kind "toll" from people who were using its kitchen to make preserves, and now the Demonstration Farm isn't even there anymore.

Back in history, Lincoln County's local gristmills and flour mills had always charged their clients an in-kind toll. The local mills scooped out their toll before they ground people's grain for them—so why couldn't the government's agricultural extension service do the same thing with berries? "Taking a cut" is an American tradition, so why can't the government take a cut?

It all made me realize the Primary Care Center could only become an economic-development multiplier for Lincoln County (beyond its providing of jobs) by being part of a larger local trading network. It couldn't just be half of a two-way trade-off with the (now extinct) Demonstration Farm.

To increase the amount of economic activity in Lincoln County, the county could set up something like what Arthur Morgan as chairman of the Tennessee Valley Authority suggested to people in the Upper Tennessee River Valley. I've already mentioned that regional supplemental-currency idea which Arthur Morgan proposed in 1933. Here's how he later described its context:

> At that time, in the midst of the Great Depression, legal tender in rural Tennessee Valley areas was exceedingly scarce. . . . A large

part of the economic life of many Tennessee Valley communities was stopped because the local inhabitants did not have the legal tender to pay each other for services. The [traditional] habit of barter had disappeared, and a money economy prevailed. The farmer could not go to the dentist because he could not pay his bill. The dentist could not have leaky plumbing repaired because he had no money with which to pay his bill. The plumber could not buy fruit and vegetables, the farmer could not hire labor, and so forth. Much of the local productive capacity was idle.[38]

In his November 1933 speech, Arthur Morgan outlined an idea that *wasn't*, as it turned out, destined to be tried in Tennessee Valley but which could have been. And later, it could have been tried in Lincoln County, West Virginia. It could be tried today for that matter, in Lincoln County and many other places. Arthur Morgan said:

I believe that to a certain limited degree this region might well set up its own local economy. It can produce its own goods and deal with itself. But if a region is going to build up a new economy by making things it needs at home [locally], it will in a limited sense have to build up a whole economy and not a fragment of an economy. . . . I would build a cooperative of some sort. I would have a central purchasing organization, a central sales organization, a distributing organization, and I think I'd have that cooperative organization have its own tokens of credit,—a sort of local money.[39]

Arthur Morgan was suggesting a way to supplement the U.S. dollar. At that time in the depth of the Depression, hundreds of local currency systems *were* in fact supplementing the U.S. dollar, including one run very successfully by the city of Knoxville where the TVA had its headquarters. In mid-June 1932, Knoxville had started paying its city employees with its own newly-invented "tax warrants," which were claims on the city's future tax income. They were not "legal tender" (only the U.S. dollar is legal tender in the U.S.) but almost all of Knoxville's merchants accepted

38. Arthur E. Morgan, *The Making of the TVA* (1974), p. 58.
39. Arthur E. Morgan, "Group Industries' Problems and Their Solution," speech on November 9, 1933; TVA Technical Library, Knoxville, Tennessee.

the city's "tax warrants." Since they were not legal tender, they could not be deposited in banks, and therefore they circulated faster than dollars circulated. After six months of paying its employees' salaries with its tax warrants, Knoxville's city government found itself receiving more of them as tax payments than it was paying out as salaries. So the city no longer had to print any *new* tax warrants in order to keep paying its employees' salaries with them.[40]

Knoxville's "tax warrants" stimulated that city's economy and rescued its city-government's finances. Simultaneously hundreds of other supplemental currencies were similarly in use across the U.S. About $1 to $2 million of such local "scrip" currency was circulating in the U.S. as of early 1933 (which now in the year 2020 would be $20 to $40 million dollars' worth). But none of those currencies came close to circulating heavily throughout a region as large as the TVA region of the Upper Tennessee River Valley.

In fact, well before the U.S. Depression finally ended in 1941, a lot of those supplemental currencies were no longer circulating. But if the U.S. dollar ever goes completely haywire, such currencies are obviously what regions, states, counties, cities, etc. will need to improvise. How? Here's one more passage from Arthur Morgan's November 9, 1933 speech at Knoxville:

> If a local shoe manufacturer should sell shoes to a [local or regional] cooperative, he would get cooperative money, not United States money, at least for part of his payment. The same would be true of the clothing manufacturer, and of all the others. If a man should go to buy shoes he could use this kind of local money in which the shoes were paid for. That money would not be good at a distance, and so those who sell things for home [local] consumption could be paid only by buying other things made for home [local] consumption. . . . [So] I would have everybody who was producing for home [local] consumption as a part of this cooperative paid at least in part in the money of the cooperative, so there would be a kind of money that would buy the things we made ourselves but not buy the things outsiders make. In that way we would be compelled to buy from

40. Irving Fisher, *Stamp Scrip* (1933), pp. 32–33.

each other. Not all business would be done in this way. Legal [U.S.] money would also be necessary. [But] I believe this compulsion to buy from each other may be necessary in order to break across the deep worn channels of trade which all lead into and out of the great commercial centers.[41]

A few years earlier, Republican president Herbert Hoover had failed to end the Depression during its first year. So the off-year elections of November 1930 saw the number of Democrats pull even with the number of Republicans in both houses of Congress. Then Hoover's continued failure to end the Depression not only led to the landslide election of Franklin Roosevelt in November 1932 but also gave the Democrats decisive majorities in both houses of Congress.

During the following four "interregnum" months after Roosevelt was elected and before he was finally inaugurated, the U.S. economy sank deeper than ever and supplemental local currencies proliferated all across the U.S. That's why, when Franklin Roosevelt was finally inaugurated as president on Saturday, March 4, 1933, one to two million dollars' worth of local scrip currency was circulating in the United States.

Right after his inauguration, at 1 A.M. on Monday, March 6th, Roosevelt closed all the banks in the U.S. for at least four days. At Roosevelt's first presidential press conference, on Wednesday, March 8th, the first question from a reporter asked when the banks would be allowed to re-open. Roosevelt said he wasn't sure yet, but that things were looking favorable. The *second* question from a reporter asked Roosevelt whether he supported or opposed a one-billion dollar supplemental national U.S. currency proposal that was then before Congress. A few days earlier, Congress had seemed likely to pass that and Roosevelt had seemed likely to sign it into law immediately, thereby telling the U.S. Treasury Department to immediately create $1 billion of a new kind of legal-tender U.S. currency—a currency which would lose its value at a rate of 2 percent a week.

In the U.S. Senate, the legislation for that new type of national supplemental currency had been introduced on February 17th. It was sponsored

41. Arthur E. Morgan, "Group Industries' Problems and Their Solution," speech on November 9, 1933; TVA Technical Library, Knoxville, Tennessee.

by John Bankhead, a Democrat from Alabama, so it was called the Bankhead Amendment. In the House of Representatives it was sponsored by a Democrat from Indiana, Samuel Pettengill, who gave an eloquent speech about it there.

Bankhead's proposal was an "amendment" because it was attached to a billion-dollar work-relief bill that was already before Congress, sponsored by two progressive senators—namely Bob La Follette Jr., a progressive Republican from Wisconsin, and Edward P. Costigan, a progressive Democrat from Colorado. Bankhead's proposal for a national supplemental currency was made an amendment to the La Follette-Costigan work-relief bill because half of Bankhead's new kind of U.S. currency was to enter into circulation by being paid out as La Follette-Costigan work-relief wages.

Prior to Bankhead's amendment, back in *January* 1933, Roosevelt as president-elect had come out in favor of the LaFollette-Costigan work-relief bill and had urged Congress to pass it. Since it is the president's signature that turns a bill passed by Congress into a law of the land, the work-relief bill was held back by Congress until after Roosevelt was inaugurated on March 4, 1933.

But first, on February 17, 1933, two weeks *before* Roosevelt's inauguration, was when the Democratic senator John Bankhead of Alabama generated widespread excitement by sponsoring his ingenious amendment to the La Follett-Costigan work-relief bill. Some of America's leading economists predicted that Senator Bankhead's amendment would flat-out solve the U.S. Depression. The amendment directed the U.S. Treasury to immediately issue $1 billion in official U.S. "money certificates" and to use half of them to pay people for doing the work-relief jobs that the La Follette-Costigan bill would create. That resembled what the city of Knoxville and many other cities and towns across America were already doing by paying their employees with their own tax-warrants. It looked so likely that Bankhead's amendment would pass that the U.S. Treasury started printing those large-sized dollars immediately, and had $10 million of them printed before the government's plans veered in a different direction. (Thus they were never used.)

The other half-billion dollars' worth of the proposed U.S. "money certificates" were to be given away free to the forty-eight states to disperse however they wanted to disperse them.

The exciting part of Senator Bankhead's amendment was that the entire billion dollars of new U.S. "money certificates" were to be issued as large-sized $1 bills that would lose their value at a rate of 2-cents a week. Their $1 face value would have to be shored-up every week with a new 2-cent stamp affixed to their back side. And because their value would keep dropping 2 percent a week, no one would put those new special dollars in a bank as savings, or hoard them in any other way ("under a mattress"). Almost everyone who had any of the new "money certificates" would spend them before they spent anything else.

The certificates were to be large enough in size to hold fifty-two 2-cent stamps on their back side. By each Wednesday morning, another 2-cent stamp would have to be affixed to the backside of each certificate, otherwise it would cease to be U.S. legal tender and no one would be required to accept it as payment for anything. But if the 2-cent stamps were up-to-date on the back of a certificate, then the certificate *would* be U.S. legal tender and every store, etc. in the United States would be required to accept it. After a certificate had all fifty-two 2-cent stamps on its back side, it could be exchanged for a regular one-dollar bill at any U.S. post office. Thus, those special dollars would have been self-liquidating, since the postal service would have acquired $1.04 by selling each certificate's fifty-two 2-cent stamps.

How would this have solved the Depression? When Roosevelt became president in March 1933, about $41 billion of U.S. money existed, but the average dollar was changing hands less than 1.4 times per *year*. Senator Bankhead estimated that his proposed new "money certificates" would change hands, on average, two to three times a *week* and thus about seventy-five times faster than regular U.S. dollars were changing hands.

No one could think of any good reason why Bankhead's amendment would *not* solve the Depression inside the U.S. The dollar-certificates might sound inconvenient, but actually they wouldn't have been since every retail merchant in the U.S. would have kept supplied with 2-cent postage stamps, particularly on Wednesdays. Storekeeper: "Excuse me, ma'am, your certificate is missing a stamp. Do you have 2 cents?" (Incidentally, two cents back then would be worth 40 cents today, and a one-dollar bill in 1933 was equal to $20 today.)

So that was why, at President Roosevelt's first presidential press conference on Wednesday, March 8, 1933, reporters avidly wanted Roosevelt to tell them whether or not he supported Senator Bankhead's amendment to the La Follette-Costigan work-relief bill.

First at that press conference, a reporter wanted to know when banks would be allowed to re-open. Then second, a reporter asked Roosevelt "Do you favor national scrip or scrip issued by clearing houses?" ("National scrip" referred to the Bankhead Amendment's "money certificates." Never mind the clearing-houses idea.)

Roosevelt answered: " . . . About Monday, the day before yesterday, a very, very wide use of scrip seemed necessary and by last night it looked possible to avoid such a general use of scrip. But it does not mean that scrip will be eliminated by any means. Scrip may be used in many areas pending the working out of a sounder plan and more permanent plan to get additional currency into use. Now, I can't tell you any more about that, because we are still working on the details, but essentially it means an addition to the available currency."

The next question from a reporter asked if an additional one-and-a-half billion dollars of Federal Reserve Bank notes were "already being printed." (Those were regular U.S. dollars, not Bankhead Amendment ones.) Roosevelt said he didn't know, and then the press conference went on to other matters, but a few minutes later currency came up again and Roosevelt said,

> On Friday afternoon last [March 3rd] we undoubtedly didn't have adequate currency. No question about that. There wasn't enough circulating currency to go around. . . . We hope that when the banks reopen a great deal of the currency that was withdrawn [from the banks] for one purpose or another will find its way back [to the banks]. We have got to provide an adequate currency. Last Friday [March 3rd] we would have had to provide it in the form of scrip [presumably meaning the Bankhead Amendment's depreciating "money certificates"] and probably some additional issues of Federal Bank notes. If things go along as we hope they will, the use of scrip can be very greatly curtailed and the amounts of new Federal Bank issues we hope can also be limited to a very great extent.[42]

So, what had changed between Monday, March 6th when the national bank holiday started and Wednesday, March 8th, the day of Roosevelt's first presidential press conference? Something had indeed changed. More

42. Press conference #1, At the White House, March 8, 1933, p. 11. Online at Franklin D. Roosevelt Presidential Library; Press Conferences, 1933–1945. Transcripts.

precisely, something had *been* changed. Most of the banks in the United States were already shut down by state governors before March 6th when Roosevelt started the national bank holiday. (All forty-eight state governors had declared state bank holidays by then, but in eleven states those bank holidays had ended and banks had been allowed to re-open.)

So how, by March 13th, were bank inspectors able to pronounce the majority of U.S. banks to be "solvent" and ready to re-open? That was done by quietly adding the assessed value of "sound assets" (including real estate) to the gold and non-fiat money which banks were allowed to count as part of their required reserves. Since banks had been foreclosing on their customers' mortgages for the past three and a half years of the Depression, they held title to billions of dollars' worth of real estate. Their brand-new right to count all of their "sound assets" (including real estate) as part of their reserves usually brought their reserves up high enough to let them re-open and even start making new loans, which in turn automatically added to their assets (à la double-entry bookkeeping). Their new loans didn't add directly to what they could count as their *reserves*, but they did add to their non-reserve assets because the money that banks loan out is newly-created money. It doesn't exist *until* a bank loans it out. It's that bank's asset because the borrower is supposed to pay it "back" to the bank even though the bank created it from thin air simply by loaning it out.[43]

As it turned out, Roosevelt never did throw his weight behind the Bankhead Amendment and it was never passed by Congress. Why? Apparently not only because some new regular money was again being created by banks thanks to the newly-expanded definition of their reserves, but also because the Bankhead Amendment was part of the work-relief bill which everyone associated with a progressive *Republican*, Senator Bob La Follette, Jr. of Wisconsin. Roosevelt was progressive too, but he wanted *Democrats* to get the credit (and the future votes) for solving the Depression, not Republicans—even if they were progressive Republicans.

In other words, even though Senator Bankhead of Alabama was a Democrat, his imaginative proposal for a national "stamp scrip" apparently wasn't tried because 1) it was part of progressive Republican senator Bob La Follette's work-relief bill, and 2) *it probably would have worked*

---

43. Regarding the "sound assets" of banks being added in early March 1933 to the definition of banks' reserves, see "Bank Holiday of 1933" by Robert Jabaily; online at the official "Federal Reserve History" website.

and then Republicans would have received most of the credit for solving the Depression. Shortly after that, Roosevelt sponsored much larger relief bills than the La Follette-Costigan one—bills appropriating 3.5 billion regular dollars rather than just one billion self-liquidating dollars—and those were the relief bills which Congress passed. ($3.5 billion in 1933 would equal $70 billion today.) The $3.5 billion relief bills did *not* include the Bankhead Amendment and they didn't solve the Depression—nor did the equally large-scale WPA that the government started in 1935. It too didn't solve the Depression, partly because work-relief on that large scale created a de facto "public sector" of the U.S. economy which competed with the private sector, especially in the South. The Depression in the U.S. continued until World War Two finally "solved" it eight years later in 1941.

Meanwhile, as we saw at Roosevelt's press conference on March 8, 1933, Roosevelt had down-graded not just the Bankhead Amendment but also *local* scrip currencies by implying that scrip was not as "sound" as regular money, and by saying that he looked forward to enough (regular) currency soon being in circulation so that, as he put it, "the use of scrip can be very greatly curtailed." Most damaging of all was probably Roosevelt's insinuation that scrip was *illegal* under normal conditions. That was insinuated by Roosevelt's press-conference sentence "scrip *may* be used in many areas pending the working out of a sounder plan and more permanent plan to get additional currency into use."[44]

Actually, supplemental currencies (often called "scrip") were, and are, fully legal in the U.S. in denominations worth $1 and up. Their continued use in 1933 and beyond would have helped the U.S. even after the rapid "turnover" (the "velocity") of the Bankhead Amendment's *depreciating* scrip would have helped pull the U.S. out of the Depression. But instead, even most of the early Depression's localized scrip currencies started to atrophy after Roosevelt threw a wet blanket on scrip in his first presidential press conference by making their legality sound iffy.[45]

In a way, local currencies are wider versions of neighborly bartering and

44. Press Conference #1, At the White House, March 8, 1933, pp. 5, 11. Online at Franklin D. Roosevelt Presidential Library, Press Conferences 1933–1945, Transcripts. Emphasis added.

45. For more details, see Irving Fisher, *Stamp Scrip* (1933), pp. 67–75, 79–83, 104–113. Fisher was a Yale University professor and, at the time, was America's leading economist. On a small scale, depreciating (and thus self-liquidating) scrip was successfully

borrowing networks. The reason they're again needed *now* inside the U.S. is in order to reduce the creation of new dollars. Every new U.S. dollar is a potential new claim on the overall assets of Americans. Dollars give anyone and everyone a claim on whatever someone offers for sale in the U.S. Dollars, in other words, give Russians, Chinese, Saudi Arabians and everyone else a claim on whatever someone offers for sale in the U.S. Since the U.S. dollar is "legal tender" in the U.S., you cannot legally refuse to accept it if someone—anyone—offers to pay you with it for something you are offering for sale. That's what "legal tender" means. All other currencies (e.g. "scrips," euros, rubles, yuan, riyal, etc.) are *non*-legal tender inside the U.S. and you can refuse to accept them.

At this point in 2021, the large-scale issuing of new dollars is threatening the ownership of America by Americans. We can cut back on issuing new dollars by starting to offer each other *non*-legal tenders, American ones—local supplemental currencies, regional ones, "time dollars," whatever people will accept in payment because they can turn around and spend it themselves, locally or regionally if not nationally. (The 1933 Bankhead Amendment's "money certificates" would have been a *national* supplemental currency.) Without new supplemental currencies, we may find ourselves being yanked around like a Third World country—yanked around by non-Americans who acquire more and more billions worth of assets inside the U.S., including ownership of our mounting debts—purchased by them with U.S. dollars.[46]

Meanwhile, our economic challenges hugely overlap with our environmental challenges, including climate change. An economic anthropologist named Alf Hornborg has devised a way to deal with those two

---

used to pay the wages of work-relief employees in several places, including in 1933 at Mason City, Iowa to build a state-of-the-art riverside parkway connecting two sections of Mason City. (It was called "Scrip Parkway.") The circulation of Mason City's scrip was hindered, however, because it required a new 2-cent stamp each time it changed hands rather than requiring a new 2-cent stamp once a week whether *or not* it changed hands.

46. By now, lots of Bitcoin and other computerized "Altcoins" are in use. But using Bitcoin and other computerized "Altcoins" won't help to keep America American-owned, because sellers who accept payments in Bitcoin don't necessarily know who they are selling to. So, even though Bitcoin is a supplemental currency that reduces the need for U.S. dollars, it won't help keep America owned by Americans.

challenges in tandem. Hornborg's proposal fits Europe best, so here I'll modify it to make it fit the United States.

One-fourth of the world's human-generated greenhouse gasses are emitted by transportation. *Long-distance* transportation can be drastically reduced by convincing people to buy local.

How? How about making their U.S. dollars worth 10 percent more when they buy local products than when they buy non-local products? The 10 percent savings could apply whenever they buy new products that were produced within (let's say) thirty miles of where they are shopping.

The 10 percent potential savings would apply to in-person purchases of anything brand-new which requires transportation. In other words, it would apply to all new *commodities* at the point of their first retail purchase. The products' barcodes would include the GPS-generated (and embedded) identification of the exact location where the product was produced.

What about products assembled someplace using components that were produced elsewhere? In that case, the place of production should be designated as the place the product was assembled. But the official place of production of any *food* product should be the place where it was grown or raised, *not* the place where it was processed, packaged, or canned.

The check-out counters of retail stores could be partitioned into two parts. The standard red scan-light would tell check-out clerks when the barcode of a product says it was produced more than thirty miles away, and those purchases would go into the "long-distance" part of the check-out counter—whereas products that were produced within thirty miles would trigger a blue scan-light and would go into the "nearby" part of the check-out counter. (Blue, not green, because 8 percent of male humans are more or less red/green colorblind.)

By partitioning check-out counters, customers would see their purchases physically separated into two categories, with the "nearby" category 10 percent cheaper. Likewise, the customer should receive two separate receipts, because one of the two categories could be paid for with a new type of U.S. dollars called eco-dollars (E.D.s)—whereas the "long-distance" purchases could only be paid for with regular dollars (R.D.s). (Of course, buyers should have the option of paying for their long-distance purchases with eco-dollars, thereby sacrificing 10 percent of the value of their eco-dollars if they're short of regular dollars.)

To prevent more inflation, eco-dollars should enter into circulation only through people and companies using regular dollars to buy eco-dollars from banks. The exchange rate would be $1 regular for $1.10 eco-dollars. Banks, in turn, could buy eco-dollars from their regional Federal Reserve Bank at the same exchange rate. And in both directions—R.D.s for E.D.s and E.D.s for R.D.s—all banks would be required to fulfill all exchange requests. But banks could not *create* eco-dollars from thin air by making loans in them—which is how regular dollars are created.

I'm aware that if the United States starts issuing eco-dollars, then banks might have to start issuing eco-dollar credit cards—but maybe not. Maybe our existing credit cards could be programmed to register regular dollars and eco-dollars both. In that case, the separation between E.D.s and R.D.s could simply be displayed on our monthly credit-card bills. But our bank *would* still need to maintain two separate accounts for us, one account for regular dollars and the other for eco-dollars.

The only way to get around having a new additional form of U.S. dollars would be to create a two-tier pricing system, and then to trust retailers to automatically charge 10 percent more when a product was not being purchased within thirty miles of its barcode-embedded point of production. To me, such a two-tier pricing system sounds hard to regulate and monitor. But I'm not an expert.

Regular dollars and eco-dollars would be fully exchangeable back and forth with each other not only through banks but whenever both parties to an exchange agree to do it. The official exchange rate at banks would be $1.10 eco-dollars to $1.00 regular dollar. People could make transfers between their two back accounts just like they now make transfers between their checking account and their savings account. Up to a certain dollar amount, post offices should also provide exchanges between the two types of dollars, just as post offices now provide money orders and cashier's checks.

Incidentally, I propose all this for in-person retail purchases only. No online purchases, or any other type of mail-delivered or commercially-delivered purchases should qualify for payment with eco-dollars. And, to repeat, only the *first* purchase of *brand-new* products should qualify for purchase with eco-dollars, and only if the product required physical transportation to reach its point of sale.

Further details can be worked out by viewing the pre-Brexit relationship in Great Britain between the pound and the euro. Britain was never in the Eurozone. Only the pound was legal tender in Britain, but all large banks and companies did business also in euros. The system was so stable that the exchange rate between pounds and euros never needed to float—it was merely tweaked every three months. In case eco-dollars are indeed issued in the U.S., even that much adjustment wouldn't be necessary. It should take a federal law to change the exchange rate of $1 regular to $1.10 eco-dollar.

This proposal for United States eco-dollars might sound unprecedented, but it isn't. The Legal Tender Act of 1862 authorized the U.S. government to issue millions of special U.S. Notes that were soon called "greenbacks." They helped to keep the U.S. government solvent and the economy functioning during the Civil War and until the 1880s.

So (in summary) the right to use regular dollars (R.D.s) would stay the same as it has always been. Regular dollars would remain able to buy *anything* offered for sale in the United States. But the new eco-dollars (E.D.s) could be used *instead* of regular dollars to buy anything retail which is (1) brand new, and (2) requires physical transportation, and (3) was produced within thirty miles of where it is being bought.

Last and I guess least, eco-dollars would give us something fun to lobby the government about—namely, whose picture should be on which denomination of E.D. currency. All of their lettering should be black but all their coloring should be *pastel*. Personally, I'd like green for the $1 eco-bill and old Ralph Waldo Emerson on it. Orange for the $2 eco-bill and Thomas Jefferson on it. The $5 eco-bill blue with Rachel Carson on it (blue because she loved the ocean). The $10 eco-bill purple with Henry David Thoreau because he wrote purple prose. The $20 bill red with Eugene Debs. The $50 bill maroon with Harriet Tubman. The $100 bill grey with (—do I hear Robert E. Lee?) Susan B. Anthony, since Quakers wore grey too. The $500 bill chestnut-brown with Frederick Douglass. The $1,000 bill silver with John Muir. And the $10,000 bill gold with Ralph Borsodi. Borsodi would have relished being on the highest denomination. And he loved gold since he hated inflation. When I helped him issue noninflationary Constants in 1972, he had me drive him around New Hampshire to sell Constants to groups that wanted the gold standard reestablished. We always brought along his bar of silver and bar of gold (both secretly fake). He'd start his talks by slowly unwrapping the velvet silver cloth from around the fake bar of silver, and we'd hear oohs and ahs from out in the audience. Then he'd start slowly unwrapping the velvet gold cloth from the fake bar of gold and as he finished we'd hear gasps from the audience. Old Dr. Borsodi could be quite a showman.

You may be wondering "Is this realistic?" Is it even remotely possible? Let me quote Alf Hornborg's final point about his similar proposal for Europe: *"Is the proposal realistic, considering the colossal power interests that it challenges?* At the current historical moment, it is not at all realistic, but there are many reasons to anticipate that conditions will change. Within the course of the twenty-first century, the world may experience social, ecological, and financial crises so severe that leading politicians will have to devise ways of safe-guarding their electorates that are radically alternative to relying on economic growth and the global market. In such a situation, I hope that some of them will be prepared to reconsider the kind of ideas presented here."[47]

---

47. Alf Hornborg, *Nature, Society, and Justice in the Anthropocene* (2019), p. 246. Emphasis in original. Hornborg's full proposal is set forth in that book's Chapter 13: "Conclusions and Possibilities," pp. 231–247. Also see Hornborg's 2017 article "How to Turn an Ocean Liner," online at Hornborg Money—Journals at the University of Arizona.

CHAPTER 16

Return to Lincoln County, West Virginia

My most recent return to Lincoln County for a substantial visit was for the summer of 1988 right after I received a history PhD from Brandeis University. Unfortunately, it was *only* for that summer.

When I arrived in May 1988, I found out Henry and Anna Baker had moved halfway down Little Laurel Hollow and Henry was dying. Henry had become a deathbed convert and was attended daily by the elderly retired pastor of Myra Methodist Church, who listened as Henry confessed his sins and prayed with Henry for inner assurance of salvation.

A few years earlier, Henry had been traumatized. He and Anna had saved up enough money for Anna to revisit her native Czechoslovakian village, and Henry had driven her to Washington, DC and dropped her off at the airport. While driving home, Henry heard on the radio that Anna's plane had crashed soon after take-off and that no one had survived. Henry continued driving home but stopped several times at roadside bars to drown his sorrow in alcohol. Finally home, he was trying to unlock the door when it opened from inside and there stood Anna.

Henry passed out.

Anna had missed her ill-fated plane. With no way to contact Henry to come back and get her, she caught a flight to Charleston and had her son Matij Triska pick her up at Charleston Airport and drive her the rest of the way home. She was sound asleep when she heard Henry trying to open the door. When Anna got up and opened it, Henry collapsed at her feet.

A mountaintop removal in southern West Virginia in the 1970s. Photo by Paul
Sheridan of the Appalachian Research and Defense Fund (AppalRad).

While visiting Henry and Anna in 1988, I couldn't help noticing that
Henry's deathbed quest for salvation was very emotional. Perhaps his
fairly recent Anna-trauma had affected his nerves. But I also remember
Spec McComas's deathbed sessions being very emotional. Those were at
Spec and Ginny's home in Sandlick Hollow with the same elderly retired
Myra Methodist preacher. I knew both Spec and Henry fairly well and
was glad the local ministers cared about everyone's hereafter whether
or not they attended any church. The local ministers all felt "called" and
most of them ministered unpaid. And they all agreed what to do about
deathbed fears—confess and ask God for mercy.

Meanwhile, a trauma loomed ahead for *terra firma* as well. A company
named Black Gold Inc. had applied for a state permit to strip-mine the
ridge directly across Mill Branch Hollow from Sand Gap Ridge, home of
my brother John and his family. The distance between the two ridgetops
as-the-crow-flies is about two-thirds of a mile. When I arrived in May
1988, my sister-in-law Jan Salstrom told me Black Gold Inc. had just *received* its permit to strip mine that ridge and it might start destroying it
any day. But then, instead of cutting down the trees and blasting open
the ridge, the company drastically revised its mining plan.

My brother John's place had once been my own. It was the "twelve acres more or less" I bought in summer 1972 for $400. While I owned it, working there always felt somehow special. For cabin logs I cut down the trees that most obstructed the view across Mill Branch to the next ridge, the ridge Black Gold Inc. now planned to blast and bulldoze down into Mill Branch Hollow.

Black Gold Inc. had first appeared in Lincoln County six months earlier. Right away, my brother John and my former land partner Charley Bates founded an opposition group they named Home Place, Inc. and announced a public meeting at the county library in Hamlin to discuss Black Gold's mountaintop-removal plan. But the meeting was inundated by 150 strip-mine workers from neighboring Boone County who received free alcohol from their bosses for attending. Early on, a fight almost erupted between Black Gold's intended strip-mine operator Delbert Burchett and a young federal mine inspector named Jack Spadaro who knew about Mr. Burchett's bad record in Kentucky, where Mr. Burchett had declared bankruptcy a month before.

As Jack Spadaro revealed Mr. Burchett's Kentucky troubles, Mr. Burchett's friends were barely able to restrain him from physically assaulting Mr. Spadaro. Whereupon my brother John, aware that the Boone County strip-miners had been drinking, adjourned the meeting.

Later we found out Jack Spadaro, although smaller than Delbert Burchett, had been co-captain of his high school's state-championship football team from a southern West Virginia coal town, so he probably could have fended off Mr. Burchett—but 150 *other* mad strip-miners?

Then more information began surfacing about Mr. Burchett, who had strip-mined for many years in Kentucky and had just declared bankruptcy there because he owed the federal government $1.5 million in back taxes. He owed another half-million dollars in fines for failing to "reclaim" his strip mines, and was in the midst of several expensive lawsuits against other coal operators, and according to his son, suffered from a gambling addiction.

With adverse information surfacing about Mr. Burchett, the actual head of Black Gold Inc., a woman from Indianapolis named Sandra Perry, started calling Black Gold's opponents communists. She said she had proof they were communists, but when a reporter asked her "What proof?" she said Lincoln County Public Library had a book entitled *What*

Construction of John and Jan Salstrom's large self-built
house on Sand Gap Ridge, with its turret of ill-repute.
Courtesy of John Salstrom.

You Should Know About Communism and Why, and the book had been
checked out five times since the early 1970s when newcomers had started
moving into Lincoln County. Besides which, she added, my brother John
was receiving orders from Communist Russia via two-way short-wave
radio equipment in the turret of his self-built house on Sand Gap Ridge.

By the date of the next public meeting, March 17, 1988, public opinion in Lincoln County started turning against Black Gold Inc. The state
itself sponsored the March 17th meeting and held it in the gymnasium
of Guyan Valley High School, located near the Guyandotte River a few
miles south of the town of West Hamlin. About 400 people attended
and six state policemen stood guard. Ten people spoke in favor of Black
Gold Inc. and thirty people spoke against it, mostly natives rather than
newcomers.

The night before the meeting, my brother received a death threat by
telephone. When his turn came to speak at the meeting, he climbed up
on the stage, looked out at the crowd and said, "Would the man who
called me at four o'clock this morning and threatened to kill me and my
family, please step forward?"

He moved a few feet from the podium and waited, watching the crowd—which remained silent. No one stepped forward. Later, my brother (who isn't loquacious) described the meeting as "very, very intense."

Two months after that March 1988 meeting was when Black Gold Inc. received its strip-mining permit—but then it revised its mining plan so much that two opposition groups, not just Home Place Inc. but also Save Our Mountains, went to court and convinced the state government to cancel the mining permit it had issued. This cancellation made Black Gold re-start its permit-application process from the beginning, and, as a result, the state announced yet another public meeting. By then I had been back in Lincoln County more than a month, so of course I attended.

The new public meeting took place on June 28, 1988, again in the gymnasium of Guyan Valley High School. Again, tension was palpable. Seventeen people spoke against Black Gold Inc. and four people spoke in favor of it. The state made tape recordings of all the statements, which I then got tape copies of, and transcribed and typed and photocopied, and donated one set to Special Collections at Marshall University Library in Huntington.

The early 1970s newcomer Jim Chojnacki, a Kent State shooting survivor (in Taylor Parking Lot) who had married Marjie Shew's younger sister Connie Sayles and farmed with her in Lower Big Creek Hollow, set forth his personal prediction about Lincoln County's future. Jim said: "Basically our choice is this: If we patiently accept our poverty of today, we will be rewarded with prosperity for our children. . . . But strip mine our county now, bring in garbage from out of state, bring in toxic industries, and sell our forests to Ohio and Japan—and we will be leaving this beautiful land locked in poverty forever."[48]

A lady named Lynn Ernest who had moved to Lincoln County after earlier leaving her native McDowell County, explained why she changed counties:

> I left McDowell County originally to escape the industrial debris, the foul air, the coal trucks, the noise, the coal dust, the destroyed roads, and the damage to community water. Now we have no community water at all in McDowell County. It's all seeped underground—but

---

48. Jim Chojnacki testimony. West Virginia Department of Energy Public Hearing, Lincoln County, June 28, 1988; Oral History of Appalachia Collection, Marshall University Library, Huntington, W.Va.

also the strip mining allows it to run off quickly. . . . So don't be fooled. Keep your quality of life. Keep the kind of *people* that this life attracts here. You're good—if only you knew how good you are. You have to see the other stuff—the slander that goes on of humanity in a mining community.[49]

Several of the statements that evening were beautiful, especially an extemporaneous statement delivered by Julian Martin, a science teacher at one of Lincoln County's other high schools. He said,

My daddy was a coal miner—lost his eye in the mines. He wasn't a communist. He wasn't an outsider. And he didn't deal in drugs— though he did drink a lot of coffee. . . . All my life I've watched the destruction of my native state. I watched Bull Creek disappear. When I was a little boy forty years ago, I used to walk up Bull Creek over on Coal River. Bull Creek's not there anymore. Any of you guys that have ever worked on strip mines know it's not there anymore. It's gone. My Uncle Kin used to work timber up in the head of that hollow with a mule, and he did the least amount of destruction you possibly could do. That place was beautiful. It's not there anymore. It's just simply gone. It's been destroyed by a strip mine. . . . The first time I saw a strip mine it absolutely stunned me into silence. I was sad and I was sick. I couldn't believe what people could do with a bulldozer to a piece of land that used to be beautiful. . . . You can't reclaim a destroyed mountain—you can put something back there but you can't put the topsoil back on—just try it. You never, never can walk though that little glade where the ferns are growing. And enjoy those cliffs the way they were—the way they were meant to be. . . . And if you think strip mining is going to bring jobs, look where they've got strip mining in West Virginia and look where they've got the most unemployment. Mingo County. McDowell County. You go to the counties where they have strip mining—that's where they have the worst of everything. They've got the worst roads, they've got the worst schools, they've got the highest unemployment rate.

49. Lynn Ernest testimony. West Virginia Department of Energy Public Hearing, Lincoln County, June 28, 1988; Oral History of Appalachia Collection, Marshall University Library, Huntington, W.Va.

Everything is wrong with those counties. Is that what we want this beautiful place to become? . . ."[50]

After the meeting, I told Julian Martin he seemed to be testifying "in the Spirit" and asked him if he'd been brought up Pentecostal. He said he had, yes, been brought up Pentecostal.

After that June 28, 1988 meeting, public opinion continued turning against Black Gold Inc. Soon, Home Place Inc. had an array of lawyers and geologists helping to keep Black Gold's new strip-mining application tied up in court cases and legal hearings, but it wasn't easy and the tension in Lincoln County abated only slowly. My brother had to collect a lot of water samples where Delbert Burchett was "exploring" and then those samples had to be used as evidence against Black Gold's new permit application. Finally two years later, in 1990, Black Gold gave up trying to get a new permit to strip-mine the ridge across from my brother's place or anywhere else. Sandra Perry who headed Black Gold moved back to Indianapolis and the strip-mine operator from Kentucky, Delbert Burchett, left the U.S. for Venezuela to see about strip-mining prospects there.

Meanwhile, during that 1988 summer, I received a $1,000 grant from the West Virginia Humanities Council to research and write about economic alternatives in Lincoln County. My research took two directions, one of which is called "sweat equity"—in other words, paying for something with work rather than with money. Since that's a form of alternative economics, I already wrote about it at the start of the previous chapter as a possible way for patients of the Lincoln Primary Care Center to pay their medical bills. (Which never happened, if you recall.)

Mostly my other economic-development thoughts that summer ran to wood products, especially since furniture-quality lumber was extremely cheap in Lincoln County—compared to northern Illinois anyway. My uncle Phil Salstrom offered to come down from northern Illinois and help us set up a production branch of his wood-carving company, or help us set up our own separate company if we preferred. I had often worked for Uncle Phil over the years, and many of central Lincoln County's other

50. Julian Martin testimony, West Virginia Department of Energy Public Hearing, Lincoln County, June 28, 1988; Oral History of Appalachia Collection, Marshall University Library, Huntington, W.Va.

newcomers had likewise worked for him to make money for land buying, so we did have woodworking experience, perhaps a bit rusty by 1988. But we didn't have anyone in Lincoln County who could reliably operate the Salstrom wood*carving* machines.[51]

Operating those machines takes six months to even begin to master. Tony Norris had tried, but after he wrecked several sets of wood stocks (with twenty-four wood stocks in each set) my Uncle Phil re-assigned Tony back to the sanding department. Personally, rather than learn the machine woodcarving, I had always preferred the less life-embroiling job of sanding-department foreman. And as it turned out, *particle-wood imitations* of real wood soon took over almost all the "carved" furniture market, leaving nowadays mainly duck decoys, cane heads, harp columns, and grand-piano replacement parts for my uncle's son and heir Phil Salstrom II to carve. Phil II now usually carries on single-handedly in the shop along Rock River near Oregon, Illinois where well over 100 employees used to block out, carve, and sand Queen Anne furniture legs and other furniture parts. (Blocking-out stocks of wood to be carved into furniture legs, etc. was done by band-saw. Band-sawing to make stocks had been my own first assignment in the shop's opening months in fall 1960 when I was still the sole employee.)

After particle "wood" took over the market for mass-produced "carved" furniture, my Uncle Phil told me even he couldn't tell some of the particle "wood" from real wood without taking a saw to it.

A banjo-making branch of my Uncle Phil's company had also flourished thanks to the young production manager of that branch, David Markle. Making banjos might possibly have had a future in Lincoln County, but my uncle had long since sold that branch in 1966 to Fender Electric Instrument Company of southern California—to where David Markle then moved and continued to manage the banjo-making several more years. Fender kept calling the banjos Salstroms for a year or two but then started calling them Fenders. In 1969, David Markle left the Fender company and in the mid-1970s Fender lost its banjo market share to less expensive Japanese-made banjos. All the "Salstrom" banjos still

51. More details on the woodcarving machines, with photos, are on-line at "On Industrial Wood Carving in America, 1780–1980; and the Development of the Salstrom Wood Carving Machine," by Mary Salstrom, 2005.

Phil Salstrom II (*left*) and the author (*right*) at
Heathcote Mill in 1972. During the next two decades,
Phil II gradually inherited the management of Rock
Wood Carvers Company from his entrepreneur
father Phil I. Photo by Lois Salstrom Chertow.

out there should be of highest quality, and most of the Fender banjos as
well. The best-known musician to perform with a Salstrom banjo was
John Hartford.

So to make banjos in Lincoln County in the 1980s, we would have
had to start over again from scratch, which didn't seem feasible without
David Markle as the production manager. David had long since limited
his work to custom inlays of pearls and gems on the headstocks of banjos,
guitars, and other string instruments.[52]

As for normal everyday woodworking, such as lathe-turned work,
Lincoln County by the mid-1980s had two shops already doing such

52. More on the Salstrom Banjo Company is at Paul Salstrom, "Banjos were made
in Oregon," *Oregon [Illinois] Republican Reporter,* January 9, 2014, pp. A1 and B1.
Sometimes that article shows up on the website "Banjo Hang-out." More available
but less detailed is Michael Wright, "Fender Artist Bluegrass," *Vintage Guitar,* May
2014, pp. 26–28.

woodworking. And as for carefully hand-crafted wood furniture similarly without much carving, two of the county's newcomers had each opened a shop making such furniture.

I wasn't the only person looking into more wood-product possibilities for Lincoln County. The mayor of Hamlin, Clarence E. Monday (a fellow opponent of strip mining) was doing so as well. But as of the mid-1980s, Lincoln County had the lowest "enterprise ratio" of any of West Virginia's fifty-five counties. In other words, the amount of money on loan *from* Lincoln County's banks was a smaller proportion of the amount of money on deposit *in* Lincoln County's banks than in any of West Virginia's other fifty-four counties—that's the "enterprise ratio." Not to mention that West Virginia's "enterprise ratio" as a *state*—the ratio of bank loans to bank deposits in West Virginia overall—was lower than the ratio in any other state. Enterprise, thy name is not West Virginia, especially not Lincoln County, West Virginia!

But maybe the future will change that. Lincoln County's distant past was quite entrepreneurial, right up to the Great Depression. In previous chapters I've mentioned the late 1800s and early 1900s' farming, timbering, tobacco growing, natural-gas-well development and oil-well development. Besides all that, even a pair of small underground coal mines flourished in Lincoln County 100 years ago. Together they employed about 100 miners. They were located near the C&O railroad tracks that ran alongside the Guyandotte River on the county's western side. As for the oil wells, they were almost all in the county's northeastern corner. So much oil was pumped from the ground there that an oil pipeline was built to Ashland, Kentucky's oil refinery. And as for Lincoln County's numerous natural-gas wells, those were scattered all over the county. With so much enterprise underway then, the county's population shot up by 5,000 people in the decade from 1900 to 1910.

The county's nineteen-teens kept the momentum going. The fossil-fuel start-ups peaked about then, while timbering was still going strong and when burley tobacco fields became common as well. The 1920s did all right too. In 1925, for instance, a million pounds of tobacco left Lincoln County. Huntington's large tobacco market warehouse had opened for business in 1910 and burley tobacco then became the main cash crop on Lincoln County farms—a leadership that it retained almost until

Huntington's tobacco warehouse closed its doors in 1997. As late as 1992, Lincoln County still produced two-thirds of a million pounds of burley tobacco.

During all those decades (most of the 1900s) locally-owned commercial enterprises and local subsistence farming were usually intertwined. They supplemented each other. And that was the focus of my two interviews in summer 1988 with my elderly friend Ray Elkins ("Mud River Ray Elkins") and his wife Mabel White Elkins.

CHAPTER 17

Looking Farther Back—
to Look Ahead

Ray Elkins ("Mud River Ray Elkins") was my elderly friend whose grandfather's uncle was one of the two "seconds" in the duel that killed Meriwether Lewis in 1809 at an inn on the Natchez Trace. Ray's immediate family was from the Gilbert vicinity of far southeastern Mingo County, where he was born in 1904, nine years after Mingo County was split off from Logan County. Ray's mother died when he was still small. His father owned a house in the town of Gilbert but worked as a cook on a timber company's shanty cook-boat, and in 1910, on Ray's sixth birthday, his father brought him to Lincoln County to live with an aunt and uncle. Thereafter, Ray's father came to visit him several times a year, but Lincoln County remained Ray's home from 1910 onward.[53]

In 1928 Ray married Mabel White, whose family had been in Lincoln County since the 1800s. Mabel's White family cemetery dates from 1890 at the latest, which was the year her great-grandfather Ephraim White was buried there. The cemetery lies a few miles east of Hamlin near the village of Sweetland. Prior to that, Mabel's White family had been in Maryland since at least 1781, and then had moved to Gallia County, Ohio (the site of Gallipolis) sometime between 1818 and 1842. Mabel's

---

53. This chapter is based on interviews I tape-recorded in central Lincoln County in summer 1988 with Ray and Mabel Elkins, Raymond Black, Flossie Black Lawson, and Vergie Farley. Transcriptions of the interviews are in the Oral History of Appalachia Collection at Marshall University Library, Huntington, W.Va.

great-grandfather Ephraim White came from there to the vicinity of Hamlin, [West] Virginia, sometime between 1848 and 1878. Her grandfather Enoch White was born in 1848 and bought a Lincoln County farm in 1878 that was south a few miles up Trace Creek from the Sweetland area, a farm which became the White family's homeplace. (Both its house and its smokehouse were still being used in 1988. But I interviewed Mabel and Ray that summer at their own home next to Mud River a mile south of Myra in central Lincoln County.)

Mabel's father, Wilbur White, was born in 1875 and her mother, Nora Ellen Smith White was born in 1885. Wilbur started his working life as a schoolteacher but in 1903 he switched to farming. Mabel was her parents' second child, born in 1905. In the winter of 1913–14 her father bought a thirty-acre farm in Lower Big Creek Hollow (several miles south of Hamlin and several miles north of Myra) and Mabel's family moved there on February 13, 1914. Until then, at age nine, she had never yet seen her White family grandparents because they lived a few miles south of Hamlin on Johnson Hill, near where Lower Big Creek flows into Mud River, whereas her own nuclear family had lived, until then, five or ten miles *north* of Hamlin near Lower Mud River.

It sounded strange that Mabel had never even met her paternal grandparents at all until she was nine, but she explained "they lived down here on top of Johnson Hill and we lived below Hamlin, and we had no way of transportation whatever."

Once Mabel's family started farming on Lower Big Creek, they raised as much food as they could, but things were tight what with ten children born into the family, although two died as infants. Their main cash income occurred once a year from selling "maybe an acre to an acre and a half" crop of burley tobacco that they raised on their best bottomland. The year their tobacco crop brought in $666.66, Mabel's dad immediately "left Huntington [the tobacco warehouse location] and went to Ohio and purchased him a team of horses, and came back and paid off the rest what he owed on the farm."

Mabel said "I knew all about raising tobacco. . . . I spread it [in the field] when they cut it. And I tied it when they stripped it in the wintertime. Kept me at home from school to tie up tobacco. We tied it in 'hands.'"

As for taking it to Huntington to sell, that was "usually soon as they got it stripped. . . . But ours were never stripped when the market opened.

Old barn for air-curing burley tobacco.
Date and photographer unknown.

It was usually in January when they took it in, and I think the market probably opened in December. . . . Twenty-sixth Street market of Huntington, West Virginia."

Most years, Mabel's family ended its annual farm cycle in debt, particularly the year when their tobacco crop brought them only $35. Fortunately, storekeepers were willing to "carry on the book" almost any local resident who owned land. The Myra storekeeper Raymond Black told me that Lincoln County's storekeepers "had an awful lot of stuff on the book. *And lost lots of it.*" (The *emphasis* was Raymond's.) In fact, Raymond's son and successor Ray Gene Black even carried *me* "on the book" whenever I asked him to, although the first time I did so I didn't go down to the Myra store in person, since someone else was going shopping there and could get me what I needed. The next time I saw Ray Gene he told me it was customary for a customer to come *in person* to start a credit account (hint hint).

As for farming, Mabel said "In summertime we usually were in the field by six o'clock. When mother had lunch [ready] we came home and ate and rested, and went back and worked till six that afternoon, and came home, and of course we were tired, but children—and we soon rested and played till dark a lot of nights."

Mabel added, "Mostly our biggest crop was corn and we also raised oats [presumably for horse feed]. One year we raised wheat for our bread—only one year that I can remember of. And then of course we raised a cane crop [sorghum cane] for molasses. And I remember one year we raised broom corn and had brooms made."

I asked Mabel, "Would someone press the molasses in Hamlin?" but she said they didn't have to take their cane anywhere. "They always came to the farm. The man who made our molasses lived nearby. He made good molasses too," she added. "And we kept cattle, had a team of horses, and hogs, but no sheep."

At that point, I should have asked Mabel whether, after the molasses had been squeezed out of the cane, they then used the "spent" cane for silage (fermented livestock feed). But before plastic sheeting became mass-produced in the late 1950s, you usually needed a silo to store silage in. Now, you can just lay silage on plastic sheeting in a trench in the ground and cover it up with another plastic sheet plus a foot or two of soil, or maybe just use old tires to hold down the top sheet of plastic. Making silage had been part of my own farm job at the federal prison in Missouri. The silage keeps itself warm by fermenting all winter, so cattle, sheep, and goats love to eat it. (Don't feed it to *non*-ruminant livestock, however.)

I asked Mabel, "Could the animals be loose or did they have to be fenced in?" She said they always had to be fenced in. Her husband Ray added that West Virginia as a state left the fencing question up to each county to decide for itself. He said Logan and Mingo counties had always allowed "free range" but Lincoln County didn't. He remembered rail fences being very common everywhere—regardless of whether you had to fence in your crops as in Logan and Mingo counties or you had to fence in your animals, as in Lincoln County.

Ray added that farming was a lot "rougher" in Logan and Mingo counties than it was in Lincoln County. "Farming was a pretty rough deal up in that country. They farmed, that's true, but they depended on the timber [and] dug lots of ginseng. .. And they raised horses and cattle. Lots of old rail fence then because they fenced the fields in that they farmed, and cattle and everything run out [free range]."

Mabel said, "We had our own milk, our own eggs, and things like that. We raised most everything we ate, all of our vegetables and things. We bought sugar, pepper [black pepper], soda [baking soda] and things like that at the store, and mother made our eggs pay for those things. Took eggs to the store and traded them for that."

I asked Mabel which store they traded at. "Well," she said, "we had a little store just below us when we first moved to [Lower] Big Creek, and when they did away with that we went to Hamlin, and sometimes we'd go to Sheridan over on Guyan River. [And we wouldn't take just eggs but] fryers; when fryers got big enough to eat we'd take fryers in to the store—on foot, not dressed. . . . Where my parents traded in Hamlin was Sweetland Brothers. . . . Sometimes they did come up to Myra to trade, but not too often. I don't know why, cause it would have been nearer."

Mabel's husband Ray Elkins added that Sweetland Brothers "did lots of trading in eggs, in produce of any kind." They accepted cured hams too, he said. And Mabel said "my mother caught—gathered up some old hens and took them down to Sweetland Brothers and bought one of those push lawnmowers. Cause we never had one. Our yard was just mowed with a mowing scythe all the time. And I think the lawnmower cost six or seven dollars."

Ray Elkins then mentioned that if people were renting their farms, "so much of the tobacco went for the rent, and so much of the corn. Probably a third of it was the commonest thing back then. . . . There might have been some cash rental [but] there just wasn't much cash going around."

Mabel added, "No there wasn't. I never knew what it was to have money to spend till after Ray and I were married. And then we didn't have much for awhile." To that Ray added, "You just learned to make do with what you had." (Mabel had already told me she and Ray never raised any tobacco, so presumably they didn't have much money until Ray became a natural-gas pipeline walker/meter-reader for Columbia Gas Company.)

Mabel added, "Make do with what you had, and what you didn't have or couldn't buy you just did without. [But] they borrowed. I remember we used to borrow from the neighbors and they would borrow from us, until we could get to the store, then we'd pay them back, and then they'd pay us back what they'd borrowed from us. . . . Maybe flour, run out of flour before time to go to the store. Coffee or something like that. We'd borrow from someone else."

Ray then mentioned that "they had the local grist mills [to grind corn] and there was a flour mill [to grind wheat] in Hamlin and one in Griffithsville. Most people took their own corn and had their own meal ground. Took their corn to the mill and had it ground into meal. . . . I don't know what their toll was, but they had a scoop and they'd scoop it out [to] take their toll. Any day of the week—they had a [wheat] flour mill at Griffithsville and they had one in Hamlin. But most of your local ones [were] just grinding corn."

Another interview I conducted that summer of 1988 was with Flossie Black Lawson who had been born in 1910 at Myra. Her father was one of the Blacks, and while she was growing up her father operated a gristmill that ground corn at Myra. She told me the toll charged for grinding corn (and also the same for grinding wheat at the flour mills) was one-half gallon of the grain per bushel, and that it was dipped out before the grinding started. Not only a gristmill was located at Myra, Flossie said, but the same long wooden building parallel to the river continued at a lower level along the riverbank and held a sawmill—both kinds of mill in one long building with two levels, located on Mud River's bank between the store and the river itself. (And come to think of it, that abandoned two-level wooden building hadn't yet been torn down when I lived near Myra in the early 1970s.)

Back to Mabel Elkins. I asked Mabel if she and her siblings were given any allowance, to which her husband Ray said "You just got what you ate and that's all there was." Mabel said, "I can remember when we were children growing up we never had any candy until Christmas time. My mother always managed to buy a two-pound box of stripped peppermint candy. And you talk about something good—that was. And pastries. She would always manage to bake a white cake and a chocolate cake I guess it was. She'd buy coconut and make a coconut cake—grind the coconut up and put it in the cake. Mostly she'd bake fruit pies if we had our own fruit, but never bought pie filling or fruit to bake pies with. . . . And I guess we ate bushels of popcorn when we were children growing up. We grew our own popcorn. I mean, that was a nightly thing a lot of times at our house."

I asked Mabel about meat and she said "We didn't have meat all year long, cause we couldn't keep it. We'd get it in the wintertimes, and then by the time hot weather came it was about all gone." Ray said, "For meat they had salting it, salt it down." Mabel: "What they call curing it." Ray: "Salt bacon or salt hams, they'd keep that the year around. . . . I don't know what all they put in—pepper—at home we always kept a few hams for the summer season."

"But we didn't," Mabel said, "we ate them up too fast. And also we'd make a few kettles of apple butter every year. We had an old apple orchard up on our place."

Mabel said she used to ask her mother why their family had so many children. "And she said 'so we'd have someone to help with the farm work.' And I always said 'Why?' That was what I asked her first, 'Why so many children?' Cause, see, it put a burden on me. I was the second child in the family. And I helped raise all those children from about the fourth or fifth one down below me." Mabel's parents had ten children in all. "Course, two of them, two of the children died in infancy, the fourth and fifth child. The one was sixteen months old and the other was six months old."

Mabel was almost nineteen when her youngest sibling was born. "Not only babysitting," she added, "I was washing diapers and feeding children and cleaning up after them, a little bit of everything. Took them with me when I went places. My youngest brother rode in the car with Ray and I, rode right between us when we were dating." (She stopped, remembering and starting to smile.)

I asked her if people *usually* could do better on a farm if they had more children, but Mabel said "I never could see it. The more children they had, the more [crops] they had to put out and raise, the way I looked at it."

As for gender roles, she said "We all worked a lot on the farm. We girls would up and do the housework, and the boys would up and do the feeding of an evening." As for the fieldwork, "we all worked together. I did everything on the farm except drive a team." She said she was "scared to death of horses," maybe because of a horse that "didn't like to be reined that tight and I pulled the reins real tight and he kicked up his hind heels and away I went over his head and my mother stood there and screamed. But he stopped when he threw me off. . . . If he hadn't stopped he'd of killed me."

A month later that same summer (1988) I interviewed the retired Myra storekeeper Raymond Black, and found out that he too, and his dad "Uncle Billy Black" who ran the Myra store before him, used to accept large quantities of both eggs and chickens as trade items—just like the Sweetland Brothers store in Hamlin did, and apparently all the other stores. I already knew from a preliminary interview with Ray Elkins (not taped) that Raymond Black's dad "Uncle Billy Black" had a chicken coop behind the Myra store in the mouth of Sandlick Hollow. The store's in-traded chickens were kept there until they were transported to market. As for in-traded eggs, Billy Black could move eggs from Myra to Huntington very quickly after the C&O railroad tracks coming south from Huntington reached Midkiff in the Guyandotte Valley in 1904. After that, he could deliver eggs in Huntington the day after he received them in trade at Myra.

But Raymond Black's own answer to my question focused on the eggs that his dad Billy Black, followed by he himself, sent in the other direction—south to Logan County. He told me that once the Chesapeake & Ohio (C&O) rail line from Huntington finally reached Logan County in 1905, pretty soon Island Creek Coal Company became a big buyer of eggs, and "they scattered them out amongst their [company] stores, you know." The market for Lincoln County eggs boomed in Logan County because the railroad's arrival in Logan County made coal development very rapid there, including at many coal mines owned by Island Creek Coal Company.

The eggs gathered at the Black family's Myra store were packed in wooden cartons holding about thirty dozen eggs each, and were hauled by horse- or mule-drawn wagons from Mud River Valley, up and over McComas Ridge to one of the C&O train stops along the Guyandotte River. That trip might sound hard on eggs, but Raymond Black said they didn't break. "Never had no complaints on that," he told me.

Eventually, Raymond told me, a private storekeeper from Amherstdale in Logan County started to visit Myra driving his three-quarter-ton van. "He'd buy up all the chickens you had, all the eggs, potatoes, or anything like that he could haul without refrigerating. . . . He'd haul a right smart load of stuff in it. . . . He bought that stuff and took it up there and retailed it."

So that meant Logan County's coal-company stores faced competition from at least one independent merchant (and probably more). It also means the C&O railroad faced some shipping competition after Upper Mud River Road was finally graded in the mid-1910's and then was improved again in the 1930s by having rock pounded into it by New Deal WPA workers. Sometime after that, it was paved.

Raymond Black's family had been rooted at Myra since 1894 when his granddad William and his dad Billy partnered together to buy out a tiny 12 × 14-foot store located there. The next year they built a much larger store in its place. Raymond himself was born in 1897. Then in 1905, his dad and granddad were instrumental in starting Myra Methodist Church, partly by donating land for it a hundred yards down Mud River from their store. The road to the church was just dirt, and it continued (in poor condition) two or three more miles downstream along the east bank of the river. The good road, Upper Mud River Road itself, had crossed Myra's rickety metal-frame bridge to the other (west) bank of the river and continued downstream on that side of the river all the way to Hamlin, climbing up and over Johnson Hill en route.

Raymond's dad, known by everyone as Uncle Billy Black, not only expanded Myra Store but was also buying timber for Armstrong Timber Company. Eventually about 1930 he set up a sawmill to the west across McComas Ridge, down in Sixmile Hollow. He acquired considerable land over there, including land that bordered my own first land parcel of 12 acres that I sold later to my younger brother John. Those 12 acres lay mainly along Sand Gap Ridge but they stretched all the way down to the bottom of Mill Branch Hollow (a branch of Sixmile Hollow) and way down there in the narrow hollow, beside Mill Branch Creek, I found a long-abandoned house basement made of concrete. Personally I wouldn't have wanted to live down there, tightly closed in by both sides of the hollow, but the few narrow acres of creek-side bottomland apparently made it feasible to live there—perhaps along with sawmill work for Raymond's father Uncle Billy Black?

Raymond told me "My dad dealt in land all the time he owned it. At any time nearly he'd own half a dozen farms. He'd buy a boundary of land that had a lot of timber on it, and work the timber up, and turn around and sell the land to someone who wanted it for a home, you know, a farm. That's the way he dealt in it. He bought it and sold it."

Lincoln Countians cut thousands of railroad cross-ties in the early 1900's while the C&O railroad was laying tracks south along the Guyandotte River through Lincoln County to reach Logan County's vast reserves of high-grade bituminous coal. Raymond told me a lot of those rail-bed ties were hand-hewn by farmers right in the woods where they felled the trees. But, he told me, "the old farmers didn't have very good wagons. 'Bout seven or eight ties was all they could haul to a load, and they wouldn't get very much for 'em when they got 'em there." And of course a lot of ties for the C&O were also being cut at sawmills.

Raymond Black also told me details about Lincoln County's natural-gas boom, which started about when the C&O railroad from Huntington to Logan was being built. Natural gas could be tapped throughout Lincoln County. Raymond said one of the ox-teams that hauled natural-gas drilling rigs and pipes up into the hills consisted of 100 oxen yoked two-by-two in a long chain. "When they was drilling gas wells in this country," Raymond said, "you didn't have to look for a job, they were looking for *you*. . . . If you was willing to work and make an account of yourself, there was a job for you."

Commercial *timbering* had started long before—at least sixty or seventy years before the flurry of oil and natural-gas drilling and of railroad building. Commercial timbering was already well underway by 1848 when a Guyandotte Navigation Company was chartered and over the next few years built dams and locks on the river. Springtime's high water on the Guyandotte always brought hundreds of log rafts floating downstream on their way to sawmills, usually with a raftsman standing at each end of the raft (or *chain* of rafts). The front raftsman wielded a long, curved pole with a six or seven foot board attached to the end of the pole and held in the water. That pole-with-board was used to dunk floating obstacles so they'd go underneath the on-coming raft. When the river was running high and fast, however, if the pole of the "fore" raftsman hit a hidden underwater snag, it could flip him up like a pole vaulter.

In the spring of 1861 while the Civil War was starting, a monstrous flood washed away all the dams and locks on the Guyandotte. They had been flimsy to start with. They were never rebuilt and as a result, log jams became common during low water. One photo from about 1910 shows a log jam that filled the entire Guyandotte River as far as the eye could see.

Additionally, after 1905 an immense amount of Logan County coal floated down the Guyandotte, piled on barges. One of my elderly friends of the 1970s had spent his entire working life operating a small coal-dredging vessel on the Guyandotte, making a good living by drying and selling the coal he dredged up off the bottom of the river.

Even on far smaller Mud River, the high water of springtime floated sizable logs to market. *Single* logs were often floated on Mud River, but when two or more logs were nailed together on top with a few boards, the logs became a raft and couldn't roll over, so those makeshift rafts could be ridden and steered.

Thousands of logs were floated out of Lincoln County every year for many decades. The "boom" that caught Mud River's logs was located far down-river in Cabell County, right before the Mud flowed into the Guyandotte, which wasn't far before the Guyandotte itself flowed into the Ohio River at the east edge of Huntington. There, a large "boom" across the river (and made out of logs itself) stopped the on-coming logs, and teams of draft animals pulled them up on the riverbank. Each log had been pre-marked with the brand of its owner. Flossie Black Lawson told me the fee charged at the Mud River boom for "catching" was 25 cents per log. A lot *more* logs came down the Guyandotte itself and that river's boom crew charged one dollar per log for "catching." A large sawmill was in operation close by that boom—sometimes more than one sawmill. But it all ended—either when a 1920s flood washed away the Guyandotte River boom or when it was disassembled on purpose (—different people tell different versions). Anyway, it was never replaced. By then the C&O railroad was already transporting many of the Guyandotte Valley's logs.

So, Lincoln County's by-gone days were replete with a variety of small and medium-sized enterprises that accompanied the county's continuous subsistence farming. Perhaps future years will see new enterprises springing up, but regardless of whether and how much that happens, I'm convinced a lot more subsistence farming *definitely* lies ahead, not just in Lincoln County but all over the United States. That's why I've written this book about past Appalachian Americans who thrived living close to the ground with very little money. Not *all* of them thrived, of course, but almost all of them "got by," natives and newcomers alike.

Of course, looking ahead, it would be nice to have breathing space enough to learn by trial-and-error which "alternatives" work best under current conditions. An array of small "green" enterprises are popping up lately, including quite a few in the heavily strip-mined part of West Virginia just south of Lincoln County. Various new "green" enterprises are also underway in eastern Kentucky. Land devastated by strip mines, including mountaintop removal, is often for sale cheaply these days even if some minable coal still lies down below it (coal which will hopefully *stay* down there). If you're buying land, be sure to ask whether a mineral deed (or mineral deeds *plural*) exist for all or part of the same acreage as the surface deed, and be sure to check whether any other rights besides mineral rights have been separated from the surface deed.

The agricultural historian Steven Stoll has suggested that Congress pass a "Commons Community Act" appropriating funds to purchase Appalachian land that would then be held communally by local commons-management committees. In the same Act he'd like Congress to appropriate funds to facilitate the home purchases of people who live on or near commons land, and even to finance the higher education of children who live there. On such "commons" land, only the land would be communally owned, not the buildings or other improvements. Those would be privately owned but would be subject to the environmental standards of the local commons-management committee.[54]

Creating such "commons" land need not wait for Congress to act. The entire initiative could be local. Several local Community Land Trusts already exist in Appalachia, the best known of which is Woodland Community Land Trust in northeastern Tennessee. It was founded in 1979 by Marie Cirillo and as of now it owns 450 acres of land in twelve separate parcels. The land trust has made each parcel available for privately-owned buildings and other improvements that meet its environmental guidelines. Its dozen land parcels hold a variety of small businesses, education projects, permaculture projects, and gardens.

Without involving any "commons" land, some interesting new projects are underway in heavily-strip-mined southern West Virginia. In fall 2017, West Virginia University (WVU) partnered with the Van School District in Boone County and together they launched an Early-College and STEM Academy in that school district. (STEM stands for Science, Technology, Education, and Mathematics.) One aspect of the Van School District collaboration with WVU is that all the public-school students in the district are automatically partners in student-initiated projects of the local 4-H Clubs. At the high-school level, the project has joined forces with the local community college so all the high school students can earn a college Associates Degree at the same time they earn their high school

54. See Steven Stoll, *Ramp Hollow: The Ordeal of Appalachia* (2017), pp. 272–277.

diploma, which leaves them only two college years away from their Bachelor's Degree. To help the graduates stay close to home after they graduate, the high school's college-credit courses emphasize preparation for careers in agriculture, forestry, and natural resources.[55]

Boone County where that's happening is one of West Virginia's six southern counties exceptionally devastated by strip-mining/mountaintop removal. As of 2014, all six of those heavily strip-mined counties were also among the twenty-two counties in the overall United States with the highest rates of drug-overdose deaths. Of 3,142 total counties in the United States, in other words, as of 2014 the twenty-two counties with the highest rates of drug-overdose deaths included all six of southern West Virginia's counties that have been exceptionally devastated by strip-mining/mountaintop removal. Boone County was #22 out of all 3,142 U.S. counties in drug-overdose deaths per capita, Logan County was #20, Raleigh County #18, Wyoming County #16, Mingo County #7, and McDowell County was #2 in U.S. drug-overdose deaths per capita.[56]

West Virginia University (WVU) has a long history of providing more of its outreach projects to northern West Virginia than to southern West Virginia, but that seems to be changing. WVU's educational partnership in Boone County is just one of many recent WVU initiatives in southern West Virginia. WVU is now touting the fact that, as a state, West Virginia leads the U.S. in the number of small farms per capita, and WVU is actively trying to help more small farms get started.

A recent issue of WVU's agriculture magazine says "of the 10 million acres of land damaged by extractive industries in Appalachia, about 500,000 lie in the borders of West Virginia." One researcher at WVU's College of Agriculture is experimenting with a perennial plant named "Miscanthus X giganteus" which is known for its fast-growing biomass and can be turned into burnable pellets. Besides which, its sugars can be fermented to produce ethanol fuel. One plus about Miscanthus is that its photosynthesis pulls carbon-dioxide out of the air and puts the carbon part of it into the ground, thereby reducing carbon in the atmosphere

55. For more about this, see Lindsay Willey, "A Roadmap to Success," *Davis College of Agriculture* magazine, West Virginia University, Fall 2018, pp. 22–27.

56. "West Virginia Overdose Deaths 2014," *Davis College of Agriculture* magazine, West Virginia University, Fall 2017, p. 10.

(like trees do) and replenishing strip-mined land with some of the carbon that strip-mining removed.

Technically, Miscanthus X giganteus is an "invasive" perennial plant since it comes from the bamboo sub-family of Asia, but because it's a perennial *hybrid* plant it is sterile and therefore it can't spread—unlike kudzu and multi-flora rose. WVU's report doesn't mention marketing Miscanthus's air-to-soil carbon "offset" on California's carbon offset market, but that's another obvious source of income for Miscanthus growers.[57]

Perhaps strip-mined land can also grow Kernza, which is a perennial "wheat-like grass whose massive 'beard' of roots help draw down carbon" from the air. Kernza was developed by the Land Institute near Salina, Kansas. The Patagonia Provisions branch of Patagonia, Inc. is promoting Kernza as part of its "regenerative organic" initiative.[58]

Another WVU researcher has documented that from 1900 to 2019, winter shortened twenty days in West Virginia (as well as warming overall) and meanwhile West Virginia's growing season grew longer by thirteen days. This researcher expects corn and alfalfa to suffer because of West Virginia's climate change, but he expects soybeans, winter wheat, specialty vegetables, specialty teas, and basil (among others) to do better in West Virginia because of the climate change.[59]

These projects aren't the only ones WVU is sponsoring. Among the others is a small experimental farm on strip-mined land in southern West Virginia that is emphasizing dairy goats. If it turns out dairy goats can thrive on what strip-mined land can grow (including maybe the first-year shoots of Miscanthus X giganteus? or perhaps the perennial wheat-like grass Kernza?) then West Virginia as a state might conceivably become the goat-cheese capital of North America and eventually rival the cow-cheese output of Wisconsin. This lover of goat cheese is waiting.

57. Pam Pritt, "Digging In," *Davis College of Agriculture* magazine, West Virginia University, Fall 2019, pp. 20–21.

58. *Patagonia* journal, Spring 2020, p. 90. More information is in Liz Carlisle, "Feeding the Soil," *Patagonia Provisions*, issue #1, Spring 2020, pp. 10–19. The full history of Kernza is at www.landinstitute.org.

59. Jake Stump, "The Positive Implications of Climate Change?" *Davis College of Agriculture* magazine, West Virginia University, Fall 2019, pp. 4–7.

The very best forage for dairy goats is comfrey, which I know can flourish on mineral-rich soil—such as on the Hebrides Islands off the west coast of Scotland—but whether comfrey can flourish on old strip mines' *acidic* mineral-rich soil I don't know. (Only parts of the Hebrides' mineral-rich soil are very acidic.) So far, it has already been proven that Miscanthus X giganteus can flourish on strip-mined land. Hopefully comfrey (and Kernza) will be test-planted on old strip mines as well.

One of West Virginia's largest new alternative projects is Sprouting Farms, located in Summers County just east of the state's worst-off coal counties. Marshall University helped Sprouting Farms win a $1.5 million start-up grant from the Appalachian Regional Commission. Founded in 2017, Sprouting Farms offers farm apprenticeships lasting six months, and also rents out the use of half of its thirty high tunnels, meanwhile offering free on-site agricultural counseling and virtually free use of its tools and equipment. It's giving many young people a low-cost way to become small-farm entrepreneurs, helping them not just with organic food *production,* but also with marketing what they grow.

On the marketing side, Sprouting Farms has helped create a food hub named "turnrow" located right on its 83-acre farm. Before widespread COVID-19 reached the U.S. in March 2020, West Virginia already held a plentitude of farms—200,000 of them—but of the $8 billion worth of food annually retailed in West Virginia, only one-tenth was produced inside the state.

About nine-tenths of West Virginia's farms are rated as "small farms," but that shouldn't stop them from becoming more productive and profitable. The mission of Sprouting Farms and the "turnrow" food-marketing hub is to help facilitate a small-farm renaissance in West Virginia. And in fact, suddenly since the onset of COVID-19, thousands of West Virginia shoppers have begun "buying local" for the first time.[60]

As for Lincoln County specifically, in 2017 the Lincoln Economic Development Authority issued a 70-page draft of a "Lincoln County

60. About Sprouting Farms, see its website www.sproutingfarms.org. About turn-row marketing collective, see its excellent website www.turnrowfarms.org and also see the article "COVID-19 Changes Everything: Farm Collective sees customer base grow from 40 to 400 in five weeks," by Michelle James, Beckley (W.Va.) *Register-Herald,* May 2, 2020.

Comprehensive Plan." It said that only one farm in Lincoln County was still producing commercial tobacco, but that 980 natural-gas wells remained in production and 139 oil wells. As for food growing, the report said

> some Lincoln County farmers are on the cutting edge [of] the farm-to-table movement where locally grown produce and [meat] are sold directly to users. Lincoln County farmers have started a small niche in this movement, especially by using high tunnels to extend the growing season. . . . The high tunnels are unheated greenhouses that allow farmers to improve their production and profitability primarily for food production. . . . There are 30 high tunnels in Lincoln County, two of which are being used at Lincoln County High School in the Career Technical Education (CTE) program related to agriculture and farming, giving future farmers an opportunity to understand how a simple structure can boost food production.[61]

I suspect that some of those high tunnel vegetable growers and farm-to-table innovators are Lincoln County in-migrants. (In another connection, the report does mention that in the 1970s numerous newcomers moved to Lincoln County "to enjoy its rural lifestyle.")

In spring 2020, the Natural Resources Conservation Service office in Huntington told me that high tunnels are more popular than ever in Lincoln County, with about forty-three now in active use and a swelling number of applicants waiting for financial help with high-tunnel funding. Meanwhile, direct farm-to-table food marketing takes place at a farmers' market in Hamlin, the county seat.[62]

When I asked the Hamlin-based environmental consultant Jack Spadaro if forty-three high tunnels in Lincoln County sounded about right, he told me there are far *more*. He said forty-three must merely be the number of high tunnels the government's extension service has helped to finance. He said there's now a new wave of young back-to-the-land

61. "Lincoln County Comprehensive Plan 2017," Draft. Lincoln Economic Development Authority, 2017, pp. 24, 29.

62. Author's telephone conversations, January 29 and March 26, 2020 with Natural Resources Conservation Service, Huntington, W.Va.

farmers in Lincoln County and "most of them have high tunnels." The county's economic future suddenly looks brighter.[63]

The local climate trend is disturbing, however, even if corn and alfalfa might be replaceable by other crops. A new U.S. Corps of Engineers study estimates that, because Lincoln County is downstream from massive strip mines to the south of it (downstream via the Guyandotte and Mud rivers), ongoing climate change will increase "stream flow" in Lincoln County up to 15 percent by the year 2040. Meanwhile, climate change will also make precipitation more erratic, thereby increasing the size of floods and the size of *flood plains* by much more than 15 percent. And looking farther ahead, the new Corps of Engineers study predicts that by the year 2100 Lincoln County's stream flow will be 25 percent greater than it is now.[64]

63. Author's phone conversation with Jack Spadaro, April 9, 2020.

64. James Bruggers, "Appalachia's Strip-Mined Mountains Face a Growing Climate Risk: Flooding," *Inside Climate News,* Nov. 21, 2019, accessed online January 29, 2020. By the way, estimates from the U.S. Corps of Engineers are almost always *low* estimates.

CHAPTER 18

Why *Hillbilly Elegy* Isn't Really About Traditional Appalachia

In the 1950s, Harriette Arnow wrote a great novel entitled *The Doll-maker* about a mountain family during World War Two. They leave their remote farm in eastern Kentucky and move to an apartment in a war-time housing project in Detroit, Michigan, where the father had traveled ahead and found work in an industrial plant. The rest of the family then follows him to Detroit.

The Dollmaker's plot focuses on a clash of values. It chronicles a relentless erosion of rural Appalachian values in the inner life of the family's mother, Gertie Nevels, until she finally gives up and surrenders completely to the values of urban Michigan. Gertie is an amateur wood whittler who specializes in carving dolls. She begins to sell her dolls to help meet her family's living expenses. Then she begins blocking out doll stocks with an electric saw to minimize the necessary carving, even though this ends her dolls' previous beauty. Finally, with her family in financial trouble, she sacrifices her life-sized work in progress, a wooden statue of Christ (or possibly of Judas Iscariot, she hasn't decided which). She saws it up to make more dolls to sell. Demoralized, her surrender to urban values has become total.

Here's another case, this one non-fiction. In the mid-1960s, General Motors Company was recruiting workers from Kentucky for its Chevrolet Corvair assembly plant at Willow Run, Michigan, near the city of Ypsilanti. One woman who taught first grade in Ypsilanti at the time tells me that, for its new workers from Kentucky "General Motors rented a home to the family for a deposit of $80, with the deposit and monthly rent to be taken from the worker's paycheck." But unfortunately,

> while the family now had a home, they had not been given any education about how to get utilities connected and how to use appliances they had never operated before. I wondered why these children had lunches of mostly junk food early in the week and nothing to eat later in the week. The families probably did not know how to budget their paychecks so that family necessities were taken care of and bills paid. Some of the families purchased cars they could not afford because General Motors offered to take the payments for a new GM vehicle out of their paychecks. In the winter, some of my students couldn't come to school because they didn't have and probably couldn't afford warm coats or boots.

This teacher, recalling her mid-1960s year of teaching first graders in Ypsilanti, says she "wondered why General Motors didn't feel an obligation to orient their Kentucky employees to suburban living, including budgeting, credit purchasing, time management, nutrition, and health care. If they did, it certainly was not evident to me when I worked with the children."[65]

Question: Is what happened to those rural Kentucky families living in urban Michigan about traditional rural Appalachia? My own answer is "No, it's not about traditional rural Appalachia because it didn't happen to them *in* traditional rural Appalachia." Is what happened to J.D. Vance's family living in urban southwestern Ohio—described by Vance in his 2016 book *Hillbilly Elegy*—about traditional rural Appalachia? Again, my answer is "No, because it didn't happen to Vance's family *in* traditional rural Appalachia."

Appalachia is a place and traditional rural Appalachian culture is place-based. You can take a fish out of water and talk all you want about what's wrong with the fish, or even what's wrong with the air, but the only thing really wrong is that the fish isn't in water. Fish evolved to live in water. Traditional rural Appalachian culture evolved for people to live

65. Personal email communication from Lucy Wieland of Greencastle, Indiana, July 24, 2019.

and thrive in traditional rural Appalachia, not in Ypsilanti, Michigan or Middletown, Ohio.

J. D. Vance's book *Hillbilly Elegy* isn't about traditional rural Appalachian culture (the "water" of my metaphor) because it doesn't deal with people *in* that culture, but rather with people who left that culture behind when they moved to urban Middletown, Ohio. No matter how much they may have internalized mountain culture, they left the culture itself behind when they moved away from its location.

If J. D. Vance's message were simply that traditional rural Appalachian culture tends to be disadvantageous *outside* of traditional rural Appalachia, I wouldn't pick a bone with him. In the 1930s the TVA chairman Arthur Morgan said that in rural Appalachia "there are millions of people living in families where even in prosperous times the total cash income is less than one hundred dollars a year. . . . For children in such families economic opportunity is primary and vocational training is the first essential, but unless it is accompanied by the cultural growth of discrimination and self-discipline, the waste of personality which will accompany the increase of [cash] income, may be very great."[66]

In other words (to re-phrase Arthur Morgan) young people need to develop self-discipline to replace traditional community discipline when traditional community discipline loses its authority because of money. People with money, particularly if they're young, often can't be influenced enough by other people to save them from themselves. They'll have to save *themselves* from themselves, with *self*-discipline. That's what Arthur Morgan was saying.

Then, you might ask, what about the meth and opioid crisis inside Appalachia? But is that happening in *traditional* Appalachia? Or is it happening where the hills have been blasted and decapitated, the streams and groundwater have been contaminated, and hardly any opportunities remain for gainful employment or self-employment? As for the drug of choice, opioids have triumphed partly because they are downers. They can bring you down to the level which nature and all its wholesome

66. Arthur E. Morgan, "Some Suggestions for a Program to Promote Better Opportunities for Rural Young People Especially in the Southern Highlands," unpublished, no date, p. 2.

emanations have been reduced to, and then you won't feel so "on edge." There's nothing traditional about a strip-mined rural Appalachia.

The basic reason why I disagree with J.D. Vance and his book *Hillbilly Elegy* is because he implies traditional Appalachia's culture is disadvantageous even *inside* traditional Appalachia. He thinks getting ahead, acquiring a career and assets, is what Appalachia's native young people should be doing if they want to thrive, even if they still live in Appalachia. J.D. Vance thinks mountain young people can thrive by doing what he himself has done—achieving a white-collar career and accumulating assets.

J. D. Vance and I obviously expect different scenarios ahead in Appalachia's and America's future. Have you asked yourself what *you* expect the future will be like? Personally, for fifty-some years now, I've been expecting our centralized food and energy systems to eventually falter, hopefully not suddenly if they do indeed falter. My expectation about the future is what drove me in summer 2019 to write this book—because decentralism and neighborhood self-reliance can thrive if we make them our goals, but they can't thrive if we keep making individual acquisition our goal—if we keep trying to "get ahead" of each other.

But why do I think future Americans who localize their economic lives and pursue neighborhood self-sufficiency can *thrive*? Because it's been done many times before, even though most writers of history ignore such history. We seem to have a one-way mindset about "progress," thinking it's all about more material goods, centralization, and individual*ism*, whereas actually progress depends on the conditions under which life is being lived. In Darwin's terms, nature doesn't automatically select for what's strongest or gaudiest, but selects for what proves most adaptable to the conditions which it is living under. Nature selects for lives that can find and occupy an "ecological niche" in the conditions they're living under.

I've written this book because I expect our society's future "ecological niches" will be closer to the earth than the way most Americans are currently living. I think our future ecological niches will depend less on centralized systems of food and energy supply than our present-day lives depend on such centralized systems. We have risked our present *centralized* "ecological niche" by burning too much fossil fuel, and we've contaminated our centralized political system, our national American democracy, by letting money pull it in destructive directions.

Where coronavirus-19 fits into this picture, who knows? But West Virginia was the last U.S. state reached by a case of coronavirus-19 because West Virginians tend to (1) live spread out, and (2) stay close to home. (As of October 14, 2020, West Virginia had still seen only 19,000 confirmed coronavirus-19 cases and only 393 deaths caused by it. By then the U.S. overall had seen almost 8 million confirmed cases and over 217,000 deaths caused by it. Thus, by then, West Virginians had been about two-fifths as likely to acquire the virus as Americans overall, and less than one-fifth as likely to die from the virus.)

J. D. Vance's individualistic answer to "hillbilly" culture may continue working for some individuals, including for some individuals like J.D. Vance who can only get there by transforming themselves. But what our *society* needs now aren't individualistic goals. It needs social goals—personal and voluntary ones, mind you, not top-down involuntary goals. We need young people who *don't want* to find their niche in today's mainstream society but instead want to help mainstream society decentralize enough to find its *varied* niches in America's future living conditions.

When hundreds of young newcomers from mainstream America moved into Lincoln County, West Virginia in the early 1970s, they didn't transform Lincoln County's culture. Instead their own culture was transformed by Lincoln County's. If they had come there with millions of dollars to invest, who knows what might have happened. But they came with very little money. They were borrowing tools and trading favors with each other, and exchanging workdays with each other, before they realized such networking was pervasive all around them among the natives. They did know that subsistence farming and gardening were going on, and they knew raising small plots of burley tobacco as a cash crop was common, but their exchanging of favors with each other was well underway before they realized such networking was pervasive all around them. By necessity, to get done what they had to get done, they had "reinvented the wheel" by reinventing voluntary reciprocity—and *then* they caught on that it was pervasive all around them.

Like the natives, the newcomers even started listening in on the "party line" sometimes—depending who it rang for—thereby keeping up with opportunities to help and be helped. The telephones thereabouts were still on "party lines" in the 1970s. The ring pattern told who was being called. The arrival of telephone service had created gaps in people's customary networking because news of people's needs was no longer traveling mainly between *adjacent* farms strung in a row up a hollow or out along a ridge. The arrival of telephones had created gaps in the farm-to-farm information network. But listening in on the party line helped re-fill those gaps.

Whatever our expectations were when we came to rural Lincoln County, we newcomers immediately began living the *rational* way to live under the conditions existing there. And if, as I expect, America's future living conditions will often resemble rural Appalachia's living conditions in the 1970s, then the way of living practiced in rural Appalachia in the 1970s will become the way to get by and thrive under America's future living conditions.

What I personally think is going to need an elegy isn't traditional rural Appalachia's solidarity and sharing, but instead it is mainstream America's career-building and self-centered acquisition.

CHAPTER 19

Summing Up

S umming up doesn't feel easy. It might seem easy to list positives and then list negatives and then weigh them against each other, but it's not easy for me. Some gerontologists say that people go through a "compulsive remembering" phase in their elderly years. They say many older people *compulsively* remember their life's events and try to evaluate their life overall, often magnifying their successes and minimizing their failures (not to mention their sins)—trying to convince themselves they've done more good than harm overall.

Being now 80 years old, I've been traversing such a phase in my own later life but haven't seemed to reach any on-balance verdict.

There were definitely missed opportunities. Not ones like trying to cross Davis Strait from Labrador to Greenland in a two-kayak catamaran with Bill Coperthwaite. No, but I wonder if there might have been a way to stay put in Lincoln County—if not on the beautiful McComas Ridge farm, then on the high Plum Knobs land where the new cabin Miriam and I started was never finished.

By now in the year 2021, that high pasture is probably no longer a pasture at all. It has probably grown sizable trees by now—some of them surely persimmon trees, which softens my regrets. And by now those trees will surely have shaded out the nasty multi-flora rose bushes, another plus.

No doubt the deer resumed sleeping in the high grass after Miriam and I quit working on our cabin. Over the years and decades, I've often remembered that hilltop and wondered if it's reverting to forest. In springtime I wonder which birds have arrived back and where they'll nest. Catbirds and brown thrashers of course and various sparrows.

Charley and Virginia Bates, with their daughter Naomi, at the McComas Ridge
cabin about 1978. Note the cabin's square-hewn logs and dovetailed corners.
Back right: Charley's noncommercial plot of burley tobacco, which
he told me took "way too much work." Photo by Tony Norris.

Some warblers and vireos if woods are indeed reclaiming the hilltop,
and surely some flycatchers. Down in the forest basin, springtime means
waterfalls rippling down the dark slate outcroppings, woodpeckers ham-
mering on tree trunks, and blue jays yelling in the treetops.

I visualize McComas Ridge too. When Miriam and I arrived there in
spring 1974, a pair of phoebe flycatchers were nesting inside the cabin on
the mantle over the fireplace. The previous year I'd been there six months
but they didn't expect me back? One egg had already been laid.

We moved the nest to a ledge out under the eave of the back porch and
the phoebes returned and raised a brood of nestlings there. In the case
of that McComas Ridge farm, it's hard to imagine its two long meadows
of thick grass growing up in trees, but along their edges the woods are
surely encroaching quite far by now into the lush green grass.

After Miriam and I bought the Plum Knobs land and sold Charley
Bates my half-share of that beautiful farm, Charley lived there thirteen
years with his wife Virginia and their daughter Naomi. They built a

modern kitchen-dining room on the back of the cabin that fit well with the cabin's rusticity. They put two solar panels in the front yard and thus had telephone service and two electric lights. Charley also took my advice and pulled off the sheet-metal roof and replaced it with boards and regular shingles. Negative ions accumulate under metal roofs and can make you sleep more than you need to. I noticed that early-on and always slept out front unless it was raining.

Much later, in the summer of 1988, I was back in Lincoln County after receiving a history PhD from Brandeis University near Boston. That's when I recorded interviews with old-timers, hoping to gather information to bolster my dissertation, which took five more years to turn into a book. Charley and Virginia Bates and their daughter Naomi had recently left the McComas Ridge Farm and moved to the vicinity of Franklin, West Virginia in Pendleton County, so Charley was glad to have me caretake the place while they put it up for sale.

It was still beautiful. But I couldn't afford to buy it from Charley, and definitely couldn't live there again since I had to make money out in the world.

Well, one day a fairly young couple arrived from Ohio to look at the farm. They admired its beauty and thought they wanted to spend their two-week summer vacations there, so they bought it. The next several summers they did spend their vacations there, but that was all. Then they had the farm timbered to make some money off it. It wasn't clear-cut but it was *considerably* cut. My brother John said it was torn up rather badly by the loggers dragging logs out to McComas Ridge Road beyond the front gate. (A large swinging gate stood where you turned in to the farm from the rarely-used dirt road along McComas Ridge.) I never went to see the farm after it was torn up by loggers. Then a few years later my brother said an arsonist had burned the cabin and its addition to the ground. Again, I never went to look. So I'll always and only remember that beautiful farm the way it once was.

Sorry to add, I haven't a clue what happened to Bob the blind mine pony. He seemed to do fine on his own there with the two benches' plentitude of fescue grass. By the time I came back and spent the summer of 1988, he was gone, that's all I know.

And despite my nostalgia for the beautiful McComas Ridge farm and the high Plum Knobs land, it doesn't seem likely I'd be writing this book if I hadn't gone back into the world and become a professor. Not that this book will change anything, but global warming and coronavirus-19 combined make its point about small farms more urgent. America doesn't yet have the millions of small farms it's going to need. And most of the small farms America does have lack the energy self-sufficiency they might also need. But lately, *because* of climate change and coronavirus-19, viewpoints are shifting. Millions of Americans are growing interested in local food security and many of them are also interested in local energy production. And they're putting two and two together not just about climate change and coronavirus-19, but about the direction American politics is veering.

Decentralized food and energy security are only achievable incrementally. Not just a lot more solar and wind energy but also a lot more "farming" in urban and suburban places are hopeful trends. My graduate-school friend Brian Donahue's book *Reclaiming the Commons* (1999) describes a voluntary and decentralized way to use suburban farming educationally, and it's useable in urban and rural settings too. The key is for schools to award academic credit to students when they volunteer after-school hours to the farming of yards, vacant lots, and neighborhood gardens. And to pay teachers for doing that with students. Doing it as sharecroppers of the property owners, and working whenever possible *with* the property owners (or the renters) and with other local residents, and with master gardeners, all learning and teaching together. Schools can combine academics and hands-on gardening by using the "service-learning" format many U.S. college courses already use for other purposes. If the schools want textbooks, there are dozens of new handbooks lately about "backyard farming."

Getting back to my personal balance sheet of lifetime pros and cons, at the top of its positive column (and of Miriam's as well) is our daughter Eve Ananda. After age five she grew up bi-cultural, which has helped her understand diverse people and see things from varied points of view. Then too, even before Miriam and Eve moved to Tunisia in North Africa when Eve was five, Eve was imbibing *executive* tendencies from her West Virginia cousin Seoka who is five months older. From the beginning, each of those two cousins has been able and willing to set her own agenda, which has taken them far in their respective fields of psychology and emergency management. So "watch out world" if they ever re-join forces with a shared agenda. That's what we adults had to contend with on Sand Gap Ridge when they were small.

Basically, this book's theme is the traditional way that people lived in rural Appalachia as a forecast of the direction I think most Americans' lives will need to shift in the future. It's a neighborly way of life that can achieve significant local sufficiency by low-budget farming and gardening, combined with neighborly networking (a.k.a. "mutual aid" or "voluntary reciprocity").

Before it hit me out-of-the-blue in 1968 that future Americans would need millions of small farms, I did know America once *had* millions of small farms. But it didn't occur to me that the Appalachian part of America still had a lot. Some part of my mind must have known so after I hiked in Appalachia in 1960, but that didn't connect with my sudden conviction in 1968 that future Americans would need millions of small farms, which simply hit me "out of the blue."

Then in 1971 when I first visited West Virginia, the dots started connecting, and more and more dots kept connecting as my 1970s unfolded. Living as I did in rural West Virginia in the early 1970s made me better able to (later) write a scholarly book interpreting Appalachia's distinctive regional history as a sequence of changing situations which Appalachia's people helped to create but also had to adjust to.[67]

So the arc of *this* book is that my early life prepared me for a light-bulb moment in 1968 when I suddenly felt sure future Americans were going to need millions of small farms, and then in the 1970s rural Appalachian people showed me how millions of small farms could in fact succeed— by subsistence farming and gardening combined with giving and receiving neighborly favors. That lesson in grassroots economics then shaped my scholarly interpretation of how *adversely* most of rural Appalachia's people were affected by major rurally-sited industrialization starting in the 1880s. Having participated in Lincoln County's rural lifeways made me realize those lifeways had all along subsidized the coal industry by partly feeding mountain miners and their families. My thinking had also benefitted by learning a lot of Appalachia's labor history while working at Appalachian Movement Press.

---

67. Paul Salstrom, *Appalachia's Path to Dependency,* University Press of Kentucky (1994).

People tend to enhance their economic resilience when their subsistence farming subsidizes *their own* commercial enterprises, such as cash-cropping, or making things while self-employed or family-employed (like the old-timers I interviewed in Chapter 17 on "Looking Farther Back—to Look Ahead"). But sadly, many Appalachians' subsistence farming didn't subsidize their *own* enterprises but subsidized destructive large-scale coal mining and industrial logging. People's grassroots subsidy of such industries departed from their local area, and mostly left the whole Appalachian region to enrich people elsewhere.

During these past forty years while I've been teaching college history and writing on why I think rural Appalachia has had the history it's had, something has hovered over all my teaching and writing. Namely, my conviction that millions of Americans in the predictable future will have to "return to the land"—either on land where they already live or elsewhere. Having that expectation, the workings of rural Appalachia's traditional sharing economy haven't just been historical facts for me. They've also been my best-case hope for the future.

APPENDIX
LIST OF PERSONS

Adams, Ansel (1902–1984)—Iconic black-and-white nature photographer based in California.

Arbus, Diane (1923–1971)—Innovative black-and-white portrait photographer based in New York City. Died by suicide.

Arnow, Harriette Simpson (1908–1986)—Appalachian author of the novels *Hunter's Horn* (1949) and *The Dollmaker* (1954).

Baez, Joan (1941–)—Well-known singer and nonviolent activist.

Baker, Anna [Triska]—Czech tightrope acrobat who landed in central Lincoln County, West Virginia, after marrying Henry Baker.

Baker, Henry—A native of Ranger Ridge in southwestern Lincoln County, West Virginia just west of the town of Ranger on the Guyandotte River. Second husband of Anna [Triska] Baker (above). Starting in 1970, Henry and Anna enormously helped newcomers in central Lincoln County.

Bates, Charley—A native of the Cincinnati, Ohio area who moved to central Lincoln County in 1971. Built the county's first yurt. With this book's author, he co-bought the beautiful farm on McComas Ridge, and lived there thirteen years with his wife Virginia and daughter Naomi. In January 1988, with John Salstrom, he co-founded Home Place, Inc. to oppose strip-mining by Black Gold, Inc. in Lincoln County.

Beck, Julian (1925–1985)—Co-director with his wife Judith Malina of the Living Theatre, based in New York City. Befriended the author in Danbury Federal Prison, 1964–65.

Berry, Charlie—Offset press operator at Appalachian Movement Press in Huntington, W.Va. in the mid-1970s.

Berry, Chuck (1926–2017)—Well-known rock 'n roll musician, songwriter, and chess whiz. Befriended the author in the federal prison at Springfield, Missouri, during the second of Berry's three imprisonments (in 1962–63).

Bhajan, Yogi [his title] (1929–2004)—A turban-wearing Sikh from India's Punjab region. Founder of the 3HO movement in the U.S. which teaches kundalini yoga.

Black, Billy—Called "Uncle Billy Black." Long-time Myra, W.Va. storekeeper. Son of William Black. Father of Raymond Black (next). Grandfather of Ray Gene Black.

Black, Raymond (1897–?)—Long-time storekeeper-postmaster at Black Brothers General Merchandise store located on Upper Mud River at Myra, W.Va.
in central Lincoln County. Early in 1973 Raymond retired and his son Ray
Gene Black became Myra's storekeeper-postmaster. Both the store and the
post office closed in 2011.

Black, Ray Gene—Son of Raymond and Frieda Black. Ray Gene became Myra,
W.Va.'s storekeeper-postmaster when his father Raymond Black retired in
early 1973.

Borsodi, Ralph (1886–1977)—Writer. Founder in 1934 of the School of Living.
Issuer of The Constant (1972–74), a supplemental currency based in Exeter,
New Hampshire which employed this book's author as its first Comptroller.
Somehow Borsodi's symbol for the Constant—€—ended up symbolizing the
Euro, probably via Bernard Lietaer.

Boyle, Tony (1904–1985)—A Montana miner. Hand-picked in 1963 by John L.
Lewis to become president of the United Mine Workers (UMW). In 1969
Boyle ordered the murder of his leading UMW opponent, Joseph 'Jock'
Yablonski. He was tried and convicted of murder in 1974 and died in prison
in 1985.

Burchett, Delbert—Stripmine operator from Kentucky. He planned (in 1988–
1990) to strip mine in central Lincoln County, W.Va. for the company Black
Gold, Inc. Local opposition was led by Home Place, Inc. and defeated the
strip-mining plan.

Caranante, Greg—Co-founder with John and Michael Fanning of *Mountain
Call* magazine, which they edited at Kermit Knob, near the town of Kermit
in Mingo County, W.Va., and had printed at Appalachian Movement Press
in Huntington, W.Va.

Chojnacki, Jim—A survivor in Taylor Parking Lot of the Kent State shooting
who subsequently farmed in Lower Big Creek Hollow in central Lincoln
County, and married Connie Sayles, the younger sister of Marjie Sayles
Shew. Jim testified against strip mining by Black Gold, Inc. at the June 1988
public hearing at Guyan Valley High School in Lincoln County, W.Va.

Chouinard, Yvon (1938–)—Born in Maine, moved to southern California as
a child with his family. Befriended the author in the Tetons and Yosemite
Valley (1950s-60s). Co-founded Patagonia Inc. in 1973. Now usually lives in
Ventura, California near Patagonia's headquarters.

Coberly, Lenore McComas (1925–)—A writer from Lincoln County, W.Va. who
grew up in the county seat of Hamlin during school months and on Big Ugly
Creek during summer months. A childhood friend of the late Chuck Yeager.

Coperthwaite, Bill (1930–2013)—A native of Aroostook County, Maine.
America's pioneer yurt builder. Lived on 500 coastal acres that he called
Dickinsons Reach (after Emily Dickinson) near Bucks Harbor, Maine.

Traveled widely. Died in a November 2013 single-car crash caused by icy road conditions.

Day, Dorothy (1897–1980)—Founded the Catholic Worker movement in 1933 with the French immigrant Peter Maurin (who popularized the phrase "A new society growing in the shell of the old"). Founded various urban Houses of Hospitality and rural communal farms, and "mothered" many more of each. Likely to be canonized a saint by the Roman Catholic Church.

Douthat, Stratton—Associated Press (AP) journalist who lived in Huntington, W.Va. and in fall 1977 wrote a popular feature article about Miriam Ralston and *MAW Magazine*, illustrated by a photo of Miriam holding her pet white dove.

Dyke, Maude Hunter—(ca. 1891–?)—Heir of a farm and sawmill near Ashton, West Virginia. Midwife, community activist, and treasure-store of traditional knowledge. Interviewed in the book *We Didn't Have Much, But We Sure Had Plenty* (1981) by Sherry Thomas.

Edwards, Edith Pridemore—A close friend of the author who lived with her husband Hallie Edwards on a large farm on the west bank of Mud River, one mile south up-river from the tiny hamlet of Myra, in central Lincoln County, W.Va. As a tobacco-grower, Edith felt conscience-stricken.

Edwards, Hallie—Husband of Edith Pridemore Edwards. Farmed along Upper Mud River one mile above (up-river from) Myra, W.Va.

Elkins, Chester Ray—A farmer who lived in central Lincoln County, W.Va. at the head of Little Laurel Hollow. Owner in 1971–1973 of the blind pony Bob. Often called by all three of his names to distinguish him from "Mud River Ray Elkins."

Elkins, Mabel White (1905–?)—Wife of "Mud River Ray Elkins" (next). In 1988 the author interviewed this couple, Ray and Mabel Elkins, at length (see Chapter 17).

Elkins, Ray (1904–?)—A close friend of the author. Often referred to as Mud River Ray Elkins. Lifelong natural-gas pipeline walker and production-meter reader in central Lincoln County for Columbia Gas Company. Heir of family lore about the duel death of Meriwether Lewis in October 1809 at an inn on the Natchez Trace in Tennessee.

Ernest, Lynn—A native of McDowell County, W.Va. who subsequently settled in Lincoln County. She testified against strip mining by Black Gold, Inc. at the tense June 1988 public hearing at Guyan Valley High School.

Fanning, John and Michael—Twin brothers from near Kermit, W.Va. (in Mingo County). Co-founders and co-editors with Greg Caranante of *Mountain Call* monthly magazine, which flourished in the mid-1970s and was printed at Appalachian Movement Press.

Gavin, James (1907–1990)—U.S. Army general during and after World War II.

Later served as U.S. Ambassador to France and as CEO of Arthur D. Little Company. He opposed the Vietnam War and devised the (never used) Enclave Plan to end it.

Gibbs, Tom W.—Poet. Author of *No Willows for the Zen Cowboy* (1978, 1986) and *The Water Gospel* (2011). *No Willows for the Zen Cowboy* was the only book published by the Appalachian Writers Project of Appalachian Movement Press. Later, Sullen Art Press re-printed it (1986).

Goldsmith, Joanie—With Lawrence Goldsmith (next) migrated from Heathcote Mill in Maryland to central Lincoln County, W.Va. in spring 1970. Mother of Alice Goldsmith.

Goldsmith, Lawrence—A resident of Heathcote Mill back-to-the-land center in rural Maryland who in 1970 started a substantial migration of young people from Heathcote Mill to central Lincoln County, W.Va.

Greenberg, Nancy—A 1971 newcomer to central Lincoln County, W.Va. who invited Tony and Sue Norris to share her rented "Possum House" in Little Laurel Hollow. Mother of Jennifer Greenberg and owner of Barigoat, a Toggenburg nanny goat.

Greenhill, Gobel—Ex-underground coal miner with advanced black lung disease who lived in retirement on Twomile Creek in central Lincoln County, W.Va. Gobel used his federal black-lung compensation checks to buy each of his four children a new pick-up truck.

Hartford, John (1937–2001)—Unique American songwriter and folk musician. Also a steamboat pilot. Interested in southern Lincoln County's Guyandotte Valley feud history. Author of the song "Gentle on My Mind."

Hechler, Ken (1914–2016)—Democrat. Activist U.S. Congressman from southern W.Va., 1959–1977. West Virginia's Secretary of State, 1985–2000.

Hornborg, Alf—A Swedish professor of economic anthropology and human ecology. Known for "Hornborg money."

Jenkins, Albert Gallatin (1830–1864)—Planter and lawyer. U.S. congressman 1857–61. Confederate brigadier general who commanded the 8th Virginia Cavalry. Wounded at Gettysburg, then severely wounded at the May 1864 Battle of Cloyd's Mountain in southwestern Virginia and died two weeks later.

Lack, Larry—A one-year newcomer resident of central Lincoln County, W.Va. who returned from there to Heathcote Mill in Maryland and greatly contributed to *Green Revolution*, the monthly magazine of the School of Living, during the year and a half in 1975–76 when I edited and printed *Green Revolution* at Appalachian Movement Press in Huntington, W.Va.

Lair, John (1894–1985)—A pioneer theme-park entrepreneur. Created Kentucky's Renfro Valley Barn Dance in 1937 in his native locality near Mount Vernon, Kentucky, about thirty miles south of Berea, Kentucky.

Lawson, Flossie Black (1910–?)—A member of the Myra (West Virginia) Black family, Flossie by the 1970s and '80s had long resided a mile north of Myra at the spot where Upper Mud River Road crosses over Little Laurel Creek near that creek's confluence with Mud River. In 1988 I interviewed Flossie there.

Levidow, Les—A movement journalist based in Philadelphia. Author of an excellent booklet, still unpublished, about eastern coal miners' wildcat strike of summer 1975.

Lewis, Almon and Glenna—Natives of Lincoln County, W.Va. who lived in Horse Fork of Little Laurel Hollow and greatly helped young newcomers learn self-sufficiency skills and become successful homesteaders.

Lietaer, Bernard (1942–2019)—Belgian economist. Advocate of supplemental currencies. At the National Bank of Belgium, he devised and implemented the convergence mechanism which created the Euro. Co-author of *Rethinking Money* (2013).

Loomis, Mildred (1900–1985)—Long time *de facto* head of the School of Living founded by Ralph Borsodi in 1934, and resident benevolent matriarch of Heathcote Mill back-to-the-land center in Maryland.

Lynd, Staughton (1929–)—Lifelong peace, civil rights, and labor activist. One of the two leading organizers of the pacifist-Far Left anti-war coalition (1965–1975) which sponsored mass "mobilization" demonstrations against the Vietnam War, often lacking nonviolent discipline. Lynd quietly distanced himself from that coalition in 1968. The coalition's other leading founder, Dave Dellinger, never did so.

Markle, David—Production manager of all the Salstrom banjos ever made, first at Oregon, Illinois (1962–66) and then at Fender Electric Instrument Company in California. By 1968 the banjoes were called Fenders.

Martin, Julian—An eighth-generation native of Coal River Valley (W.Va.). Taught high school science for several decades in Lincoln County. Testified eloquently against strip mining by Black Gold, Inc. at the tense June 1988 public hearing at Guyan Valley High School.

McComas, Spec and Virginia (Ginny)—Elderly couple who resided in Sandlick Hollow behind Myra, W.Va. Almost the only Sandlick residents, they lived in a cabin about a quarter mile below (downstream from) Chuck Yeager's birthplace. Ginny was often ill but she outlived Spec.

McDowell, Ric—A newcomer-photographer who lived on a northern Lincoln County, West Virginia farm near Lower Mud River from 1968 until recently. In 1973 he and others founded Save Our Mountains, which soon became West Virginia's most active anti-stripmining organization.

Mikels, Elaine (1921–2004)—Social activist. Founder in 1960 of San Francisco's Conard House, an innovative network of halfway-houses and residence hotels where mentally-challenged patients live among ordinary renters. Also founder (in 1969) of a dairy-goat farm and organic store on the north rim of Arroyo Hondo, New Mexico.

Miller, Arnold (1923–1985)—A West Virginia underground coal miner afflicted by arthritis who in December 1972 was elected president of the United Mine Workers (UMW) union. Resigned late in 1978 and then in early 1979 was designated the first "president emeritus" of the UMW.

Monday, Clarence E.—Long-time activist mayor of Hamlin, West Virginia who opposed strip mining and worked to establish wood-product alternatives in Lincoln County.

Morgan, Arthur E. (1878–1975)—Hydraulic engineer, educator, and small-community advocate. President of Antioch College, 1920–36. Chairman of the Tennessee Valley Authority (TVA), 1933–38. Advocate of permaculture, supplemental currencies, and many other prescient innovations.

Mosley, Woodrow—Underground coal miner from Logan County, W.Va. who retired to central Lincoln County and lived with his family at the outer (western) end of Sand Gap Ridge, one mile west of the 12-acre land parcel that I bought in 1972 and sold to my younger brother John in 1973 or '74. Woodrow worked part-time as janitor of the Branchland, W.Va. elementary school in the Guyandotte River Valley.

Murie, Margaret E. (Mardy) (1902–2003)—A conservationist who lived near the village of Moose in Grand Teton National Park. Widow of Olaus Murie (1889–1963). Together, Olaus and Mardy Murie, along with Supreme Court Justice William O. Douglas and others, inspired President Eisenhower's 1960 creation of the Arctic National Wildlife Range (now Refuge).

Murie, Olaus J. (1889–1963)—A wildlife biologist in central Alaska 1920–26 specializing on caribou. Began studying elk in Jackson Hole, Wyoming in 1927. Head of the Wilderness Society, 1945–1963.

National Hospital Workers Union—Founded in 1932 by Leon J. Davis in New York City as a local of a pharmacists' union. First known as "1199." In 1989, most of this hospital-workers union merged into SEIU, the Service Employees International Union, and Tom Woodruff of West Virginia later became SEIU's vice-president for the organizing of new SEIU chapters, helping to make it one of America's fastest-growing unions.

Nelson, Wally and Juanita—Civil rights pioneers. While a Howard University student, Juanita helped pioneer lunch-counter sit-ins in 1942 in Washington, DC. Wally was one of the 1947 Freedom Riders on CORE's interracial "Journey of Reconciliation" into the South, for which he and fifteen other participants served jail sentences. In the 1950s, Wally was the only full-time field representative of CORE (Congress of Racial Equality).

Norris, Tony and Sue—Newcomer migrants in summer 1971 to central Lincoln County, W.Va. around whom other newcomers' social lives largely revolved.

During winter 1974–75 they left for financial reasons. Tony eventually found durable success in Flagstaff, Arizona as a cowboy musician and impresario. Most of their children and grandchildren live near them in Flagstaff.

Perry, Sandra—Head of Black Gold, Inc., a company formed to strip mine coal in central Lincoln County, W.Va. (1988–1990). The plan was defeated by local opposition led by Home Place, Inc..

Petzoldt, Paul (1908–1999)—Founder in 1926 of the climbing-guide service in what would soon (in 1929) become Grand Teton National Park. And founder in 1965 of the National Outdoor Leadership School (NOLS) in Wyoming's Wind River Mountains. Over 200,000 young people have graduated from NOLS' annual month-long wilderness immersion.

Plott, John C. (ca. 1917–1990)—A professor of philosophy at Marshall University in Huntington, W.Va, and author of a five-volume *Global History of Philosophy* as well as several other fine books.

Ralston, Miriam—The author's former spouse. Mother of Eve Ananda Salstrom Ralston. Creator of *MAW: A Magazine of Appalachian Women*, which was the Appalachian movement's first women's magazine.

Rockefeller, John D. IV (Jay) (1937–)—Democrat. Governor of West Virginia 1977–1985; then U.S. Senator from West Virginia 1985–2015.

Sakaki, Nanao (1923–2008)—Japanese military radar specialist who on August 9, 1945 tracked the northbound B-29 bomber which A-bombed Nagasaki that morning. Nanao subsequently became a hermit and poet. He spent about ten years in the western U.S. starting in 1969 at a cave on Greenhorn Mountain above Libre Commune in Colorado.

Salstrom, David—My father's youngest sibling. A communally-minded Quaker pacifist who lived for many years at Celo Community in western North Carolina, then attended Berea College in Kentucky, earned a Master's degree at Kent State University, and taught education first at Lock Haven State College in northcentral Pennsylvania and then at Baldwin-Wallace College near Cleveland. Later retired back to Celo Community (pronounced "see-lo").

Salstrom, Jan LaVoy—Newcomer to central Lincoln County, W.Va. in the early 1970s. Long-time nurse midwife, gardener, and craftsperson. Spouse of John Salstrom (next).

Salstrom, John (1952–)—The author's younger brother who followed him to Lincoln County, W.Va. and became a self-employed carpenter there. Now also the keeper of Lincoln County's official property-line tax maps on behalf of the county assessor.

Salstrom, Lois (1950–)—Cousin of the author who took him to the Woodstock Festival in 1969. Daughter of Phil Salstrom, the author's woodcarving-business uncle. Lois was almost shot by National Guard troops on May 4, 1970 while she was a student at Kent State University in Ohio.

Salstrom, Matthew (Matt)—Son of John and Jan Salstrom. Matt now lives in North Carolina.

Salstrom, Phil (1912–1992)—My entrepreneurial uncle who created Rock Wood Carvers Company and its branch the Salstrom Banjo Company, based along the east bank of Rock River four miles north of Oregon, Illinois. Myself and many other central Lincoln County in-migrants worked for Phil Salstrom's company Rock Wood Carvers off and on in the 1970s, thereby acquiring money in order to buy land in Lincoln County, W.Va.

Salstrom, Seoka—Daughter of John and Jan Salstrom. Seoka now resides in Vermont.

Salstrom Ralston, Eve Ananda—Daughter of Miriam Ralston and the author.

Schumacher, E.F. (1911–1977)—German-born English economist. Pioneer of appropriate technology. Wrote the book *Small is Beautiful: A Study of Economics as if People Mattered* (1973).

Shew, Pete and Marjie—A young couple who moved to Lincoln County in spring 1971 (—Marjie from Heathcote Mill in Maryland) and adopted traditional farming practices, including the use of draft horses. Parents of two children. Now Pete and Marjie farm without horses near Athens, Ohio.

Smith, Chuck—VISTA volunteer in Boone County, West Virginia. Then founder in 1969 of a Catholic Worker Farm near Lower Mud River in northern Lincoln County. Subsequently a political-science professor at West Virginia State University located in Institute, W.Va.

Sobell, Morton (1917–2018)—American spy for the Soviet Union. Tried with Julius and Ethel Rosenberg in 1951. Sentenced to thirty years and served eighteen of those until his good-time release in 1969. Befriended the author at the Medical Center for Federal Prisoners in Springfield, Missouri (1962–64). In 2008, Sobell confessed to having spied for the Soviet Union, implicated Julius Rosenberg as his courier, and declared Ethel Rosenberg innocent.

Spadaro, Jack (1948–)—Former federal coal-mine health and safety inspector, and former superintendent of the National Mine Health and Safety Academy in Beckley, W.Va. Now a private consultant on mining health and safety, and on the environment. Based in Hamlin, W.Va.

Staats, Valerie—A native of Huntington, W.Va. Assistant editor of *MAW Magazine*, and then founding editor of *Iowa Woman*.

Stewart, Danie Joe—Co-founder in 1969 with Tom Woodruff of Appalachian Movement Press in Huntington, W.Va. In 1974 both Stewart and Woodruff became regional organizers in western West Virginia and eastern Kentucky for the National Hospital Workers Union (a.k.a."1199") based in New York City.

Stroud, Robert F. (a.k.a. Birdman of Alcatraz) (1890–1963)—Spent his entire adult life in federal prisons. While at Leavenworth, he became an authority on caged-bird diseases. Subject of a 1962 feature film starring Burt Lancaster.

Befriended the author in 1962–63 at the Medical Center for Federal Prisoners in Springfield, Missouri. Died there of a heart attack in November 1963.

Swann, Marjorie (Marj) (1921–2014)—Peace movement organizer extraordinaire. Married Bob Swann in the mid-1940s. They separated in 1978.

Swann, Robert (Bob) (1918–2003)—A carpenter and builder. Inventor of the Community Land Trust method of landholding. Also founder in 1980 (with Susan Witt) of the E.F. Schumacher Society based at Great Barrington, Massachusetts. Heavily influenced the author of this book.

Thomas, Sherry—Northern California sheep farmer. Co-editor of *Country Women* magazine and book. Author of the book *We Didn't Have Much, But We Sure Had Plenty: Stories of Rural Women* (1981), which includes Sherry's 1979 interview with Maude Hunter Dyke of Mason County, W.Va.

Triska, Matej (pronounced ma-tees)—Tightrope acrobat. Longtime resident of Little Laurel Hollow in Lincoln County, W.Va. Son of Karel Triska and Anna (Triska) Baker.

Vance, J.D. (1984–)—Author of the book *Hillbilly Elegy: A Memoir of a Family and Culture in Crisis* (2016) which is about growing up in Middletown, Ohio. Vance feels that traditional rural Appalachian cultural values did not provide answers to urban Middletown, Ohio's rust-belt social problems.

Weinberger, Eric (1932–2006)—University of Chicago drop-out. Peace movement and Congress of Racial Equality (CORE) activist. Initiator in 1962 of the Haywood (Tenn.) Handicrafters League in Haywood County, Tennessee. After 1982, Eric focused his work on feeding homeless people through Food Not Bombs in Boston, Massachusetts.

Woodruff, Tom—Co-founder in 1969 of Appalachian Movement Press in Huntington, W.Va. In 1974 he became an organizer for "1199," the National Hospital Workers Union, most of which in 1989 merged into SEIU, Service Employees International Union, one of the world's largest unions. For many years Woodruff was SEIU's vice-president in charge of organizing new chapters. Now he's a full-time SEIU consultant.

Yablonski, Joseph ('Jock') (1910–1969)—Extremely competent union leader. The leading opponent of president Tony Boyle of the United Mine Workers (UMW). Murdered on Boyle's orders on New Year's Eve 1969. Yablonski's wife Margaret and 25-year old daughter Charlotte were murdered at the same time.

Yeager, Charles (Chuck) (1923–2020)—A native of Myra, W.Va. in central Lincoln County. Childhood friend (in Hamlin, the county seat) of Lenore McComas Coberly. As a U.S. Air Force test pilot, Yeager flew faster than sound in 1947 in southern California, thereby "breaking the sound barrier."

BIBLIOGRAPHY

Arnow, Harriette. *The Dollmaker*. New York: Macmillan, 1954.

"Ashland settles emissions' lawsuits." UPI Archives, Feb. 22, 1993. Online at: Ashland settles emissions' lawsuits.

"Ashland settles pollution claims." *Oil and Gas Journal*, Oct. 12, 1998. Online at: www.ogj.com

Bruggers, James. "Appalachia's Strip-Mined Mountains Face a Growing Climate Risk: Flooding." *Inside Climate News*, Nov. 21, 2019. Online.

Burns, Shirley Stewart. *Bringing Down the Mountains: The Impact of Mountaintop Removal on Southern West Virginia Communities*. Morgantown: West Virginia University Press, 2007.

Carlisle, Liz. "Feeding the Soil." *Patagonia Provisions*, issue #1, Spring 2020, pp. 10–19.

Caudill, Harry M. *Night Comes to the Cumberlands: A Biography of a Depressed Area*. Boston: Little, Brown, 1963.

Cherniack, Martin, M.D. *The Hawks Nest Incident: America's Worst Industrial Disaster*. New Haven: Yale University Press, 1986.

Coberly, Lenore McComas. "The Fellowship at Wysong's Clearing." In Coberly, *The Handywoman Stories*. Athens: Ohio University Press, 2002, pp. 81–91. Reprinted in Coberly, et al., *Writers Have No Age*, 2nd edition. Philadelphia: Haworth Press, 2005.

Fisher, Irving. *Stamp Scrip*. New York: Adelphi, 1933.

Forbes, Peter, and Helen Whybrow. *A Man Apart: Bill Coperthwaite's Radical Experiment in Living*. White River Junction, VT: Chelsea Green Publishing, 2015.

Ford, Thomas R., editor. *The Southern Appalachian Region: A Survey*. Lexington: University of Kentucky Press, 1962.

Gatch, Loren. "Dr. Borsodi's Constant." *Paper Money* magazine, Sept.-Oct. 2013, pp. 339–345.

Gavin, James M. *Crisis Now*. New York: Random House, 1968.

Gibbons, Euell. *Stalking the Wild Asparagus*. Philadelphia: David McKay, 1962.

Goldsmith, Lawrence. "How to Buy Land." *Mother Earth News*, May-June 1970.

Hamburger, Richard. *Our Portion of Hell: Fayette County, Tennessee: An Oral History of the Struggle for Civil Rights*. Links, 1973.

Hennen, John. *A Union for Appalachian Healthcare Workers: The Radical Roots and Hard Fights of Local 1199.* Morgantown: West Virginia University Press, 2021.

Hicks, George L. *Experimental Americans: Celo and Utopian Community in the Twentieth Century.* Urbana: University of Illinois Press, 2001.

Hornborg, Alf. *Nature, Society, and Justice in the Anthropocene.* Cambridge, Eng.: Cambridge University Press, 2019.

———. "How to Turn an Ocean Liner: A Proposal for Voluntary Degrowth by Redesigning Money for Sustainability, Justice, and Resilience." *Journal of Political Ecology,* Vol. 24, No. 1 (2017).

Jabally, Robert. "Bank Holiday of 1933." Online at: Federal Reserve History [one of the Federal Reserve System's official websites].

James, Michelle. "COVID-19 changes everything: Farm collective sees customer base grow from 40 to 400 in five weeks." In Beckley (W.Va.) *Register-Herald,* May 2, 2020.

Kains, Maurice G. *Five Acres and Independence: A Handbook for Small Farm Management,* revised and enlarged edition. Mineola, NY: Dover Publications, 1973.

Kernza. Online at: www.landinstitute.org

Kump, H. G. "Address to a Regional Meeting of County Boards of Education," Charleston, W.Va., July 21, 1933. In H. G. Kump, *State Papers and Public Addresses.* Charleston, W.Va. No date.

Lancianesse, Adelina. "Before Black Lung, the Hawks Nest Tunnel Disaster Killed Hundreds." National Public Radio, Jan. 20, 2019. Online at: www.npr.org

Lappé, Frances Moore. *Diet for a Small Planet.* New York: Ballantine Books, 1971.

Laubin, Reginald and Gladys. *The Indian Tipi.* Norman: University of Oklahoma Press, 1967.

Levidow, Les. "The United Mine Workers in the Coal Strike of 1975." *Green Revolution* magazine, Feb. 1976, pp. 11–18. (And more in the March 1976 issue, pp. 13–16.)

Lietaer, Bernard, and Jacqui Dunne. *Rethinking Money: How New Currencies Turn Scarcity into Prosperity.* Oakland, CA: Berrett-Koehler Publishers, 2013.

Lincoln County, West Virginia Interviews, recorded in 1988 by Paul Salstrom. Transcribed by Mary Thomas and Paul Salstrom. Oral History of Appalachia Collection, Marshall University Library, Huntington, W.Va.

Lincoln County Economic Development Authority. "Lincoln County Comprehensive Plan." Draft, 2017.

Lozier, John, and Ronald Althouse. "Social Enforcement of Behavior Toward Elders in an Appalachian Mountain Settlement." *The Gerontologist,* Feb. 1974, pp. 69–80.

Marshall University Library. Oral History of Applachia Collection. Huntington, W.Va.

Martin, Julian. *The Soviet Union and Lincoln County USA*. Create Space Independent Publishing, 2014.

Mills, Stephanie. *On Gandhi's Path: Bob Swann's Work for Peace and Community Economics*. Gabriola, British Columbia: New Society Publishers, 2010.

Morgan, Arthur E. "Group Industries' Problems and their Solution." Speech at University of Tennessee, Knoxville, on Nov. 9, 1933. Copy in TVA Technical Library, Knoxville, Tennessee.

———. *The Making of the TVA*. Amherst, NY: Prometheus Books, 1974.

———. "Some Suggestions for a Program to Promote Better Opportunities for Rural Young People Especially in the Southern Highlands." Unpublished paper, no date.

Morgan, Thomas B. "Doom and Passion along Rt. 45." *Esquire* magazine, Nov. 1962.

"The Mothman Prophecies." Feature film starring Richard Gere, 2002.

Nearing, Scott and Helen. *Living the Good Life: How to Live Simply and Sane in a Troubled World*. New York: Schocken Books, 1954.

O'Donnell, Lawrence. *Playing with Fire: The 1968 Election and the Transformation of American Politics*. New York: Penguin Press, 2017.

Patagonia journal, Spring 2020 (re: Kernza grass).

Patagonia Provisions, issue #1, Spring 2020. "Feeding the Soil" by Liz Carlisle, pp. 10–19.

Plott, John C. *Global History of Philosophy*, 5 volumes. Benares, India: Motilal Banarsidass, 1977–1993.

Pritt, Pam. "Digging In." Davis College of Agriculture magazine, West Virginia University, Fall 2019, pp. 20–21.

Pudup, Mary Beth, Dwight B. Billings, and Altina L. Waller, editors. *Appalachia in the Making: The Mountain South in the Nineteenth Century*. Chapel Hill: University of North Carolina Press, 1995.

Ralston, Miriam. "The Birth of *MAW: A Magazine of Appalachian Women*," *Goldenseal* magazine, Vol. 47, No. 1 (Spring 2021), pp. 58–61.

Read, Jon J., and Paul Salstrom. "The Free Cities Plan." *Humanist*, Jan.-Feb. 1968, pp. 12–15.

Richards, Edward C.M. "The Future of TVA Forestry," *Journal of Forestry* 36 (1938), pp. 643–652.

Roosevelt, F.D. Press Conferences, 1933–1945, transcripts. Online at: Franklin D. Roosevelt Presidential Library, Press Conferences 1933–1945.

Rutenberg, Amy J. "How the Draft Reshaped America." *New York Times*, Oct. 6, 2017.

Salstrom, Mary. "On Industrial Woodcarving in America, 1780–1980, and the Development of the Salstrom Wood Carving Machine." Online.

Salstrom, Paul. "The Agricultural Origins of Economic Dependency, 1840–1880." In: *Appalachian Frontiers,* edited by Robert D. Mitchell. Lexington: University Press of Kentucky, 1991, pp. 261–283.

———. "Banjos were made in Oregon." *Oregon* (Illinois) *Republican Reporter,* Jan. 9, 2014, pp. A1, B1.

———. "Big Ugly Creek, West Virginia: An Interview with Writer Lenore McComas Coberly." *Appalachian Journal,* Spring-Summer 2004, pp. 368–387.

———. Editorial. *Green Revolution* magazine, Oct. 1975, pp. 2–3.

Selective Service System, "Channeling." Online.

Slifer, Shaun. *So Much to Be Angry About: Appalachian Movement Press and Radical DIY Publishing, 1969–1979.* Morgantown: West Virginia University Press, 2021.

Sprouting Farms, website: www.sproutingfarms.org.

Stalnaker, C. Keith. "Hawks Nest Tunnel." *Professional Safety* magazine, Oct. 2006, pp. 27–33.

Stoll, Steven. *Ramp Hollow: The Ordeal of Appalachia.* New York: Hill & Wang, 2017.

Stump, Jake. "The Positive Implications of Climate Change?" Davis College of Agriculture magazine, West Virginia University, Fall 2019, pp. 4–7.

Thomas, Sherry. *We Didn't have Much, But We Sure Had Plenty: Stories of Rural Women.* New York: Anchor Press, 1981.

Triska Troupe. "IT's Triska." Online.

"Triska Troupe High Wire Acrobats." Short films of Triska Troupe performances in France. Online.

Turman, Jinny. "Green Civil Republicanism and Environmental Action in Lincoln County, West Virginia, 1974–1990." *Journal of Southern History,* Nov. 2016, pp. 855–900.

turnrow marketing collective, website: www.turnrowfarms.org.

Vance, J. D. *Hillbilly Elegy: A Memoir of a Family and Culture in Crisis.* New York: Harper, 2016.

Waskow, Arthur. *Toward a Peacemakers Academy: A Proposal for a First Step Toward a United Nations Transnational Peacemaking Force.* New York: Springer, 1967.

Weiman, David F. "Families, Farms, and Rural Society in Preindustrial America," *Research in Economic History,* supplement 5, part B (1989), pp. 255–277.

Wells, Tom. *The War Within: America's Battle over Vietnam.* Berkeley: University of California Press, 1994.

West Virginia Department of Energy. Public Hearing June 28, 1988 [re: strip-mining in Lincoln County by Black Gold, Inc.]. In: Oral History of Appalachia Collection, Marshall University Library, Huntington, W.Va.

"West Virginia Overdose Deaths 2014." *West Virginia University* magazine, Fall 2017, p. 10.

Willey, Lindsay. "A Roadmap to Success." Davis College of Agriculture magazine, West Virginia University, Fall 2018, pp. 22–27.

Wright, Michael. "Fender Artist Bluegrass." *Vintage Guitar*, May 2014, pp. 26–28.

INDEX OF NAMES

See also the "List of Persons" on pages 213–221.